Nothing Good Happens at ...
The Baby Hospital

Nothing Good Happens at …
The Baby Hospital

The Strange, Silly World of
Pediatric Brain Surgery

DANIEL FULKERSON, MD

ARCHWAY
PUBLISHING

Archway Publishing books may be ordered through booksellers or by contacting:

Archway Publishing
1663 Liberty Drive
Bloomington, IN 47403
www.archwaypublishing.com
1 (888) 242-5904

ISBN: 978-1-4808-3945-8 (sc)
ISBN: 978-1-4808-3944-1 (hc)
ISBN: 978-1-4808-3946-5 (e)

Library of Congress Control Number: 2016919497

Print information available on the last page.

Archway Publishing rev. date: 12/2/2016

CONTENTS

INTRODUCTION

Question: How does a neurosurgeon change a lightbulb?
Answer: He holds it up to the socket and lets the world revolve around him.

It's been said that if you ask a neurosurgeon to name the three greatest surgeons alive, he or she will have trouble naming the other two. When I entered medical school, I pictured neurosurgery as the domain of the stern, pompous douchenozzles with executive silver hair and a God complex. Neurosurgery was serious business, demanding exacting precision, harsh attitudes, and a complete absence of fun.

Yes, neurosurgery as a specialty can be quite full of itself. But I don't buy that model. I fell backward into neurosurgery. It certainly wasn't a career goal, and it certainly seemed very out of reach when I started medical school. However, the patients I encountered were courageous and inspiring, especially the children. My teachers were (are) good people with a fierce dedication to their craft. I've found neurosurgery to be a field filled with joy, sadness, and even a little mirth.

This is the tale of the long and winding road to train and then practice as a pediatric neurosurgeon. There's a little bit of artistic license here and there; this is not a history book. I can't remember exact conversations from twenty years ago. And some of the people are condensed. All the names are changed, as are a few key circumstances.

But the stories are true. The patients and their challenges are true—sometimes happy, sometimes sad, but always true.

Neurosurgery is a roller coaster of emotion, especially when treating children. It is a privilege to operate on the central nervous system—the brain and the spine. It's a special privilege to operate on kids. I hope you have fun on the ride!

Enjoy.

CHAPTER 1

Neurosurgery 101

*C*lick.

"This is a lady with a subdural hematoma. Notice the crescent-shaped blood clot compressing the brain." Pause. "She did shitty and died."

Well, this was different.

We were seated in a cramped classroom conspicuously devoid of air-conditioning. It was hot. I was one of about fifteen medical students listening to a wizened, slightly hunched man whose eyes never left the screen. The slide projector wheezed and clicked, shifting a grainy, often black-and-white image onto the screen. The pictures were barely visible with the bright sun glare.

Click.

"This is a guy with an epidural hematoma. Notice the blood clot is lens shaped. Dirtbag. Got hit with a baseball bat. He did shitty and died."

The Professor chuckled slightly to himself. He was wearing a short-sleeved collared shirt with a loose tie that barely made it halfway to his belt. His hair was slicked back and thinning, with not quite enough gray. He was confident, brusque, and talked like Eeyore. He clearly had given the same lecture in the same room to the same gaggle of sweating medical students many times.

Click.

I wasn't quite sure how to process this. We were just finishing our second year of medical school. The first two years were primarily spent in a classroom where we either memorized reams of data or bemoaned all the ills of society. On day 1, we gathered at a reception outside of the main academic building. There were about a hundred new students, all nervously looking around at each other. We were sizing each other up. I felt terribly out of place. To break the tension, I tried to open a conversation. I chose the most awkward-looking chap, figuring he must be as frightened as I was.

"Hi," I said, breaking the ice.

"Hi, I'm Kevin. I graduated Phi Betta Kappa from Super Snooty Ivy University with a 3.95 GPA."

Uh-oh.

"Hi, Kevin. I'm Dan."

"Oh." He paused. He seemed disappointed that I didn't volunteer my own GPA, and I was still incredulous that he blurted out his.

We trundled into the main lecture hall, an old building with small chairs and stale air. I was wondering if everybody was like Kevin. The first speaker was a lady in round glasses. She gave us a flowery welcome and then immediately began listing all the mental-health resources available for students: suicide prevention hotlines, counselors, and the psychiatry services. She spoke in froufrou language but in a disquietingly measured tone. As she was wrapping up, she said, "Remember—we are a medical school that assigns grades. But always keep this formula in mind: P equals MD. If you *pass*, you become a doctor. You don't need all 'A's.' You just need to pass." She smiled.

I couldn't help but feel that she was looking out at us in the same way a farmer may look at cattle headed to the slaughterhouse.

Click.

"This is a teenager who wrapped his motorcycle around a tree. Catastrophic head injury. He did shitty and died." The Professor paused. "Wear a helmet, kids."

Click.

That initial introduction to medical school seemed a little granola to me. After all, I had done well in school. I wondered why our introduction to medicine was a detailed exposition about mental health. Then the *real* classes began.

A bespectacled man in a lab coat with a bushy mustache stood behind the podium. He waited patiently for the murmur and movement to die, and then he projected a screen with small words, angled lines, and a lot of octagons. I was proud of myself for recognizing that this had something to do with chemistry.

"So, these are the basic amino acids. But I'd guess you all know that already."

Nervous laughter. At least I was nervous. What was he talking about? That was clearly a joke meant to break the tension. But then the lecture began. No introduction to those amino whatever-they-were.

I turned to the guy to my left. "Do you know all those things?"

He flashed a tight-lipped smile that conveyed his annoyance. He didn't break his gaze from the lecture. "I was a biochemistry major in undergrad, so, well, yeah, I know them."

Uh-oh.

I turned to the guy on my right. "Do you know all these?"

"Well, I was a biology major, so yeah, pretty basic."

An epiphany is not always a positive. I sickeningly realized that my engineering degree meant somewhere between jack and squat.

Click.

"This is a picture consistent with diffuse axonal injury, or DAI.

Notice the contusions around the corpus callosum. This guy did shitty and died."

Click.

After those initial didactic lectures, we broke into small groups and began our hippie training. Birkenstock-clad primary care doctors implored us to avoid the trap of becoming a stereotypically unfeeling, uncaring doctor. A *real* doctor pays no attention to business or legal matters. A *real* doctor cares. A *real* doctor saves the world.

I bought it hook, line, and sinker. I was ready to right all the wrongs in the world. We covered them in tearful detail—political problems, women's health issues, poverty, hunger. After each seminar, I had the disturbing feeling that everything bad was my fault. Early in our first year, I was part of a small group that met with an HIV-positive, homeless Native American Vietnam vet—the mother lode of self-flagellating guilt. Our teacher loved it! We met for about an hour. We gathered at his feet in wide-eyed wonder, fawning over his every word and secretly cursing ourselves for our part in his plight.[1] We all had a good solid cry and vowed we would fix things. Crying was not quite mandatory, but it did seem to be expected, especially for a male.

The teachers uniformly extolled the virtues of primary care and eschewed the evils of specialized medicine. We learned that it took at least an hour to interview a patient, if we were to effectively under-stand how a particular problem truly affected him or her. Medicine should be unrushed, unhurried, and with empathetic people talking face-to-face. A diagnosis is not complete without an understanding of how the patient *feels* about the problem.

Click.

"This is a fracture dislocation of the upper cervical spine. Complete spinal cord injury. Vent-dependent quad until he died."

---

[1] In retrospect, this guy was about as Native American as the pope. And I'd guess he was about twelve in 1968. We were a little naive.

I was puzzled. *Are we supposed to cry now? Why is he going on?* There was no wasted motion or words with the Professor. There was no pretense, no speculation. Just facts. It's not that he didn't care. He cared. He just got to the point and focused only on the things he could affect. Was this bad? I was confused.

The Professor's lecture was our first introduction to the last two clinical years of medical school. Each of us had to do a two-month block on a surgery service. I wanted to get this out of the way early. I requested to work with children as much as possible. I like kids.

Click.

"And this is a baby with a subdural hematoma because some dirtbag abused him." The Professor clicked his tongue in disgust and then under his breath muttered, "Off with his head." He then continued in his lecture voice, "Notice the hematoma has different densities, indicating multiple times of injury. Notice also the 'black brain' with loss of the gray-white junction. This probably means anoxic injury, and the baby is going to do shitty. I saw this kid at the Baby Hospital—nothing to do."

"Nothing to do"? You've got to be kidding me!

"Remember, kids, nothing good happens at the Baby Hospital."

The Professor was the head of the neurosurgical residency program.

CHAPTER 2

Introduction to Surgery

I passed the first two years in what must have been a mix of divine intervention with pitiful charity. By a stroke of chance, I became friends with the two best students in our class. Jack was tall and loud and confident to the point of cockiness. We had both graduated from Golden U, a school known for being loud and confident to the point of cockiness. Jack struggled in college. In fact, his college counselor discouraged him from applying for medical school. Two years working in the *real world* as a chemist gave Jack maturity and a sense of purpose. My other friend was Sam, who, as luck would have it, was a medical savant. Sam hailed from small town Milan, Indiana. You know the town. It's the town and high school from the movie *Hoosiers*. Sam graduated in the middle of a high school class of fifteen. His high school counselor suggested a trade school. Sam didn't speak English; he spoke *country*. I'm not sure he could reliably use a three-syllable word in a sentence. Like Jack, he had worked in the real world. He went to community college and then chiropractic school. A few years and one divorce later, he applied and barely got into medical school. Despite his Pokémon-level vocabulary and bumpkin looks, Sam had a remarkable ability to learn everything that was important.

We began our third year trying to learn procedures. We practiced starting intravenous (IV) lines on each other. We practiced suturing. We even practiced a gynecologic pelvic exam.

"Don't be shy." An older, very patient nurse was our practice patient. I'm sure she was paid, and I'm doubly sure that it wasn't enough. She was pinched, poked, and snapped by nervous, fumbling hands. I was petrified.

"Does this hurt?" I asked.

"No, young man. You're doing fine."

A little deeper. Oops.

"Sorry."

"It's okay. Keep going."

"Is this okay?"

"Not quite. Go deeper."

I had a flashback to the first night of my honeymoon.

Snap!

"Ouch!"

"Ohgodsorry!"

"It's okay. I'm sure you'll get better."

That brought a flashback to the second night of my honeymoon.

*   *   *   *

Sam was excited. He was starting on a general surgery rotation. We all had to serve two months on a surgery rotation. I was sure I was going to hate it. I still wasn't sure what to think about the Professor, but I assumed all surgeons were exactly what I didn't want to be—uncaring, bitter, unfeeling, cynical bastards.

"General surgery, A-team, huh? That's the big one!" I said to Sam.

He smiled. "Can't wait! What are you on?"

"Pediatric surgery," I answered.

If I had to do surgery, at least I wanted to hang out with kids. The chairman of the general surgery department was the head surgeon at the Baby Hospital.

"Ouch," Sam said. "That one's rough."

"Nah, it'll be okay. I like kids."

Sam and I went to the dean's office to pick up our assignments. He grinned again. "I'm on call the first night! Awesome!"

Hold on. I'm supposed to be there at 5:00 a.m.? Seriously?

"Good luck, buddy!" Sam grinned. "Remember—nothing good happens at the Baby Hospital!"

*   *   *   *

"Early, huh?" Andy said. Andy was a *gunner*—one of the top, hyper-competitive students who seemed destined for surgery.

"Is every day going to be like this?" I asked, closing my car door and greeting my classmate.

"Maybe they're just trying to scare us."

Andy, four of our classmates, and I trudged across the deserted parking lot. The sun was just breaking the gloom, and a fine mist was clinging to the surrounding buildings. We walked past County, the state-run hospital for the indigent. I suppose at one point it was white or maybe cream-colored. Now it was a dirty gray with cracks in the foundation. A few stragglers from the night before stood smoking under the main entrance awning. We didn't make eye contact. To our left was the U, the main teaching and academic hospital. The lighting made the red brick look brown. In front of us was the Baby Hospital.

A distracted, disheveled, and generally annoyed-looking resident met us at the door. A *resident* is sort of like an apprentice. A residency is a training period after medical school where new doctors learn under the supervision of faculty doctors or *attendings*. Residents in their first year are called *interns*.[2] Residency lasts anywhere from three to seven years, depending on the specialty. Surgery residencies are the longest. A neurosurgery residency lasts seven years. Some doctors then do a *fellowship*, extra training for the most specialized fields. Those people are called *idiots*.

"Ped surgery?" he asked, not bothering to look up from the list he was reading.

"*Yes!*" we all answered in unison.

The noise seemed to bother him.

"Great. Come on."

We marched past the only other person in the lobby—a small woman at the information desk. She had a pointed noise and glasses dangling from a chain on her neck. She smiled curtly as we passed.

The lobby of the Baby Hospital was nice. There were sounds of a fountain, large stuffed animals on the walls, and a relief sculpture of Ryan White[3] crossing his fingers. We hustled past the large glass elevators and entered the surgery suite. The resident never bothered to look up.

"Go sit in there," he said, and then he hustled along his way. We all exchanged nervous glances.

"Hope I don't get stuck with him," I muttered under my breath.

"Dude, I'll kick his ass if he pulls any crap with me," Andy said, puffing out his chest.

We were in the chairman's office. Every square inch of the walls was covered by some diploma or plaque of recognition. There were pictures of the chairman, a big, burly white-haired man, shaking

---

[2] Confusingly, so are fully trained internal medicine doctors.

[3] Ryan was an unfortunate young man born with hemophilia. He contracted HIV from a contaminated blood sample in 1984. Ryan was instrumental in putting a human, child's face on HIV and AIDS. Ryan passed in 1990, but his story and legacy significantly advanced AIDS awareness and research. More on this later.

hands with various dignitaries. There was a ridiculously oversized oaken desk by a window and a smaller conference table surrounded by one too few chairs.

The chief pediatric surgery fellow burst into the room and sprint-walked to the table. He was followed by a troop of residents, interns, the junior fellow, and a nurse. He was a thin, ferret-like man, who moved with quick, jerking motions. He had darting eyes, a taut face, and short-cropped black hair. He didn't waste a solitary second with words or actions.

"Welcome," he said, sounding like he didn't mean it.

"I'm Mark. This is Ryan. We're the fellows. Rounds start at five. You'll each be assigned five to ten patients. Here's the list of information you gather before rounds."[4]

Before rounds?

Mark dealt out a packet of cards to each of us. "This is the line score. You give me the data in precisely the same order every day. Here's your patients." He dealt out another set of cards, each with a hastily scrawled name and room number. "ORs start at 7:30. You guys decide who goes where. You round again with the call resident, usually around 6:00 p.m. You guys make a call schedule to cover each night."

He was reading the names on the cards. He hesitated on one. "God, a transplant patient. I hate transplant. Got divorced when I was on transplant." He slid that card across to Andy with a flourish.

He finished with the cards, briskly stood, turned, seemed very annoyed that one of the junior residents was blocking his path, and sprint-walked off. His troop scurried behind him, all except the one resident who had led us to the room.

---

[4] A team "makes rounds" or "rounds" by walking around and seeing all the patients on the service. Dr. Montgomery (later) thought this should be called "squares" since the hospital rooms were in a block. And I just realized why I didn't find that funny then either.

"The chairman will be here soon." He then left.

We exchanged a nervous glance. Even Andy looked a little shell-shocked.

"So, he wants us to gather this stuff *before* rounds?" I asked out loud.

"I guess so."

I looked at the card. "I don't understand what half of these things are. How do you figure out the caloric intake on a preemie?"

No one knew.

We sat in silence for what seemed like hours.

"Should we go *do* something?" one of the female students asked.

"I'm not sure," I offered, studying one of the books in my pocket. I was trying to figure out how to calculate all the data. "This is insane. This will take hours."[5]

"Maybe we could get some breakfast?" another student asked. "There's no one in the office."

"I'll do the hernia surgery today," Andy volunteered. "I'll ace it. I've seen it before."

"Seriously, *hours!*"

We looked around again, too nervous to move.

Andy was getting his swagger on. He could tell I was disturbed and the other students were nervous. He was sure he was going to stand out.

The chairman strode through the suite's main door, walking in with an office worker. He glanced into the office where we all peered out, wide-eyed. He chatted with the office worker for a while, well aware that we were waiting on him but actively and thoroughly not

---

[5] Today, all this data is automatically calculated on the computers. This was also before wide spread hours restrictions on medical student work hours. Kids these days are spoiled. I also had to do my homework on the back of a shovel with a piece of coal.

caring. Then he walked into the office and sat behind that ostentatious desk. He leaned forward.

"We have two fellows on the service. Mark is the senior. He runs the show. He's good. Ryan is the junior fellow. Idiot broke his leg skiing. It's what he gets for taking vacation."

Are we supposed to laugh?

"I realize you are supposed to go to lectures on Wednesdays. Be on time for those."

He had a deep voice, and his white hair bundled around his head and thick neck like a mane. He looked and sounded like Mufasa. I had the uneasy feeling that he could actually kill and eat me.

He went on, alternately leaning forward and back. He gave us a brief history of surgery at the Baby Hospital. He spoke about the other faculty. He waxed into old stories of when he was a resident. We weren't sure if we should be taking notes.

"So remember—if you're on call every other night, it means you're missing half the cases." He sighed with contentment. I think the word *resident* came from doctors back in the day who actually lived in the hospital. Now, residents go home once in a while. Except Mark. I don't think he ever left the Baby Hospital. He certainly couldn't be bothered with things like dinner out, movies, drinks, or charisma classes.

"I'm sure Mark told you about the line score. Get it right."

Chairman Mufasa was ready for his big finish.

"A student asked why I make you get here so early. It's so you can all find good parking spots."

Pause. Were we supposed to laugh? No indication.

"I was asked why I make you stay so late. It's so you don't have to drive home in traffic."

Another pause.

Andy giggled nervously.

Mufasa looked satisfied, like a hanging judge after sentencing someone to the gallows. We were cowed to the point of wetting ourselves.

"That's it."

We paused. He looked down. He looked up again after a second. *Oh, this is the part where we leave.* We realized it all at once and scurried for the door.

"Oh, and finally ..." he said, stopping us in our tracks. "Have fun."

Right.

*   *   *   *

My day on the pediatric surgery service began at three thirty in the morning. I woke up around a quarter to three, showered in a daze, found some scavenged scrubs, put on my short white coat, and foggily drove to the Baby Hospital. I would walk into the dimly lit lobby and see the same short old lady with the same hanging glasses.

She said, "Hello," to me. Every time. The best I could do was muster a tight-lipped smile and say, "Hello," back. I began in the neonatal intensive care unit (NICU) and hand calculated all the data. This was a series of dark rooms (especially at three thirty) filled with incubators for impossibly small alien babies with giant heads and underdeveloped limbs. These babies often weighed less than a pound. It was easy to forget that they were real. They were tremendously brittle. The very act of opening the incubator door could affect their vital signs. Their plastic womb was often heated with a giant light, leading to an eerie orange glow in the room. Some of the babies with high bilirubin[6] lay under blue lights with tiny baby shades covering their eyes.

---

[6] Bilirubin is a product formed from the breakdown of blood cells. It is normally processed by the body and excreted in bile or urine. Babies who cannot do this well may develop *jaundice,* a condition that, if untreated, can cause brain damage. An effective therapy is putting them under a blue "bili" light.

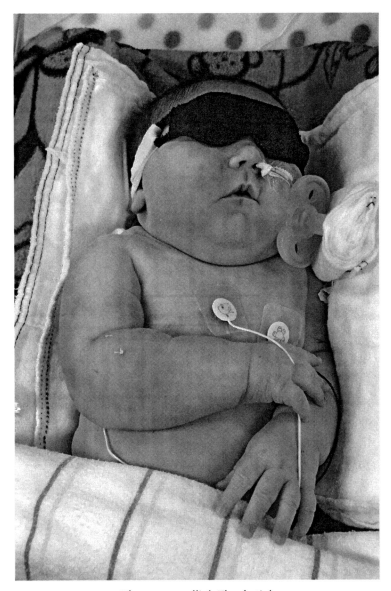

They see me rollin'. They hatin'.

One of my future residents thought the whole scene looked like a cafeteria with warming lights; the little babies reminded him of chicken wings.

I was responsible for calculating the caloric and fluid intake of about five chicken wings every day. This had to be remarkably precise, as a few extra ounces of fluid could throw one of these little gnomes into heart failure. I then recorded the range and current vital signs. After the calculations of the NICU, I repeated the process for the older kids. I had all my cards ready by five and gathered with the team for rounds.

Mark and Ryan had each graduated from a six-year residency and had volunteered to spend two more years training with Chairman Mufasa to become pediatric surgeons. Chairman Mufasa was kind of a big deal in the pediatric surgery world.

Mark was bitter and somewhat broken. On this day, Mark was a few minutes late. Ryan began the rounds when Mark stormed in.

"I'm usually *asked* when rounds start, not *told*," Mark snapped. "First patient?"

That was our cue. Each patient's student popped to the front of the crowd and dashed off the data.

"One twenty to one thirty-five, 132, 45 over 20 to 55 over 27, 24 cc ..."

The line score. Numbers only, no modifiers or comments. Any medical student who screwed this up was instantly met with a glare, a scowl, and a dismissal to the back of the pack. We joylessly marched around the hospital, seeing about sixty patients before seven in the morning. Medical students would recite the data, the residents would quickly scrawl notes, and Mark would scowl at everything.

One morning, we arrived to find that one of the NICU babies had died during the night. One of my classmates had been following the baby, and she took the news hard. Mark glowered at me as I finished my line score. We then moved toward the next incubator, now conspicuously empty. The student began to cry. "She died ..."

Mark glanced at the incubator and then moved on. He veered

slightly to his left, grabbed a small box of tissues, handed it to my classmate, and then fixed his gaze on me for the next line score.

"One forty to one sixty-five …"

After rounds, we headed to the operating room. There, Chairman Mufasa and the other faculty would work with the fellows or residents to do amazingly elaborate surgeries on amazingly tiny babies. It was fascinating. Well, at least I thought it was probably fascinating. I usually was standing behind two other people and couldn't see squat.

Surgery is performed on a "sterile field." The patient is cleansed with antiseptic, positioned, and then draped in an elaborate fashion to block off any bacteria. It seemed that the body's bacterial contents are inversely proportional to rank. Chairman Mufasa was darn near sterile and only had to lightly rinse his hands under water to be ready for gowning. As a third-year student, I was the grossest, dirtiest creature outside of the Flukeman from *X-Files*.[7] I needed to make a huge show of washing every inch of my being before the scrub nurse would deem me worthy of putting on gloves.

The main defender of the mythical sterile field was the scrub nurse. General surgery scrub nurses are hardened soldiers. They had to put up with the ribs and grouses of surgeons like Mark. They viewed me with annoyed suspicion. I knew I had to get on their good side, and the best way to do that was to perfect the art of standing still. They would eye me like a leopard staring at a hidden antelope near the watering hole. They would act all nonchalant or even engaged in the surgery, but the instant I moved, they would pounce.

"The *student* is *contaminated!*" They made sure to announce this loud enough that the head surgeon could hear and be angry.

Surgeries could last up to ten hours. I'm not sure I learned much

---

[7] https://en.wikipedia.org/wiki/The_Host_(The_X-Files). Gross.

about technique, but I did learn that it was possible to fall asleep standing up.

After standing for hours, the student had to instantly be ready for the "pimp question." Unfortunately this was not as fun as it may sound. The answer to the pimp question was generally an arcane piece of medical trivia sometimes germane to the case. If the student answered correctly, he or she was lauded. If the student answered incorrectly, well ...

The pimp question was make-or-break for the medical student. The student would stand dutifully for hours, waiting for the sliver of hope that the attending would ask him or her an answerable question. If you get it right, the attending may ask you another. Knock out a few, and he or she will think you're smart. This exercise was sort of like a pinch hitter for baseball. You spend the entire game on the bench, checking out the crowd, wondering if you could get a hot dog, trying not to fall asleep ... wow, that gal is cute in the third row ...

"Dan!"

Yeagh! Wide awake.

"Yeah, Coach?"

"You're on deck!"

Game on the line, ninth inning, hoping not to puke, walking up to the plate to pinch hit while the ninety-eight-mile-per-hour flamethrower relief pitcher is about to send some chin music and expected to get a hit?

"What's his name again?" Mufasa growled to Mark.

"Dan."

"Dan?"

"Yes, sir?"

"This lady has a problem with her immune system."

Uh-oh ...

Mark interrupted. "Take a look at this."

Mufasa's attention went back to the case. My first pimp question was about immunology? I almost flunked that class! Great.

P equals MD, P equals MD, P equals MD.

The case droned on. Mufasa grew concerned about what Mark had showed him, got busy with the case, and briefly forgot about me. I went back to my now practiced art of standing perfectly still. The scrub nurse eyed me suspiciously.

I began to daydream about what normal people with a normal life were doing. Then I dreamed that Mufasa would ask me a question about something I knew about—like football or the *X-Files*. I fantasized that I would have the guts to be funny. One of my classmates was asked by a vascular surgeon to identify a blood vessel named after some past dead surgeon.

"Whose artery is this?" the surgeon growled, pointing to the eponymous vessel in a female patient.

"Well, it's *hers*," my classmate announced. This led to laughter and a reprieve from further slaughter.

Out of nowhere, Mufasa said, "So, Dan, what do you know about GALT?" He was asking me about the *gut-associated lymphoid tissue.* That's not what I heard. I snapped from my daze and answered, "I usually shoot around an eighty-five. Eighty on a good day."

Mufasa let out a huge belly laugh. "Not *golf*!"

Mark laughed too and instantly regretted this new, scary experience. The scrub nurse laughed mechanically, while still eyeing me suspiciously.

Saved! As with golf—better lucky than good.

Such was my day, up at a quarter to three, blurrily trudging through rounds, standing still for hours at a time, repeating the rounds thing again in the evening, and then getting home around ten at night, crashing, and repeating.

Days blended into nights. Nights blended into days. Each morning, the old lady at the desk said, "Hello"—until one morning.

"How are you, sweetie?" she said.

"Fine, ma'am. Thanks."

"I need to see your ID."

What?

She smiled expectantly.

I checked—short white coat, clueless glassy eyes, shuffling gait. Yep. Everything about me screamed third-year medical student.

"Uh, well. Here." I flashed my badge.

"Okay, have a nice day."

*   *   *   *

Every Wednesday, we met in a small room for didactic lectures over lunch. All of us would fall asleep within about two minutes. At the beginning of the rotation, we hustled for the back of the room, so we wouldn't be caught napping. By the end of the rotation, we had run out of craps to give, and we would just park in the front, spread out, and snore with abandon.

I'd see Sam at those lectures. He was in heaven. Stay there all night? Absolutely! Blood, guts, poop—awesome! Sam couldn't get enough. The general surgeons loved him. Sam had found his home.

I'd also see Sam on-call. For our call nights, we would head to County and spend our time in the emergency room (ER). County was a dilapidated mess, filled with ghosts and cockroaches. The ER had its own jail.[8] It was the haven for the drunk and the criminal. You will never find a more wretched hive of scum and villainy.[9]

The night staff ranged from the neophyte to the ancient. Nurses

---

[8] Not a joke.

[9] Wait ... Obi-Wan said that first? Darn.

were either young and ready to save the world or old enough not to give a single solitary deuce about the misery around them. One intern and two medical students manned the "surgical hallway"—a group of rooms where people needed minor surgical procedures.

One night, the chief surgical resident of the ER was Vinnie. Vinnie had played offensive line for a Division I football program. He was huge. I imagine there was a time when he was in shape. While he kept his strength, he clearly had spent his surgical residency eating. The largest available scrubs were stretched like spandex over his mammoth physique, to the point that when he sat, every wrinkle of his scrotum was intimately visible. Vinnie didn't care.

When residents screw up or offend someone, they get written up. Somebody tattles and fills out a complaint sheet. The resident is usually brought into the boss's office and scolded. Residents could be fired for particularly egregious offenses. Usually, getting written up caused significant consternation for the guilty party. Not Vinnie. The general surgery bosses' got so fed up with the daily complaints about Vinnie that they just accumulated them and met with him once at the end of the month.

"You insulted Nurse Smith."

Vinnie: "That's cause she's a stupid bitch."

"You insulted Nurse Jones."

Vinnie: "She's even dumber!"

"You can't say things like that." The attending sighed.

"The order clearly said to inject the heparin into the f——ing chest tube. She gave it IV. She could have killed him."

"You still can't say things like that."

The only thing that saved Vinnie from certain dismissal was that he was really, really good. Despite his 350-plus-pound size, his hands were as soft as gossamer. He operated with such a deft touch, that by his chief year, the attendings recognized that he was technically

21

superior to them in most surgeries. Once, Vinnie scheduled a very complex chest case that he had never done before. The patient was prepped and asleep, but the attending, for whatever reason, didn't show up.[10] Vinnie broke out a textbook, read for a few minutes, and then perfectly performed the case.

On this night, Vinnie was sitting at the main control desk in the center of the ER. He was joking with the nurses and medics who, in the ER, all loved him.

"Whoa! Look at that dude! He's totally f-d up!" Vinnie bellowed as the medics brought in a drunken trauma patient. The younger surgery residents descended as Vinnie watched, much like a dad would watch his kids play football. Every now and then, he'd shout out an instruction and then go back to gabbing with the nurses.

The patient had a laceration across his thigh that was about a foot long.

"What's your name?" Vinnie demanded.

"Dan, sir."

"*Sir?*" Vinnie and the nurses laughed. "Sir? I'm sitting in a shit hospital, looking at a shit drunk asshole, at one in the morning. Think any *sirs* do that?"

"No, sir!"

Vinnie couldn't tell if I was hopeless or a smartass. "Go sew that dude's leg up."

Okay, I can do this. This is a medical student's dream! The guy was moaning loudly despite having a breathing tube down his throat. I looked for numbing medicine. There was none to be found.

"You done yet, Dan?"

With my pediatric surgery training under the gaze of the stern leopard scrub nurses, I felt like I was a master at cleanliness. Hmmm.

---

[10] It was a different time back then.

Cleanliness was going to be hard with all this blood and—*Oh no*—poop all over the place. I took off the bandage. The wound started to bleed.

"It's bleeding."

"No shit?" Vinnie yelled from his seat without looking up. "Maybe someone should sew it up."

I cleaned it, put on a gown, and then rushed to the sink to meticulously scrub my hands before donning sterile gloves. I scrubbed and scrubbed. I became aware of a giant shadow behind me.

"What are you doing, Dan?"

"Scrubbing, si—I mean Vinnie."

Vinnie nodded and stood motionless as I finished, double-checked that I didn't have any more cooties on me, and then slowly followed the ritual to sterilely wear gloves.

"Very nice, Dan. I'm impressed." Vinnie nodded approvingly.

My heart soared!

"Thanks!"

"That was great scrubbing. Just f-ing great. Now, contaminate yourself."

"What?"

"Contaminate yourself. Get your hands dirty."

The nurses elbowed each other and giggled.

"Here, I'll help." Vinnie took my pristine gloves and wiped them on the bed and on the patient's noncleaned leg. I was aghast but helpless.

"This guy was lying in a ditch for about two hours, drunk off his gourd. There's no way his wound is clean. You did a good job removing the dirt, but his wound is contaminated. There's no way to make it clean. Right now, he's losing blood. He needs the wound closed. We'll put him on antibiotics. Wash it out and sew it up. *Now.*"

Later that night, one of my classmates was called to help a junior resident debride a diabetic rectal abscess. A diabetic rectal abscess is a painful collection of bacteria and hatred, nestled tenderly in an obese person's butt.

It's the foulest-smelling thing on earth.

Imagine a combination of vinegar, rotten eggs, and dead birds. Then take a deep breath and enjoy that intoxicating aroma because that's a rose petal compared to a diabetic rectal abscess. It smells like diarrhea mixed with evil. And the abscesses are horribly painful.

For obvious reasons, the lowest-ranking providers are sent to deal with it. In this case, the patient had long passed the four-hundred-pound mark. He could barely move. My classmate's job was the noble task of holding open the butt cheeks.

"Okay, you're going to feel a stick; then it should feel better," the junior resident said.

My friend braced himself.

The treatment of an abscess is the advanced, modern technique of sticking it with a knife. Experienced residents sit to the side. This resident did not.

"*Oooooowwwwww!*" the patient yelled.

My classmate used a leg to brace open the butt.

The reason the experienced resident sits to the side is that the foul vomitus pus is under pressure—a lot of pressure. Power-wash pressure. Pus squirted out, dousing the resident in a yellow-white shower of hell.

My classmate, losing his battle in ass-spreading, saw the mess, smelled the smell, and promptly vomited. His heave was mighty, and because of his position standing over the resident leaning into the ass cavern, most of the puke hit either the patient's or the resident's leg.

"What the ..." the patient said, feeling the splatter. He could smell the stench and feel the warmth of puke. So he started vomiting. This made the student vomit again. This made the patient vomit again.

Dear God ...

Vinnie looked up from his magazine. "What's going on in there?"

An old nurse sitting beside him sighed deeply. She paged the janitorial service, knowing that they would rush to the scene as soon as they darn well felt like it.

Sam sidled up next to me. "Isn't this great?"

He was serious.

*   *   *   *

I had survived my surgery rotation. On my last day, there was only one last thing to do. I had to ask Chairman Mufasa for a letter of recommendation. Ugh. The only time he really talked to me was that first day and the occasional pimp question.

"He's in there," the secretary said without looking up.

I meekly reentered the office with all the diplomas.

"Sir?"

He looked up from whatever he was reading.

"SirIwaswonderingifIcouldgetaletterofrecommendationforresidency."

He looked puzzled, trying to figure out what I had just said. I saw the light go on. "A letter? Sure." He looked at some memo.

"Are you junior AOA," he asked. AOA or Alpha Omega Alpha is an honors group, like Phi Beta Kappa for medicine. Making AOA as a third-year medical student (junior AOA) is extremely difficult. Less than 1 percent of the class is so honored. Jack and Sam were both junior AOA.

"No."

"Ah. Well, sure. I'll write you a letter. You did a good job on the service Steve."

"My name is …"

He went back to his journal. I was to leave then. I left the Baby Hospital, dead tired and sure that I would never become a surgeon.

CHAPTER 3

Operating with Grandpa P.

General surgery was over, but I had my surgical specialty rotation coming up. After a day off to sleep, I dejectedly trudged toward my next rotation: neurosurgery.

I was the one of two students on the service. We arrived at the neurosurgery office suite at the U and introduced ourselves to the lady at the front desk. She took us to a small conference room, guarded by a full-size skeleton model. It was filled with books and journals. There was a table in the center with a slide projector pointing at a makeshift screen.

The chairman of the neurosurgery department was Grandpa P. He was late. I idled for a few minutes, dreading the coming of another Mufasa. I dejectedly realized, with only two students, there was no place for this antelope to hide from the inevitable pimp questions.

Grandpa P arrived in a tornado of bustle, smiles, and dishevelment. He was carrying a bunch of papers, dropped them haphazardly on the table, and then grabbed my hand in a meaty, two-handed shake.

"Hi, hi! Welcome. Welcome. What's your name? Where you from?"

Grandpa P. was in his late fifties, with thick old-man glasses and an air of comfort. He had a large, genuine smile. Two of his residents followed: Rich and Cam. Grandpa P. introduced Rich; he was chief resident. Cam was the junior. Rich had a big smile and looked somewhat like a younger version of Grandpa P. Cam was tall, twitchy, gangly, and dour.

Grandpa P. asked me about my family, where I was from, and my hobbies. I told him all about the Lovely Wife. He then seamlessly transitioned to a lecture about the initial management of a patient with head trauma. He talked for about an hour. He would pause from the slides, ask us questions, teach us some lessons, and share knowledge as comfortably as if he were showing us how to fish.

"Okay," he said at the conclusion. "Have fun. Let me know if you need anything." Big smile. Strong, double-fisted handshake, and he was off in a blur.

"Okay, guys, let's go," Rich said.

He oriented us to the U and took us around to see the patients.

"What time do we prcround?" I asked.

Rich laughed. "We're not general surgery. *We* can read. We'll meet here at seven."

The next day, I showed up as scheduled, still unsure if I was supposed to gather data or not. I wasn't. Rich, the other student, Cam, Kelly, and I started the day's work. Kelly was a nurse who had seen and done it all. We bounced from patient to patient. Rich and Kelly did all the talking. Cam wrote the note in the chart. It was unstructured, chaotic, and still impressively efficient.

"How you doing, Ms. Smith?"

"Just fine, dear."

"Hold your hands out like you're catching raindrops."

Rich quickly but skillfully examined each patient. Without fail, he made all of them laugh at the end.

We finished rounds, and Rich looked at us. "You guys know what's next?"

Uh-oh, the hammer was about to fall. "Surgery?"

Rich laughed. "Breakfast!"

The surgeries were supposed to start at 7:30. It was now 7:35. Rich could see my mental conflict. "We've got time," he reassured me.

After breakfast, we headed to the operating room where Rich was scheduled to assist Grandpa P. in a spine surgery. It was the resident's job to prepare the patient for surgery. We waited for the anesthesiologist to put the patient to sleep and establish the lines in the arteries and veins, and then a nurse would place a catheter in the bladder. For back surgery, we would then flip the patient in the facedown position on a specially designed table.

Lying facedown is surprisingly dangerous. It doesn't take long for a patient's skin to break down. If there is too much pressure, part of the body could be damaged. The anesthesiologists are quite paranoid about pressure over the eyes, as permanent blindness can occur. For males, if the penis gets trapped under the body or if there is too much tension on the catheter, the penis can, well, *die*. Therefore, the final move before prepping the patient is the all-important "junk check."

Rich then prepped the back with antiseptic and headed out to the sinks to scrub. I followed. I began to scrub, with the meticulous dedication to removing at least two layers of skin that I learned on general surgery. Rich was amused.

"That's probably good. Grandpa P. will like it."

We went into the room, and Rich began the elaborate draping process preferred by Grandpa P. Most surgeons use a few drapes to block out the sterile field. Grandpa P.'s draping routine was as artistic as it was complicated—down sheet, up sheet, side sheet, side sheet, four towels then sticky, up sheet a second time, two "wings," down sheet a second time, and drape.

The residents tried to see how fast they could drape his patients without allowing a wrinkle in the sheets. As we draped, Grandpa P.

began to scrub his hands. He scrubbed long and passionately, splashing water around the sink like a toddler in a tub. He entered, smiling and dripping.

"Hello, hello!" he tooted, clearly smiling beneath his mask. "Everybody ready?"

A nurse placed a light on his head. Many surgeons wear a headlight—a light source that shines directly where the eyes focus. Grandpa P.'s light was first generation, meaning I think it was powered by coal or steam or fireflies or something.

The surgery commenced. Grandpa P. liked to get his face right down near the patient. This surgery was done through an incision about six inches long. Rich then began a practiced, nuanced dance. He bobbed and weaved, rhythmically swaying from side to side, balancing on one foot, and somehow sashayed his way to seeing the operative site around Grandpa P.'s head. Grandpa P's head movements were brutal and violent. An unsuspecting resident less facile with the dance would be on the receiving end of a surprisingly painful head butt.

"Cut. Not there, right here!" Grandpa P. instructed, as Rich swerved to see around the boss's head. He tilted, leaned hard to one side, and reached his right hand as far as his elbow would allow to finally cut the right thing.

"Good, good."

Rich made it look easy. He danced around Grandpa P. like a bird darting in and out of the mouth of a crocodile. Rich made everything look easy. And he smiled and joked the whole time.

Rich and Grandpa P. gabbed like old ladies. They talked about golf, the day's news, and whatever antic the Professor was up to at the time. Every now and then, Grandpa P. would yell, "Cut right here!" and Rich would pirouette around the giant head and headlight, snip what needed to be snipped, and continue the procedure. It was a ballet with two masters.

I assumed the position of my well-honed skill of standing perfectly still. Grandpa P. was having none of it.

"Okay, this is called the lamina."

Oh my, he wants me to look in the wound! I soon found out that looking around Grandpa P.'s head was much harder than Rich made it look. I craned my neck and balanced.

"And this is the nerve root. Say, where did you say you were from?"

I told him my hometown.

"And where did you go to college?"

"Golden U."

"Whoa!" Rich and Grandpa P. stopped, looked at me, looked at each other, and then laughed.

"Golden U? They suck this year!" Rich laughed, referring to a rough patch for my college football team. "You lost to Northwestern!"

Ouch. I see it's time for the gloves to come off. Chairman of the department or not, nobody *insults my team.*

"Where did you go to college?" I asked.

Rich answered with the name of a local but nationally known school that specialized in engineering and veterinary medicine.

"Do you know at your school that they don't teach driver's ed and sex ed on the same day?"

"No … why?"

"The horse gets too tired."

"*Ouch!*"

Rich and Grandpa P. laughed.

The rest of the rotation went much the same way. The next day, Rich and I joined the Professor in his case. I found out then that every resident could mimic the Professor's distinctive voice.

"How are you, Professor?"

"Oh, I am faaaaaaabulous," he said.[11]

Everyone said hi to the Professor. We all scrubbed in. I positioned myself a little closer to the action.

"Who's this?" the Professor asked, pointing at me.

"This is Dan. He went to Golden U," Rick said.

"You guys *suck*! You lost to Northwestern."

Blood pressure rising …

The Professor laughed in a wholly unexpected, high-pitched *"Heeheeheeheehee!"*

Rich laughed too.

The Professor operated in a completely different way than Grandpa P. Grandpa P. made each movement with short, controlled precision. It was quite obvious that every move he made was exactly the same as he had done a thousand times before. The Professor operated like Grandpa P. scrubbed—arms flailing, *attacking* the surgery. Rich could navigate the Professor's movements as easily as he could with Grandpa P.

Rich performed the surgery while the Professor made wisecracks to the nurses. Rich did an elegant, efficient job. Even I, as an unseasoned student, could appreciate how smoothly he operated.

The Professor brusquely grabbed an instrument, jabbed it in the wound, and bit off a large piece of bone.

"You know what that was, young man?" he asked me, holding up the instrument containing the remnants of a bone spur. "*That* was the bite that cured him. *Heeheeheeheehee!*"

He turned to Rich. *"Close!"*

Rich handed me the needle driver and the suture. The Professor scrubbed out and began to flirt with all the nurses.

"How are you, darling?"

---

[11] Not high, flamboyant, *Fabulous* fabulous. More like what Eeyore would say after finding his tail.

"Fine, Professor. How are you?"

"I. Am. Faaaaaaaaabulous."

Later in the rotation, Rich and I went to the preoperative area to prepare a young girl for surgery. She was twenty-something and gorgeous in a librarian sort of way. She had a soft but athletic appearance. Over the past month, she'd noticed some trouble moving her right hand. Nothing big. It's just that she seemed to fumble things—buttons, forks, and the TV remote. Then she had a little trouble finding the right words to say.

Initially, she thought it was no big deal. But it kept happening. She felt like something was wrong. She saw her primary care doctor, who quite reasonably asked her about stress at work. She was just out of graduate school and trying to make it in a business that was (is) a boys' club. She worked long hours. She sacrificed her social life. She fought for respect every day. Stress seemed logical.

Then she had a grand mal seizure.[12]

Seizures are surprisingly common; they will occur in about one out of one thousand people. A seizure starts when a part of the brain gets irritated, short-circuits, and then releases an electrical power surge. If the surge spreads to the whole brain, the patient will lose consciousness. Most seizures stop within seconds. If a seizure continues for more than a few minutes, it may cause permanent brain damage. Most seizures are relatively harmless but look scary. Prior generations likely thought a seizure patient was demon-possessed.

In her case, the seizure moved the diagnostic consideration from stress to something much more sinister. The primary care doctor ordered an MRI. This coldly showed an inoperable brain tumor.

Our job was to get a piece of it. It was deep and intertwined with

---

[12] A focal seizure involves part of the brain, and the person may stay awake. A grand mal seizure involves the whole brain, causing a loss of consciousness and often shaking throughout the body.

parts of her brain that kept her conscious. Her treatment options were possibly chemotherapy or radiation therapy. However, we couldn't subject her to the poisonous effects of either of those therapies without being completely sure of the diagnosis. Our job was to do a biopsy, extract a small piece, and send it to the pathologist.

Passing a needle into the deep recesses of the brain is no mean feat. We had to plan passage of the needle through parts of the brain that control movement and speech, while avoiding important blood vessels. At the time, the best way to do this was to attach a frame to the patient's head, get a CT scan, and use a computer to plot the trajectory. This is called a *stereotactic biopsy*, and the frame process was pioneered by a Swedish doctor with the awesome comic book villain name of Lars Leksell.[13]

The frame creates an X, Y, and Z space based on geometry. A target is chosen. The frame shows up on a CT scan. By measuring the distance to the target in each dimension, a trajectory and depth of the probe is calculated. The frame is attached directly to the head of the patient with screws.[14]

Rich explained this to the patient, who had a glaze of resigned terror in her eyes. I held the frame while Rich used a long needle to inject numbing medicine. She winced. We then systematically began turning the screws to an alarmingly tight degree, puncturing her skin and then drilling directly into her skull. I thought we would crack her head. We finished. She courageously thanked us (*thanked us?*), but she clearly had tears in her eyes.

"I'm sorry, I'm sorry," she whimpered, fanning herself. "It's just …"

It's just what? It's just that you are a beautiful, talented young

---

[13] He could operate on your brain and bend metal with just his mind.
[14] The technology has improved so much that now we can do the same thing with just a few stickers instead of the somewhat medieval frame.

woman whose life has just been turned upside down and now a doofus like me is screwing a metal harness into your head? That?

That.

Rich comforted her with an easy smile. "I know, that sucks. The worst part is over." He held her hand gently, and she seemed a bit relieved that we didn't think less of her. She went through the scanner and then to the operating room. She was put to sleep, and we began the operation.

Rich made everything look so easy. She was positioned and draped. Rich placed a tiny incision in a small area where we had clipped her hair. He exposed about two inches of her skull.

"Here," he said, handing me a pneumatic drill.

I looked at him skeptically. I was at the level where my classmate puked in the County surgical hallway treating a butt abscess—not at the level of brain surgery!

"Push this button and hold it steady. Whatever you do, don't let go."

Okay.

"Oh, and don't plunge into her brain."

Super.

Well, here goes nothing.

I grabbed the drill, held it like he instructed, and hit the button. It was hard to control. I can see why he warned me not to let go; it shook so much that my hands hurt. He knew my instinct was to let go, so he kept repeating, "Keep going! Keep going!"

I was pretty sure I was too deep. This was taking way too long.

"Keep going."

Now I was sure I'd see the end of the drill come out her chin.

"Keep going. Now—don't plunge!"

I was sweating, partly because this was hard work and partly because I was terrified I was about to kill my first patient. Suddenly the whole thing jerked to a stop. I was sure I had broken it and would get cast into the surgical hallway at County forever.

Rich laughed. He then explained that the drill was designed to stop the instant it got through the skull. There was very little chance of me plunging. I looked at the hole I had created. It was not nearly as big as I'd thought. I could see a few bone fragments that Rich quickly removed. Then I could see the robin's-egg-blue color of the *dura,* the outer covering over the brain. Rich cut through this with a very precise knife.

By this time, the Professor walked in.

Rich positioned the frame, passed the needle, sucked out a few millimeters of tumor, and then we waited. Now we would send that little fragment to the pathologist who would tell us if we sucked out tumor or normal brain. We waited with the needle in the patient's brain. It took about twenty-five minutes.

Rich and I sat down, arms folded so as not to contaminate our gloved hands. The Professor muttered something to himself and then personally walked the specimen to the pathology lab. He liked to look through the microscope himself.[15]

"All right," Rich said. "We've got time. This is the time where the medical student tells us a joke."

"What?"

"We've got some time to kill. So tell us a joke—or sing, if you prefer."

Well, I certainly wasn't about to sing. I told the two best jokes I knew that wouldn't get me a trip to the dean's office. I had broken the ice. Rich and I began to talk, and we discovered that we had a lot in common. In a few minutes, we were laughing and joking like we were sitting at a sports bar.

---

[15] A skill that, sadly, surgeons in my generation and after have lost.

The Professor returned. "It's malignant," he said.

Silence.

"That's too bad." He left the room.

Rich and I finished the surgery in silence.

CHAPTER 4

The Old Dogs

I met the entire neurosurgery faculty over the course of the month. I spent most of my time with Grandpa P. The Professor spent most of his time at County. That seemed natural. It seemed like he would fit in with Vinnie.

Grandpa P. replaced the Old Man as the chairman of the department. The Old Man was one of three doctors who built modern neurosurgery at our university. These three were the Old Dogs.

The first Old Dog (Dr. Mason) was tall and gruff and helped mold the Professor. He had a direct training lineage to Harvey Cushing, the father of neurosurgery. Cushing was a noted scholar, legendary surgeon, accomplished artist, and spectacular dick.[16] Dr. Mason had trained at Harvard and was one of the pioneers in brain tumor treatment. The second Old Dog (Dr. King) was the first neurosurgeon in the state to specialize in treating children. He was gentle and classy. Dr. King had to work a second job when he started as a neurosurgeon, as he had difficulty supporting a family with the grand salary of $9,000.[17]

The main Old Dog was the Old Man, who bore more than just a

---

[16] Rumor has it a group of his original trainees would meet once a year after his death just to pee on his grave. Ouch, man.

[17] I doubt I'll bring this up during our next contract negotiations.

passing resemblance to Mr. Magoo. He was a boxer for the army at, I think, ninety-five pounds. He was a small and wiry octogenarian. He would greet people with an uncomfortably hard smack on the back, muttering, "Okay, okay, eh, eh," and smiling in the way old people smile. The Old Man had practiced in a time unencumbered by rules and regulations, where surgeons tried and did everything. Anything we do in surgery today is based on the lessons learned by the cowboys from the Old Dogs' generation.[18]

Every surgery has a risk of complications. Operate enough, and there will be infections, bleeding, and damage to things you don't want to damage. That's just the nature of surgery. All the greatest complications in our university's history somehow, someway, involved the Old Man.

Every few years, doctors treating head trauma get all jazzed about iatrogenically[19] cooling the brain for therapy. There are stories of people falling in frozen rivers and somehow surviving when they, by all reason, should have drowned. Perhaps, it was thought, the cold protects the brain. Cold has been shown to protect the body in other disciplines, most notably in cardiac surgery. Despite the fact that this makes a lot of sense, putting active cooling in practice has not been proven helpful and may, in fact, be dangerous.

Early in the process, the Old Man decided he wanted to cool a trauma victim's head. It was winter, so he logically stuck the top half of the bed (with the patient in it) out the County room window. At another point, he hooked a football helmet up to refrigerator coils and placed it on a patient. Unfortunately it worked so well that the patient got frostbite bad enough to require skin grafts. This really was a time of frontier medicine.

---

[18] Dr. King experimented with a procedure called a *cingulotomy* and controlled ablation of parts of the brain for psychiatric disease. This was very off the beaten path at the time. Now, the most cutting-edge neurosurgery is working on the exact same thing he did decades ago.

[19] *Deliberately* in medical-speak.

The Professor was the Old Man's prodigy. Just like the Old Man, the Professor had some glorious complications. When the Professor was a resident, he was called to see a poor young gal who had been in a car accident. She had a piece of glass cut through her sciatic nerve. This is the major nerve that runs down the back of the leg to the foot. Without a working sciatic nerve, the foot is useless.

The young Professor and the Old Man went to work and sewed the nerve back together. One major principle of peripheral nerve repair is that it must be relaxed when it heals. It can't be stretched or under tension. So the Old Man wanted her casted with her knee and hip bent. To do this, he instructed the young Professor to get a broomstick. This isn't a euphemism for some surgical tool; he sent him to the janitor's closet to get a broom.

The Old Man cut off the bristles, leaving about a four-foot piece of wood. He tied one end to the foot and the other to her waist. He then plastered casting material around all of it, fixating her leg in the appropriate position.

"Eh, eh, now go get a saw."

"What?" the young Professor asked.

"A cast saw. A cast saw."

"For what?"

"How's she gonna shit?" the Old Man asked.

Young Professor got a cast saw. He began to cut out a chunk of the cast to allow access to the perineal area. That's a fancy way of saying he sawed out her junk. But in the process, the saw blade nicked her vagina. It was a tiny nick, but she bled profusely.

"*Ohhhh*! You've killed her! You've killed her!" the Old Man shouted. "Make sure you present that at M&M.[20] Tell everyone a neurosurgeon sliced off someone's vagina."

---

[20] *Morbidity and mortality,* a conference where doctors present complications. Stay tuned.

It was sometimes hard to believe that the Professor was ever a neophyte like me. As a medical student, I was alternately awed and amused by the Professor. It was almost unfathomable that there was time when he was a junior resident.

The Old Man replaced a neurosurgeon who, unfortunately, seemed to go off the deep end later in his career. Young Professor was assigned to that attending. The attending was doing an experimental procedure for headaches. The procedure involved opening the coverings over the spinal cord (*dura*, just like the brain), finding the parts of the spinal nerves that control sensation, and cutting them. It sounds like a bad idea now. I think it sounded like a bad idea then.

Young Professor assisted on one of these cases, hoping to cure a young woman of headaches. After the surgery, she learned the real meaning of pain. At the end of the surgery, the young Professor wanted to suture close the dura. The attending insisted that this step was unnecessary. To be fair, other surgeons have said the same thing. They're wrong.

One needs to close the dura, because this holds in the patient's spinal fluid. Predictably, the patient began to leak spinal fluid. She was miserable and soon developed meningitis, an infection of the meninges, the full covering over the brain or spinal cord. The dura is one of the three layers of the meninges.

Distraught and questioning his instruction, the young Professor sought the counsel of the Old Man.

"Eh, eh, just don't let him kill her."

Great advice. The attending began writing orders that just didn't make sense.

"Eh, eh, just don't let him kill her."

Young Professor was baffled. He then wrote one of the greatest orders in the history of neurosurgery.

He wrote, "Do NOT obey any orders from Dr _____."

It's hard to overstate the amount of guts it takes for a first-year resident to hand-write an order for all to see, basically nullifying any input from a senior surgeon and recent chairman of the department. Young Professor's guts probably saved that poor girl's life.

The Professor and the Old Man had a relationship that went beyond student-teacher. I always thought the Old Man took a bit of a fatherly role, as the Professor's dad died at a too early age. The Professor wouldn't talk about things like that, but I could tell by the way he revered the Old Man that their bond was special.

In the Professor's first year of practice, he evaluated a six-hundred-pound patient in poor health[21] with leg and back pain. The patient was too big to fit in any scanner to see what was going on. Baffled, he sought the wise advice of his colleagues. All told him not to do anything—all except the Old Man.

"Well, I'd open up the back and explore L5 to S1 with a laminectomy." This means a large incision, wading down through half a foot of fat, and then drilling off the backbone of the spine in hopes of finding an explanation. Miserable.

"If I didn't find anything there, I'd go up to L4 to 5 and do the same thing. Then L3 to 4 if need be."

This sounded horrible to the Professor.

"I don't feel comfortable doing that. I guess I'll just send him to you."

"Eh, eh, well, in that case, I wouldn't do anything."

I kind of wondered why they kept the Old Man around after his surgical days were over. He always seemed on the verge of falling asleep and rarely seemed to be listening. But I realized that he had a wealth of knowledge and experience that, every now and then, would come out. During a conference, one of the residents presented a rare and interesting case.

---

[21] Duh.

A quite prim and proper gent from the private group in town was in attendance. He was a noted and feared vascular surgeon who had trained at the same institution. He was in his sixties and not far from retirement.

The Old Man seemed to wake up a little as the resident finished his presentation. Then he turned to the vascular surgeon and said, "Didn't you make a poster presentation about a similar case when you were a third-year student? What did we do then?"

The vascular surgeon looked bemused, then confused, and then had a dawning of a memory long forgotten. "That's right! I remember the case!"

He was remembering a single presentation from this guy from thirty years earlier. His body was failing, but that mind was razor sharp.

I loved the conferences. These were attended by most of the medical students who were interested in pursuing neurosurgery as a career. I got to know the other students. One of them was Steve, who looked like he should be finding clues with Blue. Steve was about my height, but somehow always felt either taller or shorter. For an average height, he had ridiculously large hands and spindly arms. His voice was way too deep for his body. Steve was a year behind me in school, and we became fast friends.

All the Old Dogs would show up to the graduation and neurosurgical dinners. We invited guest lecturers in their honor. They molded the generation who molded me. I met with Dr. King years after his retirement. He walked with a walker and in a great deal of pain. He slowly told me stories about the old days. The Baby Hospital was different then. It was purely funded by the state, as people in those times felt charging a fee to take care of children was impolite. There were no real specialists in pediatric medicine. Adult doctors, even the private-practice ones, took their turn caring for the "invalid and infirmed." Unable to support his family on the princely $9,000-a-year salary, Dr. King hired his services out to the nearby veterans hospital. He built neurosurgery at the Baby Hospital and established pediatric neurosurgery as a legitimate specialty in the state.

He then began to train others. He took his first fellow, a quirky genius who eventually inherited his mantle as the soul of the Baby Hospital. That surgeon's name was Thomas.

CHAPTER 5

Thomas

I followed Cam into the operating room. The patient—a young, pretty woman who looked to be about thirty—was already asleep. Her legs were drawn up in a peculiar fashion and looked way too small for her already petite body. Cam tried to position her, but she was stiff as a board. He muttered something to himself. The anesthesiologist, meanwhile, was trying in vain to get a reliable intravenous line. He too was muttering.

"Did you page Thomas?" Cam asked gruffly.

"Yes," answered the scrub tech. The scrub nurse was already gowned and busily organizing things on the back table.

"What kind of shunt do you want?"

"I don't know; we'll have to ask Thomas."

Cam continued to try to move the patient, which only frustrated the anesthesiologist.

"Let me get this line first."

Cam sighed in exasperation, audibly enough for the anesthesiologist to hear.

"You want her asleep, right?" The message was clear: "Let me do my job."

The room seemed tense, and as usual, I just felt in the way.

"You did call him, right?"

"*Yes!*"

"Well—"

The door was flung open, and Thomas entered, in a frenetic flurry of skinny arms and elbows, with a surgical mask vainly trying to contain a bushy unkempt goatee that, in turn, covered a number of facial scars. Thomas was personified Brownian motion—constantly and randomly flitting from place to place. He beamed with an inescapably contagious enthusiasm. He was constantly in motion, both in gangly limbs and in mouth. Jack Skellington on speed. Thomas had high Nordic cheekbones and a taut face. He would look perfectly in place on the Iron Throne or in a homeless shelter. He smiled with his whole body. I thought he was a skinny Santa Claus.

As soon as he walked in, the room became brighter. The masked scowls became smiles.

"Sorry I paged you twice, Doctor."

"It's okay. I was hoping it was you and not my wife. At least *you* aren't asking me for money," Thomas said, eliciting a giggle. He paused and grew stern. "You *aren't* asking for money, are you?"

"No."

"How are you?" Cam asked.

"I'm just *lovely,*" Thomas said, surmising that anesthesia was having trouble getting a line. The patient was named Brittany, and she was an adult with spina bifida. She had had IVs since infancy, and all her veins were long since scarred. Thomas grabbed an IV kit, felt around gently on her spastic foot, and then smoothly popped in the needle. "Here you go!" Thomas had such a natural kindness about him that the anesthesiologist saw this as an act of helping, not as trying to show him up.

"How's Mister Smith?" Thomas asked Cam, referencing another patient on the unit.

"His spinal fluid grew *E. coli* and other anaerobes," Cam said. In other words, that patient had an infection from bacteria normally found in poop.

"I *thought* he was a shithead," Thomas mused.

With the IV started, the anesthesiologist finished his preparation and Thomas moved the patient. She had had prior scoliosis surgery, like many spina bifida patients. Somehow, Thomas had no problems getting her in the proper position. I began to wonder why Cam was having so much trouble.

"Don't shave too much hair. I don't want our incision to be her rate-limiting step at the singles' bar!"

Cam sighed. Thomas had a full and genuine laugh. When Thomas was happy, one-liners, quips, and bad puns came pouring out in a furious word salad.

"Do you want a Foley?" the nurse asked, wondering if we should place a catheter in the patient's bladder. Thomas didn't hear.

"Thomas, do you want a Foley?"

"Yes, please. And how about placing one in the patient too?"

The nurse giggled. Cam sighed again.

Cam began to cleanse the patient with surgical soap. Thomas sat down.

"Oh, I'm such a *sluggo*!" He sighed. Thomas was perpetually tired. Sleep was a passing fancy that other people enjoyed. He looked at me. "I'd try to get another job, but I'm not qualified to do anything else."

We went out to the sink to scrub. Thomas was meticulous about his hands. He wasn't so meticulous about his scrubs, which looked like they hadn't been changed in a week. Rarely can someone wear a shirt with both a blood and ketchup stain and have it not look out of place. Thomas's whole persona was one of chaos. I assumed his scrubs were changed once they could be described as "soaked." Haircuts and beard trims were accomplished on a quarterly basis.

Thomas had an ability to make the hardest concepts easy and the easiest concepts hard. As a trainee, Thomas found an abandoned closet in the hospital. He began to fill it floor to ceiling with books. Once, he was challenged about this: "Thomas, when are you ever going to read all these books?"

"Oh," Thomas replied, "these are the ones I've already read."

Residents are expected to take and pass a national written exam before graduation. Usually, the residents take this examination as an upper-level trainee. Thomas took it in his first six months of residency and recorded one of the highest scores in the history of the program.

Thomas was cursed with the disability of genius. His parents were both exquisitely educated. In fact, his father had been a physicist who may have worked on a little project that would go on to impact the world.

Yeah, that *project.*

His dad would never speak of it, but his life was later destroyed by depression and alcoholism. Suicide was rampant in Thomas's ancestry. Thomas himself was affected, and I always kind of thought he was abused as a baby. Despite his skinny frame, Thomas's head was ridiculously large. Sometimes extra fluid around the front of the brain in an infant can lead to an outlandishly large head. This can occur in babies who suffered abuse. I never directly asked him about it, but I always wondered what we would find if we put him in the CT scanner.

Thomas loved chess and was a master. He collected chess books from all over the world. Sometimes, he would buy books in languages that he didn't know. He then did what any supergenius would do—he learned the language so he could read his book.

While trivial concepts such as neurobiology, physiology, language, physics, and chess came easily to Thomas, he was baffled by the mundane. Thomas had his comfort zone, which included the hospital and that's it. I'd like to say his home was a comfort zone, but really it was the opposite.

Thomas had trouble with money. To him, money was an abstraction that seemed to be confusingly important to a variety of people in his family. Thomas's idea of retirement savings was playing the lottery. Asked about investments, Thomas said, "All my money is in consumer goods," a nicer way of saying, "Other people spend all my money at the mall."

Thomas hated to travel outside of his comfort zone. Years after I met him, I accompanied him on a trip to a national meeting held in Orlando. Steve and I walked Thomas to the plane, helped him find his seat, gave him a chess book to keep him occupied, told him where the bathroom was—*Wait ... Is this a brain surgeon or my five-year-old?*—helped him off the plane, walked him to the luggage pickup and then to the curb to await transport to the hotel. The bellhop handed us a Disney pager. It was as big as a pancake with an obscenely happy

Mickey surrounded by a Christmas string of gauche lights. Thomas stared at it with a fierce, unblinking intensity.

"Do you think it went off?" he asked, worried that he'd miss his ride.

"No, Thomas."

A few minutes of staring later, "Was that it?"

"No, Thomas. You'll know when it goes off."

A few anxious minutes later, "Was *that* it?"

Maybe I could find him some crayons.

After about ten minutes, the pager exploded in an orgasm of lights, vibration, and a shockingly loud mechanical chorus of "It's a Small World."

"That's it!" Steve and I hustled him to the cab, gave the driver a tip, and told him to walk Thomas directly to the desk.

Thomas was also cursed with the rare disease of altruism. Because of this, his patients *loved* him. Thomas gave all his patients his personal pager and phone number. He told them to call him whenever there was a problem. He was a pediatric neurosurgeon by training but seemed to collect all the tough adult patients with "pediatric" problems. This included adults with spina bifida. Adult surgeons were usually not comfortable dealing with these patients, so they all came to Thomas. Like this Brittany today.

As Cam draped the gal, he asked Thomas about another complex patient.

"We got called about Scott Jones, a thirty-five-year-old *myelo*[22] with a shunt ..." Cam started.

"Is this the guy with a catheter in the right lateral ventricle teed into a valve and another posterior fossa catheter coming from the left? Maybe a programmable valve set to 120 with a siphon guard?

---

[22] Short for *myelomeningocele*, the open spinal defect in babies with spina bifida.

Lives in Plymouth with his mom and works as a teacher's aide in the high school? Really into Sinatra? He's had seventeen prior shunt revisions?"

Cam thought for a second. "Yes—"

"Never heard of him."

Cam sighed again.

This was my introduction to Thomas. I liked him instantly.

*   *   *   *

The surgery was to revise (fix) the patient's shunt, Thomas's specialty. Thomas had some mystical power to attract patients with shunt problems. He was the Pied Piper of Shuntland.

The body perpetually creates cerebrospinal fluid (CSF). This fluid bathes the brain and spinal cord, providing support and protection and facilitating nourishment. The CSF is formed, circulates through four chambers of the brain (two lateral ventricles, a third ventricle, and a fourth ventricle), travels around the spinal cord, and then works its way around the outside of the brain where it is reabsorbed in the veins. The body makes, circulates, reabsorbs, and replaces all the CSF about three or four times a day.

There are certain conditions that cause the CSF to build up. Very rare tumors from the choroid plexus (the frond-like structures that make much of the spinal fluid) make the body overproduce fluid, overwhelming the ability to reabsorb it. Other conditions, such as infection or hemorrhage, gum up the small channels that reabsorb the fluid. Finally, there are a few narrow pathways that bottleneck the flow. A particularly narrow channel connects the third ventricle to the fourth ventricle. A small mass or tumor can easily block this channel, which is typically about one-seventh of an inch wide. If CSF begins to back up, it will eventually put pressure on the surrounding brain. If the pressure is high enough, the brain will start to get squished, a condition that, by and large, isn't good.

The brain stem is the very basic lower part of the brain that controls many of the automatic functions of the body. These things include breathing, maintaining blood pressure, and being awake. If the brain stem is rapidly squished, patients will die. The brain can compensate to a point if the pressure buildup is gradual. If the pressure is not quite enough to kill, it may still affect the brain, causing intellectual delay or blindness. In babies, the pressure may cause the head to grow to grotesque sizes. The buildup of fluid and hence pressure is called *hydrocephalus.*[23]

Surgeons can treat hydrocephalus by placing a shunt. A shunt is a set of tubing that basically allows fluid to drain to somewhere else in the body. A shunt has three basic parts: (1) a proximal tube that goes into a CSF space, (2) a valve that regulates the flow and prevents backflow, and (3) a distal tube that goes somewhere else in the body. There are many choices for this tube, but most commonly it is placed in the peritoneal space, the space in the belly that surrounds the stomach and intestines. The fluid travels through the proximal catheter, then the valve, then the distal part to collect in the abdomen where the body reabsorbs it. The three parts of a shunt are simple in concept, but there may be hundreds of variations.

There are a number of choices of valves. All have the basic purpose of preventing either too much drainage or backflow from the abdomen to the brain. Draining too much fluid too quickly may cause severe headaches or even be fatal. Draining too little fluid may not treat the problem. To flow, the pressure pushing the CSF out of the head must be a little bit greater than the resistance of the valve and wherever the distal catheter goes. Valves may have a fixed resistance

---

[23] *Hydro-* means "water" and *cephalus* means "head."

or be "programmable," where the resistance can be set or changed with a handheld magnet device. Valves may have different features, such as a resistance that changes with the position of the patient, adding more resistance if the patient is upright and reducing the resistance if the patient is lying down.

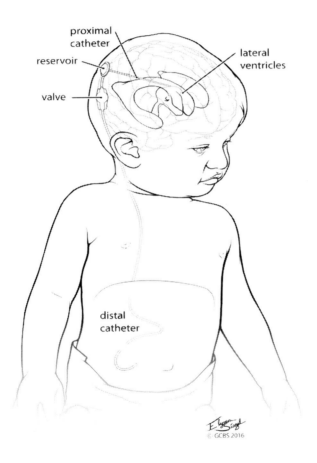

Shunts—the life-saving device for patients and bane of adult neurosurgeons.

Thomas was a master at sorting out exactly which variation a given patient needed.

Shunts are lifesaving. In fact, neurosurgeon Harold Rekate said,

"The development of the valve-regulated shunt has led to the saving of more lives and the protection of function for more patient-years than any other procedure done by neurosurgeons." Spine surgery may make a patient's back pain get better, but shunts *save lives*. So clearly, every neurosurgeon would want shunt surgery to be a major part of his or her practice? Right?

Wrong.

Shunt surgery is treated with all the respect of removing dog poop from the lawn. It has to be done, but it sure would be nice if an underpaid worker did it instead of the bourgeois master of the house. The underpaid worker was Thomas, and the bourgeoisie were the adult surgeons.

When I initially realized that all the fancy-pants adult neurosurgeons treated shunts with disdain, I thought it was because the procedure was sort of beneath them. Super-important spine or brain surgeons couldn't be bothered with mundane plumbing. As I progressed, I realized that they were really terrified of shunt surgery and would go to almost comical lengths to avoid these cases. Shunt surgery can only make the surgeon look bad. If one shows a postoperative image of a completely resected tumor or an expertly clipped aneurysm, then the surgeon looks good, puffs out his chest, and goes about his day as the single most important human who ever lived. But if you show a well-placed shunt, well, that's what you were supposed to do. If your postoperative image shows a poorly placed shunt, then you are met with scorn and ridicule by other puffed-up neurosurgeons.[24]

Shunts fail. A lot. Anything that can go wrong with a shunt has gone wrong with a shunt. I'm not sure why, but they tend to fail mostly at midnight on the weekend. A shunt failure may be fatal. So the shunt surgeon must operate emergently.

---

[24] Experienced shunt surgeons will simply sigh with a resigned, I've-done-that-too look.

One of the seminal papers in modern pediatric neurosurgery is the "shunt design" trial published by Kestle and Drake et al. in 1998.[25] This study rigorously compared three different types of shunt valves to see if any one was better. As it turns out, they all sucked. Shunts will get infected 5 to 10 percent of the time. A shunt infection is a serious, even life-threatening problem. Over the course of two years, *half* of all shunts will fail and require another surgery. A shunt is a lifelong commitment.

I was recently at a meeting where noted pediatric neurosurgeon A. Leland Albright gave a talk about shunts. Dr. Albright is a giant of neurosurgery and a certifiable curmudgeon. He had polled a number of the other most famous pediatric neurosurgeons. All had twenty-five or more years of surgical experience. All were well known and well respected. His talk was sobering. They all used different shunt systems. They placed the shunts in different anatomical locations. They used different methods to place the shunt. There was basically no consensus in how to shunt patients among the best, brightest, and most experienced surgeons in the country.

Shunt surgery does not pay well. Shunt patients are also often disadvantaged, poor, and disabled. They often come from poverty. Doctors are paid by a system that measures relative value units (RVUs).[26] This is a system designed to measure how much work a doctor does. Shunt surgery is ridiculously undervalued. A lifesaving, middle-of-the-night, pants-wetting emergency surgery is valued about one-fifth as much as an hour-long neck surgery for arm numbness.

Shunt patients are complicated and often have many other medical

---

[25] J. Drake, J. Kestle, R. Milner, G. Cinalli, F. Boop, J. Piatt, S. Haines, S. Schiff, D. Cochrane, P. Steinbok, and N. MacNeil, "Randomized Trial of Cerebrospinal Fluid Shunt Valve Design in Pediatric Hydrocephalus," *Neurosurgery* 1998 Aug; 43 no. 2 (1998): 294–303.

[26] The number of RVUs for a particular procedure is determined by your federal government.

issues. Adult spina bifida patients have limited mobility, scoliosis, Chiari malformation, bowel and bladder issues, and many develop obesity. They have a high rate of complications and infections. Shunt surgery is for the gluttons, the altruists, and the bleeding-heart fools. Shunt surgery was for Thomas.

Thomas happily accepted anybody as a patient. He cared for the downtrodden. He never looked at insurance status or performed the disturbingly common "wallet biopsy" to see if he'd get paid for treating them. He *loved* his patients. He treated them with respect and dignity. He placed their concerns well above his own.

*   *   *   *

Surgery seemed to go well. Thomas was paged incessantly through the case. Cam's pager remained disturbingly quiet in comparison.

Beeeeeeeeeeeep!

"Oh, I hope that's good news," Thomas moaned.

It wasn't.

Beeeeeeeeeeeeep!

"Maybe that one's good news?"

It wasn't again.

Cam groaned. "Is it *ever* good news?"

Thomas thought for a second. "No."

Surgery finished, and Brittany emerged from anesthesia. The first words out of her still asleep mouth were "Thank you! Thank you!"

Thomas smiled.

As I would find out, Thomas's patients *loved* him. In fact, they loved him so much that they almost killed him.

CHAPTER 6

Finishing School

Sam shined in surgery. The average medical student adds work to a resident's schedule. Good medical students will break-even. Rarely, a *great* medical student truly helps a resident. Sam was great. He functioned at least as well as the interns. Sam was able to stand out without being annoying. As good as Sam was in surgery, Jack may have been even better in medicine. By about halfway through our third year, he realized that he knew more about medicine than any of the chief residents.

The medicine service operates like this:

Arrive in the morning, meet the intern, and round.

Meet the chief resident, and round.

Meet the attending, and round.

Then lunch.

Then round. Then go to conference.

Then round again.

Sam and I found this to be soul-crushingly tedious; Jack loved it.

Jack was entertaining in the conferences. Most medical students would keep a low profile, maybe take a few notes, and try hard to look interested. Jack was intimately engaged and would often question or even argue with the faculty. A medical student who argues with superiors is playing a dangerous game. Attendings do not like to be questioned. A medical student who asks too many questions will be perceived as arrogant and shunned. Jack, however, only questioned things that he thought were wrong or out of date. He also studied the current literature so well that he could defend his position. The few great teachers loved this. The majority of non-great teachers saw him as an arrogant tool.

Jack knew his future path led to a career in internal medicine. He knew he was staying as a resident at the U, since his wife was a year ahead and already working. He also knew that the U was lucky to get him.

Once I got over the culture shock of that initial surgery rotation, I thoroughly enjoyed all my clinical rotations. And then we came to obstetrics and gynecology (OB/GYN).

There were six of us on the rotation. We came in with high hopes. At least I did. I like babies.

OB turned out to be six weeks of me apologizing for having a Y chromosome. I thought back to that fumbled attempt at my first pelvic exam with the patient nurse. It was like that all day, every day.

"Good morning, ma'am ..." I would begin hopefully.

"Are you a doctor?" uncomfortable very pregnant lady would ask.

"No, I'm the medical—"

"I need my *doctor*. I am in *pain!*"

"Well, can I ask you a few—"

"*Yougetmemydoctortobringmesomepainmedicinerightnow!*"

"Thank you, ma'am ..."

As opposed to every other service in medical school, the residents were predominately female. They hated all the male medical students. The only people they hated more than males were females. They *hated* women, especially pregnant women.

A typical clinic appointment consisted of a pregnant woman

complaining about how miserable she was to the resident, then the residents gathering and complaining about how much they had to listen to complaining. I never mustered the guts to ask them why they went into OB if they were so filled with soul-biting hatred of those with child. There's an old stereotype that surgeons are the biggest assbags in the hospital. Sometimes that's true. Mark the fellow was certainly a certifiable douchebag. But for my money, there were no more hateful people than the OB team.

Gynecological surgery was almost as gross as that rectal abscess. The surgeons were angry, bitter people. I think they felt that the (male) general surgeons condescendingly discounted their skills.

I followed my resident into a surgery. We watched the chief resident for a while. I wasn't scrubbed in and was standing far away from the table. I reverted to my now perfected skill of standing skill. The attending, a large woman with a busty voice and dripping hatred of men, stormed in. She looked like Ursula—the giant octopus witch from *The Little Mermaid*—only she was less pleasant. She practically dared anyone to make eye contact.

Not me. No way.

She hastily scrubbed and began to have the nurse put on her gown, speaking to herself but in a loud enough voice so that everyone could hear how she didn't have time for this, she was underpaid, and everyone else could just drop dead. Plus her deadbeat ex-husband hadn't shown up to pick up the kids.

Ex-husband?[27]

The gown was on, and she whirled around with the grace of a drunk hippo and inadvertently brushed up against me.

She stopped dead and glared at me. I was still standing motionless and not daring to make eye contact. The room stopped.

---

[27] Maybe *escapee* would be a better word.

"What. Is. Your. Name?" she hissed.

"Uh, Dan, sir. Uh, ma'am."

She then dramatically ripped off her gown ensuring that everyone in the room saw the spectacle.

"Well, *Dan* just completely contaminated me and now we have to start over! The case will be *delayed*, and my day is *ruined*!"

I was perfectly still! It was the only skill I had truly mastered!

She left the room, cussing to make a huge dramatic show of how she had to scrub her hands again, the patient would probably die, and men are pigs.

"We'd better go," the resident said, as she had finished answering her page. "Mrs. Smith is fully dilated."

Thank God ...

I slunk out of the room, trailing my resident, sneaking behind the scrubbing seahag bitch. I passed Jack, who was following his resident into the surgery. His resident was supposed to join the case, as, by default, was Jack.

My resident and I dashed to a pregnant lady's birthing suite. Birth is a wonderfully gross exercise in a doctor's limitations. About 98 percent of the birth process just *happens*. Doctors are there for the 2 percent.

We walked into the room, and I took in the scene. There was the wife, up in the lithotomy position—legs flexed like a fat frog trying to poop. She was red and sweating and breathing in fast, quick breaths. There was the OB nurse, who, I think, kind of secretly resented all the doctors and was sure she could deliver the baby better than they could. There was the husband, awkwardly shouting encouragement, snapping most inappropriate pictures, and desperately trying to find something to do.

"Breathe, honey!"

Great advice.

I'm pretty convinced that Lamaze was invented to get husbands away from the waiting room where all they had to do was pass out cigars. I believe a secret cabal of women decided that that job was way too easy and the husbands needed to be brought into the room where they could be punished for their role in this whole mess.

"Let's see." My resident was pretty good. She smoothly dropped down between the red wife's legs and put her gloved hands into the birth canal.

"The baby's crowning!"

"Hear that, honey? He's crowning!" the husband gleefully shouted before the red wife shot him a look of pure, unadulterated death-hate.

"Breathe, honey!"

"Okay, are you ready to push?" the resident asked.

By now, I knew my job. I would grab one leg, the nurse would grab the other, and then we would push Mom's legs up to her chest as sort of a cantilever to squirt the little brat out.

Her breathing got faster.

"Push!" the resident yelled.

"Push!" the husband yelled.

Mom screamed.

"Breathe honey! *Owwwwww.*" Classic rookie mistake. He held her hand during a contraction. He vigorously shook his now-crushed fingers.

Since it was Mom's first baby, things took a while. We danced the dance—breathing, seeing the next contraction start on the monitor, seeing Mom's desperate look as the contraction began to kick in, me holding the leg, the nurse wishing she could trade seats with the resident, and the husband uselessly yelling, "Breathe!"

Finally, in an orgasm of blood and goop, the baby squirted out and made a first gasp and then a high-pitched cry.

"It's a boy!" the resident joyously exclaimed.

I'm not sure what immediate release of neurochemicals happens at that instant, but it's always the same. Mom's face contorts into a satisfied smile-cry. Dad takes a deep breath. The baby gets placed on Mom's chest, eyes closed, little hands moving about aimlessly. Dad and Mom look at each other in a moment of afterglow and love. It's a mixture of joy and relief.

The resident began the less glamorous task of stitching up the wounds and delivering the afterbirth. Dad ceremoniously cut the cord. Mom cuddled her new baby. We left the room happy.

It was then that I ran into Jack. While we got to witness a new life coming into the world, Jack got to scrub in with the seahag who erroneously assumed he was me[28] and that he had the audacity to take up space when she twirled in her gown. Apparently Jack spent the last few hours getting berated for all the faults of every male (including her deadbeat ex-husband) who had ever lived.

He looked at nothing in particular and then said, "I don't use the 'C' word often, but she is a total c—."

We gathered, finished our duties, and trudged toward conference. I was still kind of giddy from the birth, Sam was amused at Jack, and Jack was seething.

We filed into the conference room where another attending began to speak about some of the week's surgical complications.

"So, and *anybody* tell me why the ureter was injured?"

Sam elbowed me and whispered, "Because a gynecologist did the surgery?"

I snorted, and then we both realized that one of the residents had heard. Oops.

The conference droned on.

"So then we decided to treat this patient with a beta-blocker. It's

---

[28] I couldn't tell if she thought all medical students or all males looked the same.

a beta-1 blocker. Wait, maybe a beta-2. This can affect the lungs. Or the heart. Which one does the heart?" The attending peered out to the room of residents. None knew the answer. Future cardiologist Jack found this intolerable.

"I can't learn from these people."

One day a week, we gathered with the residents and one faculty to talk about all the people on the service. It started slowly enough but invariably degenerated into the residents complaining and at least one crying. Our first-year hippie training came into full bloom—the ability for a male to cry on cue was absolutely essential for a good grade. I did my best. Sam did his best. Jack would sit, arms folded, thoroughly and demonstratively unimpressed.

The days passed. Sam and I soldiered on and kept our eyes down in a meek show of subservience to our female overlords. Jack had had enough. The residents began to notice. The residents didn't really like Sam and me, but they tolerated us. I guess we weren't so bad—you know, for *boys*.

Jack was professional but quite clearly wouldn't become the meek castrated male that the residents expected. This infuriated them. He would show up and do all the work that was expected of him and not one microsecond of work beyond. He wouldn't cry. The residents began to be harder on him.

He didn't care. He didn't respond. This just made them madder. They would call him out in conferences. They would openly criticize him in front of the other students and attendings. They would shun him at every opportunity.

Still no response.

Finally, one of the residents flat out announced in front of everybody, "We're going to flunk you." This is about as devastating a verbal volley as one can lob at a student. Sam and I looked at each other, worried for our friend.

"No, you're not," Jack said, nonplussed. His monotone dismissal was more than they could stand.

"We're all going to write terrible reviews and make sure you flunk."

Jack didn't seem fazed. They were clearly itching for some response. Any response. I'm sure they were working for a tearful admission of failure and knee begging for forgiveness. But Jack wasn't really listening. By now, he was just exasperated that we were all wasting time.

"Listen," he began.

The resident leaned in, waiting for the begging.

"I won't flunk. I'll get the highest grade on the test, and I won't flunk."

Thus ended the conversation.

The residents seethed and planned their revenge. But they had no case. He didn't shirk duty. He was there, on time, professional and courteous, every day. And as he predicted, he got the highest grade on the rotation-ending test. He also received the only honors grade of our group courtesy of the sterling test score.

Later, Sam showed me his third-year transcript. He had all "honors" grades except OB, where he got a "pass."[29] Sam later interviewed for a residency position in general surgery at one of the most prestigious hospitals in the country.

Big important Mufasa surgery chairman at Ivy League hospital: "So, I see you only got a 'pass' in OB?"

Sam: "Yes, sir."

Big important Mufasa surgery chairman at Ivy League hospital, after considering it for a while: "Good."

---

[29] Basically, a C if "honors" is an A and "high-pass" is a B.

*   *   *   *

We ended with psychiatry. While OB punished us for being male, psychiatry punished us for being rational. I *loved* my psych rotation. The attending I was supposed to work with unfortunately developed an unexpected illness just before the rotation. So it was just the chief resident and me. It was at the end of his residency; he couldn't care less and was often gone for a week at a time. Thus the psychiatry in-patient consult service at the U was me. I prescribed antidepressants for everybody! Including the patients!

Jack continued his hot streak of miserable rotations by being paired with a psychiatrist at the Veterans Administration hospital (VA), whose main academic goal was to correlate penis size with bipolar disease.[30] She asked the medical students to measure each patient's manhood and then review their psychiatric records.

One of the students rationally asked, "Flaccid or erect?"

She didn't have an answer.

Jack would argue with her.

"I think the beta-blockers are making him depressed," she said.

"He's had an extensive cardiac history, including an MI[31] within the past six months," Jack said.

"Stop them."

"Absolutely not! That's dangerous!"

Jack examined one of the patients and reported that he was worried about a blood vessel in his leg.

"He has a pseudoaneurysm. We need to call vascular surgery."

She went into the room, examined the patient for about an hour, and then came out. "He's fine. We should stop the beta-blockers."

---

[30] Sadly, this is not a joke.
[31] *Myocardial infarction*—a heart attack

"He has a pseudoaneurysm," Jack insisted. "We need to call vascular surgery."

"He's fine. We're not calling vascular surgery."

"I'm calling them right now."

"Do *not* call vascular surgery."

"I'm dialing."

"I'll flunk you if you do."

"Hello, can you please page vascular surgery for me?"

She stewed while the team waited for the vascular surgeons. They arrived, looking somewhat annoyed, went into the room, examined the patient for about two minutes, and then came out with much different looks on their faces.

"He has a pseudoaneurysm. We need to take him to the OR right now."

The psychiatrist looked shocked. She turned to Jack. "How did you know?"

Jack walked her into the room, leading her like a child. "I could hear the bruit in his leg. Listen right here." He then somewhat condescendingly placed her stethoscope on the patient's leg.

Their relationship continued to deteriorate to the point that Sam and I pulled Jack aside.

"Listen, I know you don't think much of this, but you have to *pass*."

"I'll pass."

"This isn't one of the OB residents; she's an *attending*. She *can* flunk you."

"Okay, I'll try to be nice. But she's a total moron. Seriously. Penis size and bipolar disease? Are you kidding me?"

At the end of the rotation, we were still worried. Sam and I got the top two grades on the rotation-ending test, so Jack couldn't rely on just that. Jack filled out the obligatory evaluation of his attending and was absolutely scalding. The reviews are supposed to be anonymous, but Jack put down his name, phone number, and an exhortation for the department chairman to call him.

Still, Jack passed.

I breathed a sigh of relief. As it turns out, I think she kind of liked the abuse Jack heaped on her. He must have gotten a good evaluation from her. I didn't realize how good until the end of our fourth year. At the end of medical school, there was a large fancy banquet where we celebrated, handed out awards, and received awards. I had become the class president and one of my duties was to announce and pass out the awards. I got the list of the winners a few days ahead of the banquet.

Top surgery student? Sam. No surprise.

Top medicine student? Jack. No surprise.

Top psychiatry student? Jack.

Wait. What?

This had to be a joke. I called the psychiatry department. Nope, it was real. He was nominated by his attending at the VA. I felt kind of dirty announcing that one!

As the banquet finished, the same bespectacled, bushy mustachioed biochemistry professor who had given that very first lecture of medical school asked me if he could present a "special" award. This wasn't in the script, but what the heck? Sure. The week before, one of my other duties of the class president was to write a small article for the campus paper about our experience in medical school. I mentioned my experience with those damn amino acids in that lecture hall on that first day.

The professor began, "In honor of his graduation, I would like to present this plaque containing a diagram of all the amino acids to Dr. Fulkerson."

Daniel Fulkerson, MD

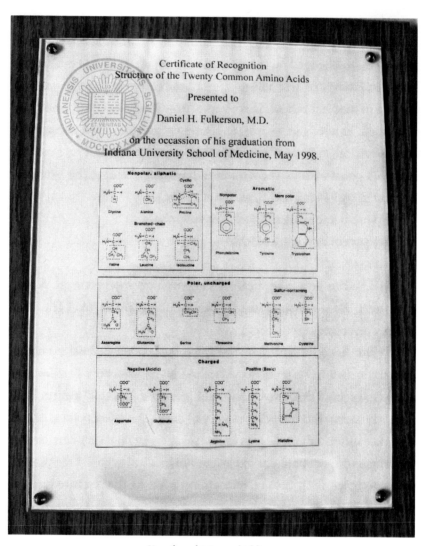

You thought I was kidding.

CHAPTER 7

Conspiracy Theory

I absolutely love the late-night cable Hitler/alien TV shows that interview people who are convinced that the government is out to get them. At any moment, black helicopters will crest the horizon and storm down because of their secret knowledge of Roswell, the impending reptilian invasion, or the super-secret plot where George W. Bush really killed JFK.[32] I love the shows, but all the people are clearly nutjobs. The government's not out to get anybody.

Except me.

Unfortunately, they aren't out to get me for any cool reason like repressed memories of my time as a high-level assassin, Bigfoot caretaker, or UFO concierge.[33] The government conspires against me purely for laughs.

My main career goal in high school was to become a military pilot. I jumped through all the hoops to apply to the Air Force and Naval Academies, including getting a letter of recommendation from my senator, a handsome young chap and future world savior Dan Quayle. Everything was going along swimmingly until the physical examination. As it turns out, I have a very specific genetic defect in my eyes.

---

[32] All of those are true, by the way.

[33] As far as you know.

It doesn't affect my vision but disqualified me from becoming a pilot. That was it. In one instant, my career path was shot.

I was still interested in the military, thought I'd get another chance at becoming a pilot, and needed money for college. So I joined the Reserve Officer's Training Corps (ROTC) and enrolled at Golden U. After graduation, the military gave me a time allotment for medical school. I didn't really think much about this again until fourth year.

I spent much of my fourth year working with the neurosurgery department and bonded with Grandpa P. The brain and the central nervous system enthralled me. I enjoyed the surgical procedures.

Neurosurgery is just *classier* than the other surgical specialties. Every surgical specialty deals with some kind of fluid. Urology deals with pee. General surgery deals with poop. ENT deals with snot. Neurosurgery deals with cerebrospinal fluid—a (usually) sterile clear liquid with a little salt and sugar. It's like champagne. It's dignified.

I talked to Grandpa P. and the Professor and declared my intention to apply for a residency spot.

"Will the military be any problem?" the Professor asked.

"I doubt it," I said. After all, they told me I could "be all that I could be."

But I was worried. I called my local recruiter. He explained the situation. First, I had to apply to the military match program for permission to apply to a residency program.

"So, will they work with me to facilitate my career goals?" I asked.

"Sure," he said.[34]

So I applied to the military match.

"I'd like to apply for a neurosurgery residency," I said to the disinterested lady on the other end of the phone.

---

[34] Followed by "*Eeeeeeexxxellent,*" Montgomery Burns style.

72

"There's only one spot."

"What do you mean 'one spot'?"

"Congress sets how many doctors can go into each specialty. They only approved one spot for neurosurgery," she explained, I presume while scanning the web for shoe sales.

"Okay, I'd like to apply for the one spot," I said nervously. In the span of a second, I felt despair and then hope. I was a good candidate. I had as good a shot as any.

"Fine. Send in your application. But the spot has already been given to someone else."

"Okay, so the application gets sent to … Wait. What did you just say?"

She sighed. I was obviously keeping her from something more important.

"Send in your application. But someone else already has the spot."

"But I haven't even applied yet!"

"So send in your application—"

"And then I'll be considered for the spot?"

"No, it's been given to someone else."

"But the deadline for applying isn't for three more months! We haven't even started interviewing!" I protested.

Sigh again.

"Send in your application, and you can then set up your interviews."

"And then?"

"Someone else already got the spot."

"So should I even send in an application?"

"Yes, we need your application."

Either she was slow or I was.

"Are you just messing with me?"

"I work for the military," she said dryly. I couldn't tell if that was a yes or a no.

So let's check the score: by this time in my life, I have had two goals (pilot and neurosurgeon), and the military crushed both of them.

♫ *Be, All that you can be!* ♫

I absorbed this blow like a stoic rock—curled up in a fetal position and gently sobbing. *What am I going to do now?* I felt I needed wisdom and advice from a master. I knew just where to go.

I walked into the Professor's office and began to explain my predicament. "I wanted to apply for neurosurgery, but the air force said I wouldn't be allowed to accept it without their approval, which they promised to someone else." I argued my case, *pleaded* really. The Professor was slightly hunched forward, watching me with an unblinking blank face. He listened intently without interrupting. I finished. I felt better. It felt good to open up to a sage, experienced teacher. It was cathartic. I took a deep breath, settled back, and waited for the inevitable wise solution.

The Professor didn't move for a few seconds.

"So ..." he started.

I straightened hopefully.

"Yes?"

"You're f——d."

Super.

I paused for a second. I guess I should have been more disappointed, but somehow the Professor could always find a way to get to the heart of the problem. He did. In one contraction and one expletive.

He was right. No point in fighting it.

The air force gave me two choices: choose a different specialty or take a "transitional" year of general surgery and then serve some active-duty time. I chose the latter.

*   *   *   *

The Lovely Wife, tiny daughter, and I packed our bags and headed to the next city for my general surgery intern year. I spent much of the year with a large, burly Czechoslovakian who specialized in removing people's gallbladders. Like the Professor, he spoke his mind. He would often tell fat people that they needed to lose weight by having more sex, all with a voice like Conan the Barbarian.

"Old still, dis will just hut fah a sekund. Wood be better if you want so faht."[35]

It was a demanding year, living in a new city with a new baby. I was on call every other to every third night,[36] and it felt very similar to that third-year general surgery rotation at the Baby Hospital. I kept a low profile and kept my nose clean.

The call rooms for the main trauma hospital were located right below the helipad. After sprinting through the service all day, we would crash in this room, hoping for about ten minutes of sleep. Then the helicopter would start up.

Whum.

Oh, great.

Whum.

This will take a few minutes.

Whum, whum, whum.

Here it comes ...

Whumwhumwhumwhumwhumwhum.

---

[35] He was actually a practicing surgeon who had to escape the country because of the threat of death during the fun-filled Ceausescu years. He came to America and, in order to practice, had to complete a full general surgery residency again. In a fight with the real Conan, I'd bet on the Czech.

[36] This was before the duty hours restrictions.

Once the chopper started going, the entire room shook with the fury of a magnitude 8.0 earthquake. It was then that I did a quick calculation—ten minutes to the scene, ten to load, ten to get back, okay, I can sleep for twenty minutes before heading down to the trauma bay.

The year passed quickly for me but less so for the Lovely Wife, who was blossoming with a second child. She radiated sunshine and happiness, while chasing a rambunctious toddler, heroically vomiting at every opportunity, and (probably) cursing the day she met me. The slightest off-texture food or smell would throw her into vomiting hate-rage. It was horrible.

I still held out hope that I could get into neurosurgery. I contacted the assignment office and explained my situation.

"So, can I reapply for neurosurgery now?"

"No."

"Can I be a pilot?" Heh.

"You can reapply for neurosurgery after you complete a general medical officer assignment. Assignments are either two or three years. If you get a three-year assignment, then you either have to take another assignment or add more commitment time."

"Okay," I said. "Where can I do a two-year tour?"

"Right now, we don't have any openings for a general medical officer."

"What?"

"We have no place to send you. I guess we'll just have to park you somewhere. Any requests?"

"Anywhere in the United States. I just want a two-year tour. Minot, Texas, Louisiana, I don't care, just somewhere in the continental US."

Pause.

"How about Misawa, Japan?"

So then I said ... Japan!

This was the exact moment when I knew they were just screwing with me.

*   *   *   *

The perpetually puking Lovely Wife and I packed up all our stuff, including an eighteen-month-old little girl, and trudged out to the airport to catch a military flight to Japan. Our first stop was in the dark dead of night in Seattle. Despite being sick, the Lovely Wife was desperately hungry. From Seattle, we boarded the "freedom bird." This was a commercial 747 converted to military use. By "converted," I mean they somehow doubled the seating and halved the legroom. They also removed any of the luxuries spoiled travelers covet, like air-conditioning and food. The temperature was boiling; the Lovely Wife kept her eyes closed in a failing attempt to avoid vomiting while the little girl squirmed incessantly on her lap.

We flew to Alaska, where the night was somehow darker. The little girl couldn't quite figure out if she was supposed to be awake or asleep, so she just cried. The Alaskan airport was even more desolate than the one in Seattle.

The flight was delayed. Apparently there was an army enlistee who couldn't be found. One hour went by. The little girl dozed off, and the Lovely Wife constructively used the time to throw up. A second hour went by. The little girl woke up in a daze and angrily protested that she was hungry. Finally, by the third hour, someone realized the enlistee was sitting with the group, asleep with headphones on.

The next stop was a dusty military hangar in Korea where the group of about two hundred fought to stand in line at the one 1960s vintage concession stand. By then, the Lovely Wife had gone into full *Lord of the Flies* mode and stalked a bag of stale Cracker Jacks like a lioness. The little girl was baffled why we had to wait so long and why it was daytime at night.

We finally arrived in Japan in pea-soup fog. The time lag in the now about thirty-hour flight made us seriously question whether it was day or night. Turned out it was about four in the morning local time. We found ourselves at billeting. The night watch lady greeted me, a delirious toddler, and a vomiting wife, who, despite the brave face, must have been questioning every personal decision that led to our marriage. We were drenched in sweat. Despite the early morning, the condensation from the fog and the heat made us feel like we were in the world's biggest sauna. The lady gave us a room key for a dorm a few buildings away. Our room was on the third floor of a Spartan stone building sans elevator.

The little girl was slaphappy and yelled out the number of stairs with each step.

"Wwwwwoonnnnnnnn! Dooooooooooooo! Treeeeeeeeeeeeee!"

At each step, she paused, yelled the number, and then hopped up the next one to repeat the process. Finally we reached our third-floor room, which, in a way that scoffs in the face of rational thermodynamics, must have been twenty degrees *hotter*.

We set up the little girl's makeshift crib and then collapsed in an exhausted pile of sweat, confusion, and morning sickness. Was it morning? Holy cow, it was morning. Soon the sun began pouring into the window, making sleep impossible and cranking the heat from "fry" to "burning hellfire."

*   *   *   *

People in the military share certain miserable experiences. It's called "the suck." An old military joke is that an air force person evaluates their situation and says, "This sucks." An army person evaluates the same situation and says, "I'm glad this sucks." A marine says, "I wish this could suck some more."

All military members experience this to some degree. I experienced small annoyances: an uncomfortable flight, a hot room, and a change in career plans. But on the whole, I was in a wonderful position. No one was shooting at me. I wasn't in any danger. Other military members experience real challenges, and it was an absolute honor to help care for them and their families.

The next day, we experienced the beauty of the military. We were trudging back to billeting to arrange our housing, when we were greeted by one of the other doctors.

"Hi, I'm Will. Welcome to Misawa."

I introduced our disheveled group.

"The hospital is over there. I suppose you'll need a car." He thought for a second. "Well, I don't live too far from the hospital. Take mine until you get your housing."

He tossed me the keys, pointed out the car, and then began to jog away. "See you at 1500!"

Just like that—someone I'd known for ten seconds tossed me the keys to his car. Everyone in the military bands together. People help each other. People realize that every other military member is going through some level of challenge. *Teamwork* is not just an inspiration poster vapid buzzword; it's a way of life. Over the next few days, we met other people on the hospital staff. We moved out of the dorm into a pretty nice little apartment. We got our own car and returned Will's. People began showing up at our door with food. People brought over clothes for the little girl.

People in the military pay it forward. One of my fondest memories was four years later, as I was leaving. I was driving a Japanese hooptie. It wasn't much to look at, but it got me from place to place. I tossed my keys to a fresh-faced enlisted man, who looked about twelve and was straight out of training.

He looked excited to have some wheels but then crestfallen as I could tell he had no money. "How much?"

"It's yours. And here's fifty dollars to cover the title transfer. That office right there can help you. Have fun. This is a fantastic place to be."

Chapter 8

Government Medicine

Japan is a beautiful country. We lived in what passes for the countryside of the nation. Within a few minutes' drive, one would be surrounded by rice paddies nestled at the foot of jagged evergreen mountains. Driving in Japan was an adventure for Americans who, generally, could not read any of the signs. Directions were passed by mouth. "Go until you see a big red pole, turn left, then forward until the Big Buddha." The "Big Buddha" was supposedly the world's largest sitting Buddha statue and welcomed drivers to Aomori. I'm sure it had a more proper name in Japanese. The Big Buddha was nestled in a crevice of a mountain range, and he sat placidly near a five-story temple. There was a small park along the path filled with small paper dolls. This innocent little park was a tribute to aborted babies. Once we learned this, the Lovely Wife could not walk past it without tearing up.

There were a number of parks nearby, including one with a small-scale replica of the Statue of Liberty next to the Egyptian Sphinx. Within an hour's drive, there was a national park with hiking trails next to waterfalls, leading to a cold glass lake. Just past that was the supposed final resting place of Jesus.[37]

---

[37] Yes, *that* Jesus, and, yes, they were serious.

The Statue of Liberty Park heralded a patch of "love motels." The Japanese could somehow take something like a seedy motel and, at the same time, both class it up *and* make it weirder. Love motels had themes and instruction books. We couldn't read them, but there were pictures. Lots of pictures. The male figure often had the torso and head of a lion and the female was often depicted as a disturbingly young maiden. And yes, there were tentacles. Payment was made on the honor system.

Our base had a movie theater that ran donated films. The playlist generally trailed the American opening by about six months. One of the great treasures in life is to see a movie on a military base. I highly recommend it if you ever get the chance. Before the film, there's the usual mill of noise and talking. Then, the national anthem starts and the whole room immediately pops to attention. It's remarkably inspiring.

The military is associated with the political right. However, I lived in government-supplied housing, shopped at a government store, and worked in a government hospital providing free health care to government employees. My work crew was truly integrated. Our crew was male, female, white, black, Hispanic, Filipino, European, and African. The military is really a leftist's paradise—well, except for the duty, discipline, and lack of facial hair.

I became an emergency medicine doctor by default. Our base was basically a small American town, transplanted to the Orient. It was much more Mayberry than M*A*S*H. I spent days and nights seeing kids with fevers, female problems, and minor orthopedic injuries. The foggy, sweltering summer gave way to a deep, soggy winter. One of our most common diagnoses was "the crud," a combination of snot and coughing that ran its course over about four months.

There were very few retirees in rural Japan, but there was one. He was an old codger named Gus, who had not one, but *five* primary cancers going on at the same time. He'd pop in from time to time in heart failure or with chest pain.

"Hey, Gus. How are you feeling?"

"With *my hands*!" he croaked, holding up his mitts and squeezing the air.

The female nurses knew to keep their boobs at arm's length.

Will would come in, tune him up, and send him on his way. He was married to a tiny Japanese woman who, like Gus, was in her late sixties. Near as I could tell, she spoke little English and he spoke even less Japanese.

There was a small population of young men out on their own for the first time, who fell in love with the first pretty girl to smile back. There was also a population of Japanese girls who, for various reasons, wanted to marry an American service member. I guess it worked out for old Gus, but generally the combination of young, dumb, and full of, well, *vigor* with a pretty Japanese gal was a disaster.

If the couple was married, the Japanese girl was eligible to come to our ER for care. This was generally obstetric care.

Me: "So, are you cramping?"

Japanese Girl: Blank stare.

Young husband: "*Cramping*?" making frantic movements with his hands to, I guess, pantomime cramping.

Girl looking at husband: Smiles meekly.

"Craaaaaammmmmmmping?"

Saying a word in a foreign language *louder* does not help in the translation. Try as I might, I could never get this across to our airmen.

Me: "I don't think her problem is her hearing."

Young husband: "Well …"

Me: "I'll get a translator. Maybe you should just wait outside."

I don't like to brag,[38] but I got pretty good at pelvic examinations. I remembered the lessons from that first patient nurse in medical

---

[38] Editor's note: total lie.

school. Men, I believe, are much more concerned with hurting the patient than female doctors. We had a compliment of thirteen doctors in Misawa; at any given time, two or three were OBs. One particular OB had a mean disposition and freakishly large hands. The ladies of the base *hated* her. As our base was basically a small town, everybody knew everybody else. I took it as a compliment when her patients would find out when I was on shift and come to the ER for their pap smear.

Lots of things can happen during a pelvic exam, and almost none of them are good. Doctors are generally comfortable with the embarrassing parts of the body. After a few tries, examining the nether regions is no different from examining the wrist. However, it may be very different for the patient. I had one husband of a multinational descent insist I perform a vaginal examination without looking.

"You want me to do what?"

"In my culture, another man is not allowed to see the wife naked."

"Your wife may have a life-threatening problem. I'm going to examine her."

"I'll—"

"You'll wait outside."

All kinds of inappropriate things may happen during a pelvic exam. Some patients want to chitchat. Piece of advice, no chitchat. For women who may be unfamiliar with "guy" rules, the pelvic exam is like guys at a urinal, eyes forward, minimal talking, finish your business, and be done.

Betty was one of my fellow ER docs. She was from New York, married to a rocker, and trained in primary care. Every ER has certain "frequent fliers"—patients who come all the time. In this case, Betty's frequent flier was a very attractive, very lazy, young female airman who always seemed get injured just before her unit was scheduled to do a strenuous training exercise. The exercises were scheduled, so we pretty much knew the cadre of slackers who would show up with varying complaints hoping to be put on medical waivers. Every time, the girl (Bubbles) would come in with some assortment of sprained ankles, vague abdominal pain, and cold symptoms. Usually the only thing missing was a note from Epstein's mother.

Today, however, she had vaginal bleeding, a legitimate ER problem. She arrived with her young boyfriend. Betty did the evaluation and determined that she needed a pelvic examination. The boyfriend was clearly unsure how to behave.

Betty: "Okay, just let your legs drift apart."

Bubbles: "Okay."

Betty: "Now, you'll feel a little pressure."

Boyfriend: "Honey, just pretend it's me."

Uncomfortable silence ...

Betty: "Let's try this again."

She shot a withering look at the boyfriend. "It's *not* you." Chastised, he looked to the floor.

Betty: "Okay, now I'm just going to insert—"

"*Ooooowwwwww*!" Bubbles screamed and grabbed Betty's hair, pulling her up. This was just doomed from the start.

I later saw Bubbles for the more routine back pain.

"So, you hurt it working out?"

Bubbles: "Yes. I don't think I can carry anything."

Me: "It should be fine. So, your unit is about to exercise, right?"

Bubbles, working up her best "sad" face: "Yes, and I-I ..." *[Sob for effect]* "I'm going to miss it!"

Me: "Yeah, shoot. Well, I'm sure your unit will *somehow* get by."

Bubbles: "Well, I guess they'll have to. I'm transferring soon."

Me: "Really? Where to next?"

Bubbles: "Officer training school."

Figures.

*   *   *   *

The Lovely Wife settled into a small-town routine. One of the beauties of the military is that there are other people going through the same suck as you. Like always, she quickly made a group of lifelong friends. As luck would have it, I met one of her future best friends before she did.

The shift started like usual. I was working nights. I got through the dinner rush and then settled in for the group of people who showed up from ten to midnight. This is a busy time for pediatric patients. I used to wonder why people would stay at home all day and then come to an ER at midnight. It finally dawned on me that the child's earache wasn't an emergency until the parents couldn't sleep.

A nurse from another section of the hospital came running down.

"Doc, we need you in labor."

I'm sorry. You want a real doctor. I'm sure there's one around here somewhere.

"Me?" I asked.

"Yes, our doc is in a C-section and the other one is out of the country."

Sounds like poor planning. Why must I be involved? I got a pass *in OB. Want to hear about my experience with a gynecological surgeon?*

"What do you need?"

"Lady is about to pop."

Oh sweet heavens …

I put on my best I-got-this face and shuffled down to labor and delivery.

Freshly off the plane, a lovely young woman was in *the* position, feet in stirrups, screaming with each contraction, her face a sweaty, panicked mess. Her husband, younger than I was, was clutching her hand. A technician was holding one leg. The nurse immediately went for the other leg and then shot me a look that said, "Get your hiney in there *now*!"

"Hello, ma'am, I'm—"

"*Are you the doctor*?" she screamed between breaths.

"Yes." *This time with confidence, idiot!* "Yes!"

Well, I can see the top of the baby's head. That's good, right?

My mind and heart were racing. It had been three years since I was on that ill-fated OB rotation, but it all came back. I remember complaining about how useless certain classes were, but now, I was frantically scanning the memory banks for any nugget of knowledge from OB. I was thankful (surprised!) everything seemed to come automatically.

I reached in and ran my fingers around the baby's head, massaging the canal to get a little more room. The nurse was watching the monitor and telling Mom when to push. Mom, God bless her, was doing everything she could. It was beautiful.

The head began to come. I cradled it, pulled gently, and then the whole lump of jelly plopped out. This was too easy—

The baby is blue!

"Is it okay? I don't hear crying!" Mom gasped.

The cord had wrapped around the neck twice. The baby wasn't breathing. Or moving.

"Fine …"

I unwrapped the cord. I'm sure this took about a second or two, but it felt like an eternity. Every cuss word in my vocabulary was right on the tip of my tongue. The nurse, looking below the drapes, was ashen white. I unwrapped the last twist and smack-rubbed the chest. Time was still. I could see everything in the room at once, motionless: Mom's anguished, worried face; Dad's quickly dropping smile; the concerned nurse … The monitor stopped in midblip …

Then, like I'd just hit the restart button, the baby let out a throaty scream and the room breathed again. Two screams later, he was pink, gooey, and kicking up a storm. I plopped him on Mom's exhausted chest. She looked at him with eyes tearing with love.

The nurse kicked back into gear. We clamped the cord. I even remembered to have Dad cut it. She hustled the baby to the warmer to clean and swaddle him. I went back to my post to wait for the afterbirth.

"Nice job."

The real OB (Grumpy) had finished his emergent case and sprinted to our room. He was a good friend and *hated* being in the military, although he would eventually serve honorably for decades. Grumpy was one of the senior doctors on our base. He despised the buffoonery of the military but was a technically outstanding obstetrician. Grumpy checked out the baby and then came over to me. He grinned. He could tell I was just coming down from a panic high.

"You want to sew this up?"

"I should probably get back to the ER." Translation: *Ah hells no!*

He grinned again. He introduced himself to the couple and took over.

Dad shook my hand vigorously. Little did I know it, but that couple would become close friends. It took me a few years to tell them that their baby came out blue! I was grateful. I was grateful for all the lessons I had learned when I thought I was wasting my time. I was grateful that the human body takes care of itself. I was grateful that everything was fine. I was grateful to have the opportunity to witness that little glop's first satisfying breath.

I was also grateful to get back to the ER and hope that such a circumstance never happened again!

*   *   *   *

Each general election, there are certain factors that become political issues for one side or the other. Near as I can tell, the purpose of politics is to remove logic and reason from any issue.

Our ER was a microcosm of government-provided health care. Again, living overseas, our population was predominately healthy and young. Patients with significant medical problems were not shipped to Japan. So one may think that an ER would have little to no use. We saw sixty to seventy patients per day.

Japan is divided into prefectures. Each prefecture has a major medical center that acts similarly to America's tertiary-care hospitals. I was fortunate enough to visit the medical center in our prefecture multiple times. I noted that the ER had six beds. I must have visited ten times, and I never saw a patient in any of these beds. One day, I asked one of the doctors why.

"Only for emergencies."

"But aren't there emergencies here?" I asked.

"Yes, car accidents, heart attacks, strokes. These beds are for emergencies only."

"Fever?"

"No, the patient goes to the clinic."

So, their emergency room is only for emergencies?

Contrast that to our ER. Here are smatterings of chief complaints that I encountered. I'm not making any of these up.

1. A patient heard that there were killer bees in Japan. She thought she had been stung by something. She came to the ER to find out if it was a killer bee.

2. A patient presented around midnight with the chief complaint that she was tired.

3. A wife brought her husband to the ER angry that he couldn't satisfy her sexually because he, well, "flew solo" too often.

4. A patient came to the ER wanting a refill on his daily medications.

> "Why didn't you call your doctor?"
> "Well, I didn't want to bother him. It didn't seem like an emergency."
> "So you came to the *emergency* room."
> "Yes."

As it turns out, people will use easily accessible emergency care for just about anything. Americans don't really want to go to the doctor for maintenance. Every person on our base had a primary care doctor who was easily accessible and free of charge. Yet our ER was consistently bombarded with the mundane. Americans go to the doctor when something needs fixed or they can't sleep because their kid is crying.

Sometimes, even with accessible primary care, people get into all sorts of silliness. One patient presented with constipation. Constipation is a pretty common ER complaint (mostly in kids), and it's only funny if you are not the one who is constipated. This lady was having trouble and dutifully saw her primary care doctor. He prescribed two enemas. She picked these up at the pharmacy and headed home.

Her husband called the ER that night.

Me: "Didn't work?"

Him: "Well, we're not sure."

Me (confused): "Not sure of what?" This seemed like something one could figure out pretty easily.

Him: "Well, she wasn't able to finish."

Me (still confused and a little grossed out): "Finish?"

Him: "Yeah. She was able to drink the first bottle okay, but she just can't finish the second one."

Me: "Well, the first one … Wait. What?"

Him: "She couldn't finish drinking the second bottle."

Stunned silence.

Me (really confused): "Did your doctor tell you to drink them?"

Him: "Well, uh, I guess we thought …" His voice trailed off.

Me: "Do you have the box?"

"Yes."

"Are there any pictures on the side of the box?"

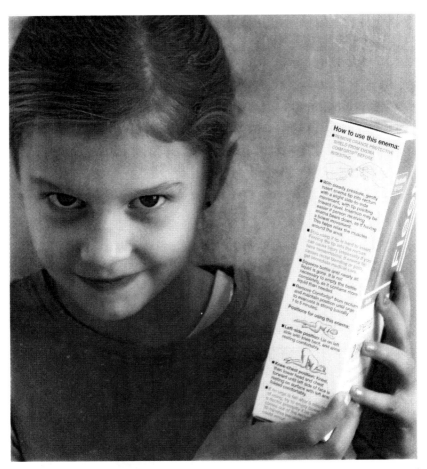

Exactly like this?

Long pause.

Him: "So is it a problem if she drank one and a half enemas?"

Me: "Let me get back to you."

I switched the phone to hold. I looked at my nurse incredulously. I had to admit, I didn't know. We decided to call poison control. After five minutes of uproarious laughter, the poison control center thought it would probably work and wasn't dangerous, but that she was in for a rough, bloaty night.

Not only did people use the ER for every little thing, they also came to expect convenience. I don't mind helping people with things that should wait until the family practice clinic. But I totally disagree with the current concept that patients are customers. Sometimes, doctors have to focus on the truly sick. Customer service is not our first priority; taking care of the sick patient is.

Old Gus finally had enough. He came in looking ashen. We began to work on him. We started IVs and got the defibrillator ready.

"What's the blood pressure?" I asked.

The nurse looked grim. "It's in the sixties."

"Did you call Will?"

"He's on his way."

"Okay, let's get a drip ready."

As I said, our hospital was a small, close-knit group. I'm sure Gus knew every doctor there. Well, maybe not Grumpy. But every non-OB doctor. Soon the ER was full with half of the medical staff.

"I'm losing the pressure!" the nurse yelled.

"Start the drip. Pulse?"

The nurse shook her head.

Gus's wife sobbed gently as one of the technicians escorted her to an empty room.

We began chest compressions. Gus was slipping.

"I'm holding compressions. Do we have a shockable rhythm?"

"Asystole."

"Resuming compressions."

Will arrived, surveyed the situation, and surveyed Gus. "Stop."

Gus was gone.

We talked to his wife with our translator. We packed Gus up and began to wheel him down to the morgue. The ER was physically a small place. Everybody in the waiting room could see through the window at the crowd of doctors frantically working on the old codger.

We were all deflated. It wasn't unexpected—he did have five separate cancers—but we were still deflated. That was when someone angrily rapped on the window of the control room.

"Excuse me, but we've been waiting for over an hour for my child's earache!"

"We've been busy," one of the technicians said, moving slightly out of the way so the body bag was in clear view.

"We've been waiting for over an hour!"

"We'll get to you as soon as we can."

Bitch.

CHAPTER 9

The Day the World Changed

There were two rules of food in Japan: the food never tastes quite the way you think, and there's always a surprise. An innocent rice ball may hide uncooked squid. A nice simple dish may look great until the waitress cracks a raw egg over the top. Bean curd can look surprisingly like ice cream.

The Lovely Wife never quite adjusted to Japanese food. One night, we ventured to a fine restaurant with another couple. We were shown to our table and began the multicourse meal. Japanese dinners generally have many courses. There's a plate of sashimi, followed by a small salad, followed by miso soup, followed by sushi, followed by varying plates of the main course. The meal is designed to be savored.

We talked quietly while the waitress delivered our plates of sushi. Presentation matters in a nice restaurant. The plate was colorful, with dainty bites of fish surrounding a freakishly large full shrimp. The armor shell on the back was removed, but everything else was intact—legs, feelers, eyes. The waitress smiled curtly and moved on. All of us nibbled around the sushi and kept talking. Out of the corner of my eye, I thought I saw one of the feelers of my shrimp move. I paid no attention, until I thought I saw it again.

"I think my shrimp is moving," I said.

The Lovely Wife gave me an eye roll and kept talking.

"I'm serious."

"Yeah, sure. It's just—Aaaaaaaaaaaauuuuuuuuggggggghhhh!"

She looked down, and her shrimp was sitting up on its haunches, staring right at her with its antennae moving and probing.

'Sup?

She screamed and pushed back from the table, nearly dumping the nearby waiter.

The restaurant came to a dead stop. In Japan, drawing attention to oneself is a vicious *faux pas*. This is especially true if one happens to be a gaijin devil. The other patrons muttered, shook their heads, and went back to their meals. The Lovely Wife was mortified. From the ocean to plate as soon as possible—the gourmet way to eat shrimp is whole: head, legs, and all. The beasts had been flash frozen and, as we talked, thawed. Japanese food always comes with a surprise.

This sounds silly until you experience it. One of the odd things about the Japanese people is that they are *all Japanese*. Even in my small Midwestern hometown, people are Protestant, Catholic, Jewish, Hispanic, African-American, Italian, and so on. In Japan, everybody is the same. This makes white people stick out like a sore thumb.

The Japanese are unfailingly polite. Our base was fairly accepted in the local community. There were very few protests. When a protest did occur, the activists gathered outside the main gate, did their business, cleaned up after themselves, bowed, apologized for the inconvenience, and then departed without a fuss.

I struck up a relationship with some of the surgeons in the main prefect hospital system. The hospital ran like a fifties television show. The doctor would arrive, usually smoking, bark out a few commands, and then move on. The gynecology clinic was a long room with two rows of ten tables. Twenty women were positioned, feet in stirrups, only a small cloth covering their abdomen. The doctor would go from one to the other, do the examination, and make a few orders to the nurse, who would bow curtly and say, "Hai!"

The neurosurgeons operated with tremendous speed and efficiency. I generally sat with the anesthesiologist to observe the procedure. Most of the Japanese professionals spoke English, and the anesthesiologist seemed happy to practice on me. He showed me all the technology at his fingertips and his phone, which was slightly bigger than a lighter. Japanese technology is just like American technology, only fifteen years ahead.

The Japanese surgeons worked hard and played hard. After the day's surgeries, we all went out on the town. A typical Japanese night out has many stops. We hit one bar for drinks, then another bar for drinks, then yet another bar for the first course. The normally uptight surgeons began to loosen up after a few Saki stops. Two ladies joined us. I couldn't tell if they were office workers, spouses, nurses, or working women. Eventually, we ended up at a smoky karaoke bar.

Their English got worse as the night and drinks flowed freely.

"Music?"

"Yes."

The surgeon looked for the words. "Who do you like?"

"I like Eric Clapton," I said. This sounded more dignified than Iron Maiden.

They shouted and clapped each other on the back. "Eric Clapton! Yes, Eric Clapton!"

Another surgeon talked to one of the women, who shook her head no. He seemed crestfallen. Then ...

"Ricky Martin?"

I wasn't sure where this was going.

"Ricky Martin?"

"I know Ricky Martin," I said cautiously.[39]

They shouted and clapped each other on the back again. "Ricky Martin!"

The girl bowed with a big smile and disappeared. The unmistakable trumpet heralded the beginning of "Livin' La Vida Loca."

"Riiiicckkeeeeeee Marrrrrrtin!" they all shouted.

Then, sloppy drunk, they began to scream sounds that I assume were their attempts at the words. One grabbed me by the arm. "Translate!"

I looked at him quizzically.

"Oooohhhh, saaaaaahhhh, ooooohhhh, saaaaaaah out! Livin' la lida locaaaaaaa," they screamed, now fully disinhibited.

The surgeon holding my arm grinned from ear to ear. "*Translate!*"

Deep in the dead of night, in a seedy karaoke bar, in the middle of a town that I didn't know, I tried hard to translate salsa into a language that I didn't speak. The group was totally snockered, and

---

[39] Heck *yes* I did!

it dawned on me that they would be back to work in less than four hours. Two of them passed out, which seemed ridiculously funny to the rest.

Oh god. They just turned on "She Bangs" in Spanish. Now I was translating one language that I didn't speak into another language I didn't speak. They didn't care. I'd make up some gibberish lyrics, and they would laugh uproariously.

We stumbled out of the bar. They laughed and disappeared into the night. I had slowed down on that Saki hours ago, but I was still totally lost in a foreign city. I was thankful one of the gals found me and walked me back to my car. I began the drive home. The drive there was confusing in the daylight but totally surreal at night. I kept telling myself that I hadn't had much to drink, but I was still silly tired. Somehow, I found my way back to the base.

Clearly, I thought, shouting Spanglish to Japlish Ricky Martin in a room full of drunk surgeons ranked up there on the weirdest experiences of my life. I found the bed and crashed. The Lovely Wife grunted at the intrusion, and I immediately found deep, deep sleep.

In what felt like two minutes later, I felt a grip on my shoulder. *Lemme lone, I need more sleep.*

The grip was hard, painful even, and quite insistent.

My eyes opened.

"You have to see this." The Lovely Wife had a strange expression on her face. I had never seen this expression before.

"What?"

"You have to see this."

"Are the kids okay?" I asked. Her gravity was scaring me.

She led me stumbling to the TV, where I saw smoke billowing from the Twin Towers. Was this a movie? What was I watching? What was happening? What started the fire?

"A second plane crashed into it. I think someone's attacking us."

I felt numb and confused and sick. Like all of America. "Don't let the kids watch."

Then the first tower crumbled. Then the second.

An alarm went off. No one spoke. I put on my uniform and headed into the hospital. We were all called to duty stations.

There was a dread calm smothering the base. Normally, one would hear planes taking off. Now, everything was silent. Pilots were ready but waiting for orders. No one knew what was going on.

We sat in silence, watching the military TV. We had one patient come to the ER that day.

"Get this thing off!" he demanded, dropping his casted arm onto the table. "I can't do my job with this cast on." He was a flight-crew chief. He didn't care about his broken arm. He cared about doing his job on the flight line.

"Get it off." It wasn't a request.

The orthopedic PA took it off.

"What's going to happen now?" my youngest technician asked.

"I don't know."

"Everything's changed, hasn't it?"

"Yes."

We were confined to duty stations and then confined to base. No one knew the scope of the threat or if we were in danger. We heard stories—another plane, the Pentagon, a field, the White House. Were our pilots leaving? Were they going to war? Where? Who was attacking? We received the orders to work in shifts. People were told to stay in their homes. Some took cover, although no one seriously thought mainland Japan was going to be attacked. Mostly we waited, confused and hurt. All the phones were down—reserved for official use only. The Internet, dial-up slow, crashed.

The first day ended. Then the second. Overnight, our sleepy little Mayberry turned into a military base. Camouflage was draped over flight line buildings. Ridiculously large guns were placed at every gate, manned by terrified nineteen-year-old soldiers away from home for the first time. People who lived off base were subject to complete auto searches that lasted almost an hour. People didn't speak. People didn't make eye contact. Then one day, we heard all the fighters taking off. War must be starting.

Would we be bombed? We were a twelve-minute (by F-16) flight to North Korea. North Korea famously "tested" their missiles by launching them just north of our base. Would they bomb us?

In retrospect, I know we were in no danger. But at the time, we didn't know the threat or the enemy. We were confused and frightened, just like, I imagine, our families back in the United States.

Gradually, we settled back into routine. President Bush gave his speech and told us to "Be ready." We were. We learned about al-Qaeda and Bin Laden. We learned about the herculean effort in the States to immediately ground every commercial flight. We learned about the kindness of people taking food and offering shelter to stranded passengers. We learned of the courage of the passengers on Flight 93. We saw stories of people giving blood (Yasser Arafat?). We heard of the deaths in New York. We grieved. We were angry. We wanted to bomb something, someone.

I hadn't thought about it in the few weeks after that horrible, surreal day, but I was scheduled to interview for residency that October. We were confined to base. I discussed the situation with the hospital commander, who petitioned the generals in charge of the Pacific. I was granted one week of leave. I figured I had four days to interview, as the trip to and from Japan took three days. Normally, the interview process takes about six weeks. Applicants generally visit around twenty programs, usually on set dates. I picked my top five choices, called each program, explained my situation, and set up interviews in four days.

There was a very palpable sense of dread on each flight. I flew commercial out of Tokyo and in the States. No one spoke. Security was everywhere. Passengers nervously studied everyone else boarding the flight. Dark people were met with suspicion.

I would check in. The attendants would see my military ID and profusely thank me.

"I'm an ER doctor. I'm not someone who ..."

"God bless you, Captain."

I felt proud and guilty at the same. I'm not a fighter. I treat earaches.

My whirlwind tour of the programs began. Every place was understanding and gracious.

I didn't realize it at the time, but this was the last time our country was truly together. Every single person was rallying together. Everyone was helping everyone else. Stories of people feeding strangers, of heading to New York to help, of giving blood, of the heroes in police or firefighter uniforms, buoyed us. Baseball came back to New York with a defiant, tearful celebration. It saddens me that the country has become more and more divided ever since. It also saddens me that my kids, too young to know what was going on at the time, only know an America divided. Dan Rather, in tears on Letterman, offering to "man a post," is but a forgotten memory.

CHAPTER 10

Starting at the U

"Dr. Fulkerson, you've got a phone call!"

"Patient?"

"No, some doctor from the States."

"What?"

It was no mean feat calling Japan from the United States. Without knowledge of the military system, calling required going through multiple international operators, many of whom did not speak English. Grandpa P. had called my intern-year surgery office, found out where I was stationed, and somehow, someway, figured out how to connect to the Misawa ER phone. We talked for a while, catching up. Grandpa P. was excited to bring me back for residency training. I was touched that he would go through this effort to contact me.

I finished my tour, said a few tearful "good-byes," gave away my car, and boarded the freedom bird for the last time. The Lovely Wife had enthusiastically moved back to the States a few months earlier. I left like I arrived—in a fog both of mind and weather. I had a few weeks to get our house settled, now girded for three kids. I began to read my textbooks, trying to shift gears from pelvic exams to brain surgery.

Due to world circumstances and my station in Asia, my interview process was quite different from everybody else's. In their final year, nonmilitary medical students participate in the *match*. This is basically the computer equivalent of Harry Potter's sorting hat. Medical students interview for residency training spots. The students then submit their "rank list" of their preference. The programs submit their rank list, and a computer somewhere decides where everyone is going to go. All the students find out on the same day.

The federal government sets the number of residency positions and, despite the growing shortfall of doctors, has not allowed much expansion in seventeen years.[40] They have, however, expanded the number of medical student spots, generating an increasingly problematic bottleneck. Some specialties now have many more applicants than available training spots. Neurosurgery remains one of the most competitive residency positions, so every detail of a student's application is important, including the face-to-face interview. Most students interview at around twenty to twenty-five programs around the country.

The interview process works both ways. Students evaluate programs. A program that hides their current residents (usually because they are bitter and miserable) is probably one to avoid. Programs evaluate students looking for red flags. Every year, there are a few students who stand out for all the wrong reasons. I didn't make a single one of these up:

1. A large, burly, single male without kids was quite open about his fondness for the TV show *Hannah Montana*, which would have been fine if he wasn't a large, burly, single male without kids.
2. A set of identical twins spent most of their time discussing how the other twin sucked.

---

[40] https://www.aamc.org/newsroom/newsreleases/374000/03212014.html.

3. A student was asked to give a PowerPoint presentation in front of the chairman and the entire neurosurgery staff. He inserted his memory stick into the computer, knowing the presentation was his big shot to get the attention. He certainly got their attention when a folder full of hard-core porn exploded[41] on the screen.

Every student is asked this question: "Why do you want to go into neurosurgery?"

The answers are usually similar. Years later, Steve and I were musing that none of these answers were truly honest.

"Just once," Steve said, "I wish someone would answer honestly."

"So what's the honest answer?" I asked.

"Chicks and money," he joked.

The Professor overheard us joking around and insists to this day that I said that during my residency interview. I think this is also how the Internet news works.

*   *   *   *

My first day as a neurosurgeon arrived. I met the team on rounds. The service seemed familiar from my medical school days, but there's a different feeling as a resident. I was terrified. Luckily, I saw some familiar faces. Kelly, the nurse who ran the service, was there and greeted me with a hearty hello. She made things happen, chewed butt when butt needed chewed, and acted as our surrogate mom. Also greeting me was Steve.

"Hey!" he greeted me in that distinctive voice more suited to extolling the power of the dark side. "Welcome back."

---

[41] Shot? Plopped? Squirted? Help me out here...

"Thanks."

"Ever done a DBS?"

"What?"

Steve laughed.

The other resident was Bryce, a certifiable genius with leading-man good looks and a very disinterested affect. "Let's get going." Bryce absolutely smoked any standardized test he ever took, including recording the highest score in the country the year he took the written neurosurgery board examination. When motivated, he was charming, engaging, and charismatic. When unmotivated, he was a spectacular ass. He knew this and sort of reveled in dickery.

We started rounds. Steve and I started gabbing like old friends. Bryce seemed annoyed by everything. When we were almost finished, the chief resident, Kendall, sauntered in, sipping coffee.

"Nice of you to show up," Bryce chided.

Kendall was nonplussed. Clearly, he had grown accustomed to Bryce's habits over the years. "I made it in time for breakfast." Kendall introduced himself to me and pretended to be interested in what we told him about the patients, and we all rolled off to breakfast. Kendall reviewed the cases scheduled for that day, divvied them up, and then dove into his pancakes.

Kendall had a raging case of *chiefitis*. This is a disease that all chief residents get at some point. You hope it doesn't happen until the last part of the year. I think Kendall contracted a nasty case about halfway through his residency. *Chiefitis* is when a person is flat out sick of being a trainee and just wants to get by until graduation.

Kendall assigned the cases, conspicuously choosing the shortest, quickest procedure for himself.

"Okay, where will I find you?" Kelly asked Kendall, in case there were any problems on the patients.

"I'll be in the call room, sitting on the couch, surrounded by a ring of Cheeto dust."

We settled into our routine. Kendall would pick the shortest case and leave. Bryce would be in his own world, and Steve and I would run the service. My schedule was pretty set. Every Friday, I operated with Grandpa P. Every Wednesday, I was assigned to the functional neurosurgeons to do a deep brain stimulator (DBS). Every Monday and Thursday, I was assigned to the spine surgeon.

Spine surgeons generate the most revenue for a neurosurgical service. A busy spine surgeon is worth multiple millions of dollars to a hospital every year. The system ridiculously favors them, and they know it. This gives them an unmistakable sense of confidence bordering on entitlement. Many seem like the rich-kid bad-guy bullies in every eighties teen movie.

Steff McKee in *Pretty in Pink*? No.

Stan Gable in *Revenge of the Nerds*? Closer.[42]

Johnny Lawrence in *The Karate Kid*? Yes! A thousand times, yes!

Kendall couldn't stand operating with the spine surgeon (Johnny), so I got the draw twice per week. Kendall's total disdain for Johnny gave me the opportunity to do a tremendous amount of surgery early in my training.

Every Wednesday, I worked with the functional neurosurgeons. Functional neurosurgeons are often prim, obsessive-compulsive, tweed-clad professorial types. There were two functional neurosurgeons in the program. One was so precise and so exacting that we actually entertained the notion that he was an android.[43] That precision is quite helpful when one is trying to target a single cell deep within the brain. The second, the Distinguished Gentleman (DG), was the

---

[42] Who am I kidding? I could never speak ill of Ted McGinley. The man's a comedy Adonis.

[43] We're over 75 percent sure he's not.

type who would go through three changes of clothes per day. He had a smoking jacket and silk pajamas. He had books lying around his immaculate living room describing the proper way to clothe the modern male. He dripped with class. He found neurosurgery to be mundane and much less engaging than math. In fact, he spent much of his time as a professor of mathematics in the associated undergraduate school. As he got older, he began to look remarkably like David Bowie.

Deep brain stimulators are remarkable devices. Years ago, Cooper serendipitously discovered that occlusion of a particular artery (the *anterior choroidal*) would induce a stroke in a deep part of the brain.[44] Normally, we consider this a bad thing. However, this happened in a person with Parkinson's disease. Parkinson's is one of the leading causes of dementia in elderly patients and is characterized by a terrible tremor of the hand. Parkinson's patients sort of look like Frankenstein—masklike faces, stiff walking, and tremor of the hands. The tremor can be especially horrible, preventing the patient from doing mundane tasks, such as bringing food to the mouth. Cooper discovered that the tremor vanished in his patient after the stroke. This led to initial attempts to cure Parkinson's by intentionally blocking this artery.[45] Unfortunately, the side effects were too unpredictable and too great for this to be accepted.

However, these efforts led to the theory that certain parts of the brain, even certain cells, may be defective and cause the symptoms. Perhaps targeting these cells could help the disease. Research has shown that symptoms are caused by a loss of *dopamine* due to degeneration of certain cells in a part of the brain called the *substantia nigra*. This loss of dopamine affects a very elegant and complex loop

[44] I. S. Cooper, "Ligation of the Anterior Choroidal Artery for Involuntary Movements, Parkinsonism." *Psychiatry Quarterly* 27 (1953): 317–319.
[45] R. W. Rand, W. E. Stern, and J. K. Orr, "Parkinsonism: Early Results of Occlusion of the Anterior Choroidal Artery," *Calif. Med.* 81 no. 4 (1954): 276–8.

in the brain and eventually leads to overactivity of certain neurons that affect movement. Medications were developed, including early efforts highlighted in the movie *Awakenings*.

Medications are still a mainstay of treatment. But eventually the benefit of medication wears off and the side effects, including a different kind of writhing motion, set in. As a side note, making fun of this side effect in Marty McFly is specifically diagnostic of being a total mouth-breathing thunderturd.[46]

The DBS electrode is precisely placed near one of the malfunctioning cells causing the characteristic tremor. This sends a small field of current that essentially deactivates the cell.

The surgery is really remarkable. The patient is awake. The surgeon may ask him or her to perform a task, such as raising a glass or even playing a musical instrument. The patient will try, but the tremor will interfere. Then the electrode is turned on. The patient's tremor *disappears*. Completely. The patient goes from severely disabled to normal *instantly*. DBS also works for other types of tremors. It has been tried for seizures, refractory obsessive-compulsive disorders, and even obesity. Current cutting-edge surgeons are working on using DBS to do the same surgeries that Dr. King performed decades ago.

DBS is conceptually fascinating. The surgery, however, for me was terribly boring. I would make a small incision and then drill a hole. Then we'd spend about six hours slowly listening to every cell in the path of the electrode. The android surgeon loved it. The whole process took about eight hours. Surgery had a remarkable effect and tremendous benefit, was conceptually challenging, but was cosmically boring. Thus Steve told me DBS stood for "Done by second-year" (me).

We'd finish breakfast and head off to the OR. Kelly would head

---

[46] David Montgomery, "Rush Limbaugh on the Offensive against Ad with Michael J. Fox," *Washington Post*, October 25, 2006. To be fair, Rush probably does know a thing or two about medication side effects.

back to the wards to take care of whatever needed to be done, and Kendall would head back for seconds.

About once a week, Bryce would get in trouble. He rivaled Vinnie in the number of write-ups and only the consistent loyalty of Grandpa P. kept him from getting fired. When he wanted to be, Bryce was dashingly charismatic, in a Benedict Cumberbatch[47] supergenius sort of manner. Eventually the evil would come out, often in hilarious ways.

New high-definition view screens had recently been installed in the U's operating rooms. This was a stellar advance. We would use the computer to call up the relevant images of the surgery and have it in glorious wide-screen display. The computers were Internet compatible. As expected, the administrators kept close watch for anything inappropriate.

Bryce was in a good mood. He was operating away, chatting up the nurses. Everyone was at ease. Megan, the circulating nurse, was discussing her teenage son's newfound affinity for snowboarding. Bryce casually mentioned that he too was a snowboarder and started telling her about the various resorts within a reasonable driving distance. Megan soaked up the advice.

"I really want to get him a new board for his birthday, but I have no idea where to start."

Bryce began to outline the various types of boards. He asked her a few questions about her son's skill level and started to make some recommendations. Megan furiously began writing down everything he said.

"How much do one of those boards cost?"

"Expensive."

Megan was dejected.

---

[47] *Star Trek:* ~~*Crappy Wrath of Khan*~~ *Into Darkness* Benedict Cumberbatch, not *Sherlock* Benedict Cumberbatch. There's a difference.

"*How* expensive?"

"Very." Bryce paused and then offered a ray of hope. "But I do know a place that's having a big sale."

Megan brightened up. "Really?"

"Yeah, Dick's Sporting Goods." This large chain sporting shop had recently opened in the area.

"In fact," Bryce continued, "you could probably buy it from their website."

Megan was giddy. "Okay, how do I do that?"

"Just go to the 'extreme sports' section of their website."

Megan was not particularly savvy with computers. She pecked away at the keyboard but with no luck. "I can't find it."

"It's easy!"

Still no luck.

Bryce feigned exasperation.

"All right, just go to Google. Type in 'extreme dicks.'"

"E ... X ... T ... ... Okay, I think something—Oh my God!"

Bryce chortled.

"Escape, escape. It won't let me escape!"

*   *   *   *

"You can't be a skull base surgeon," Kendall said to me flatly, after I commented on a patient with a particularly impressive brain tumor. I was offended. The skull base surgeons were the cowboys, the mavericks, and often the bigwigs of organized neurosurgery. They considered themselves the "true" neurosurgeons with egos big enough to match their skills.

"Why not?" I asked, kind of hurt.

Kendall stuffed a handful of corn chips into his mouth and aimlessly clicked the mouse.

"Why not?" I demanded.

"Because skull base surgeons mess people up. That'd bother you too much." He sighed. He pulled the patient's MRI up on his computer. She had large *acoustic neuroma*—a benign tumor that grows from part of a cranial nerve heading to the inner ear. The eighth cranial nerve has components that transmit signals important in hearing and balance. The tumor technically arises from the superior part of the balance fibers of the nerve—the superior vestibular division. The tumor is properly called a "vestibular schwannoma," but the other name is pretty entrenched. This lady's tumor was large enough to deform the nearby brainstem.

"She looks good now. But once we get ahold of her, she's going to need at least a PEG, maybe a trach." He meant there was a high likelihood that surgery would damage or irritate the cranial nerves that basically control the face and throat. He thought she wouldn't be able to swallow safely and would thus require a permanent feeding tube.[48] She wouldn't be able to move half of her face, and she may need a tracheostomy for breathing. Really, she could die.

"It's part of the game. Skull base surgeons mess people up. You have to hate the tumor more than you like the patient. Anyway, you'd feel bad if you messed someone up. You shouldn't do it."

Kendall had an understated wisdom. He was right. He sighed, ate a few more chips, and then trudged down to the OR for what would be a full-day surgery. He was working with Dr. Montgomery, the senior brain surgeon. Dr. Montgomery was a Poindexter of a man, with a screechy voice, a hump in his back, and quite possibly teamed with Smithers to manage the town's nuclear power plant.

We rounded on the patient the next day. She had been recently extubated but was still pretty sleepy. Kendall aggressively rubbed her sternum.

---

[48] PEG, percutaneous endoscopic gastrostomy—a feeding tube.

"Show me your teeth!" he yelled.

She tried to open her mouth. The left half of her face worked.

"Close your eyes!"

The left eye closed. The right eye rolled back in her head with the lid still open.

"She'll need drops and lube at night." Kendall's voice was level and passionless. "Speech therapy, keep up the steroids, keep her head elevated." He was barking out orders to me; I dutifully recorded them. "Probably need ENT to weight that eyelid at some point."

We moved on. Later that day, her incision would start to leak spinal fluid. We then put her to sleep and placed a temporary drain to remove spinal fluid. A few days later, the general surgeons placed a PEG tube. A few days after that, we placed a permanent shunt. Each morning, we would wake her up, shake her, figure out what complication was going on that day, write down a few orders, and move on.

The lady's life was changed permanently. We dealt with it in a few minutes at six each morning. After a few weeks, Kendall paused after we left the room. He sighed and then looked at me.

"The bitch of it is her surgery went great. We took out her tumor smooth as silk. She's cured but wrecked.

"Man, if I had one in my head, no way would I let anybody operate. Either radiation or nothing. Her tumor was too big for radiation, so she was screwed. But if you did that," he said, gesturing to her room, "it'd bother you. Skull base guys have to hate the tumor more than they like the patient."

He was right.

We kept rounding. We made our way through the third-floor ICU. Bryce disappeared. Steve, Kendall, and I then headed up to the seizure floor. There we encountered a very irate neurologist who vehemently disagreed with our attending's plan.

He met us at the entrance and began to yell at Kendall, who stared at him placidly. He looked impressively professorial, with pompous glasses, a neatly trimmed goatee, and a large trailing crowd of medical students, residents, and nurses. Like all neurologists, he was able to use lots of big words to describe problems he couldn't fix. I'm sure he wanted to put on a show for his troops.

Kendall, as always, seemed unconcerned. However, Kelly was bristling. She started to sway back and forth like a prizefighter. She was slight in build, but I'll bet good in a fight. The neurologist kept yelling on and on about how our plan was not indicated and standard of care and so forth. He became more and more animated, gesticulating his arms to prove the immediacy of her concerns. His trailing medical students all had furrowed brows, sharing their leader's dismay, even if it was quite clear that they had no idea what he was saying.

Kendall didn't move, blink, or even react. For a split second, I thought he had fallen asleep.

The impressive neurologist finished his verbal barrage and stood there, panting.

Kendall's eyes stayed locked on his. He slowly reached up to the lapel of his coat and held up his ID.

"My badge says *resident*."

The neurologist's eyes widened.

Kendall continued, "If you have concerns, call the attending."

He turned on his heel, and we were off. Kelly was grinning. Kendall had masterfully brushed off the assault with the fact that he was just doing what he was told. The neurologist had wasted all that energy for nothing.

We heard a weak "I will" coming from behind.

Steve elbowed me. "We just load the trucks."

* * * *

We settled into our morning routine. Steve and I loaded the trucks. Bryce took care of his own patients but didn't have much interest in anybody else. Every now and then, we'd encounter one of the attendings on morning rounds. Dr. Montgomery was always quite prompt, and we would review his patients. Grandpa P. occasionally bounded in and made all the nurses laugh. Johnny Spine sometimes showed up to grouse, bitch, and continue his noble quest to remove joy and mirth from the hospital. The resident team then congregated for breakfast, looking for the elusive and somewhat arbitrary Kendall sighting.

"What's on the schedule today?" Kelly asked.

Steve glanced over the list.

"Temporal lobectomy, I'll take that one. Lumbar fusion. Bryce?"

Bryce nodded agreement and grumbled something about Johnny and rectal tubes. I was a little confused on how that assignment skipped me.

"At any rate, one aneurysm. Kendall?"

Kendall arrived, looking a little annoyed. "Fine."

"And one Thomas shunt."

Everyone looked at me.

"Uh, sure."

Steve laughed. "Like you have any choice."

"Who's the patient?" Kelly asked.

"Jocelyn."

"Oh *God*," Kelly groaned. "Not again!"

Jocelyn had become well known to neurosurgery service. She was originally treated in a different state but quickly burned through every doctor in a one-hundred-mile radius. Jocelyn was a drug seeker. She arrived with various unprovable symptoms of pain—back pain, headaches, and so on—and basically whined until she was given narcotics.

One of the difficulties with pain management is that it is impossible to prove that someone *doesn't* have pain. One can check lab, EKG, or imaging studies to prove that someone is *not* having a heart attack. But there's no way to prove that someone is *not* having a headache. The doctor is left with his or her judgment and the patient's word.

A few years ago, there was a big push for pain control. According to some brilliant politicians and groups that accredit hospitals,[49] uncaring doctors were ignoring their patients' suffering and, never to waste a potential popular gain, there became increasing pressure from above to treat pain as a vital sign. So doctors began to liberally dispense narcotic pain medications. To the surprise of absolutely no one in medicine (and everybody outside of medicine), we created a tremendous prescription narcotic abuse problem.[50] It seems Americans love them some narcotics. Over 75 percent of narcotic pain medications are consumed in America.[51] That's a staggering fact. One person dies of a narcotic overdose in America every nineteen minutes.[52] Some are famous. Most are not. Neurosurgeons are in the middle of this, as exposure to narcotics often starts with a patient treated for back pain.

Jocelyn had gone doctor-shopping frequently. She would go to one doctor, complain about her various pains, and then go to another, complain again, and work hard to get prescriptions from both. Eventually, all the locals caught on and people refused to see her.

Tragically, at some point, she had a shunt placed. So she found Thomas.

If asked to give a talk about Adolf Hitler, Thomas would emphasize his good points: "He really rocked a jaunty moustache. We haven't seen someone pull off that look since!"[53] Thomas always believed

---

[49] I'm looking *squarely* at you JACHO.
[50] CDC Issue Brief: "Unintentional Drug Poisoning in the United States."
[51] As of 2011. I'd wager it's actually higher.
[52] http://www.cdc.gov/mmwr/preview/mmwrhtml/mm6450a3.htm.
[53] Michael Jordan notwithstanding.

the best in everybody. So if Jocelyn had a headache, maybe her shunt needed fixed again ...

And again ...

And again ...

For someone so good at chess, pattern recognition was not one of Thomas's strong suits.

Kelly groaned. "Is it too early to have a drink?"

Steve laughed. He then addressed me: "So, it's time you learn about Thomas's patients. He's the pied-piper—as soon as he gets into town, all the rats flock."

I had to say, I was a bit offended by this characterization.

Kendall nodded.

Kelly kept muttering, "Just kill me now."

"Most of his patients are good people. But some are dirtbags. There are a few danger signs. Number one, if the patient calls him 'Thomas' instead of 'Doctor.' Two, if the patient came from over an hour's drive away. Three, if they have allergies to anti-inflammatories, Tylenol, aspirin ..."

"Usually they have allergies to every drug but the one they want," Kendall interrupted laughing.

"It's funny for you guys. I'm the one who has to get them out of the hospital!" Kelly interjected.

"How long do they stay?" I asked.

"For this surgery? Overnight. For this patient? We'll be lucky to get her out this week."

We broke up and headed to the preoperative area where I met Jocelyn. She was in her early fifties and had makeup that bordered on vaudeville. Divine would think her taste in clothing was too gauche.[54]

---

[54] https://en.wikipedia.org/wiki/Divine_(performer).

I checked her past medical history and allergies. There were over twenty.

"I called Thomas last night and told him I was *dying* ..." Jocelyn said, raising her hand to her head for dramatic effect.

"Well, we'll try to get that shunt fixed," I offered. "On a scale of one to ten, how bad is your pain right now?"

"Oh, honey, those pain scales don't apply to me. My pain is *beyond* that scale. On that scale, my pain is a *twenty*! I have a *really* high tolerance for pain. So normal pain medications don't work on me."

"Really?"

"Very high! Plus I'm allergic to so many. Really, only Dilaudid even *touches* the pain. It may bring it down to a nineteen."

Dilaudid is a very powerful narcotic. It is approximately ten times stronger than morphine.

"Nineteen out of ten?"[55]

She nodded, face screwed into a position of ultimate suffering.

"Also, all your other little residents always try to kick me out of the hospital *way* too early. I need at least a week."

"You know that already?"

She nodded ruefully. "I *suffer*," she said, drawing out the last word and searching for Mr. DeMille for her close-up.

"Well, we'll do our best ..."

"Is Thomas here? I'd like to speak to him," she said.

"I haven't seen him. Do you want him paged?" I asked.

"I just want to make sure he's in charge of my pain. All you residents don't care that I'm suffering. *Thomas* is the only one who cares."

I couldn't argue with that. "He takes very good care of his patients."

"Oh, I know! He's such a saint. I'm so happy he cares for me.

[55] A tip: if a doctor gives you a ten-point pain scale and you say something higher than ten, the doctor will invariably think you're crazy and suck at math.

Normally he's taking out brain tumors in babies! All my doctors at home are terrible. But then I found *Thomas*!" She smiled.

"Super. Sign here."

I wandered back to the operating room, feeling hauntingly like I needed a shower and a shot of penicillin. I met Thomas. He stretched out his gangly, cachectic frame and sighed deeply. He seemed sad.

"I'm such a *sluggo* today." He looked pensive and stared off into space.

After a pause, he said, "You know, there is a real possibility that she's overdraining." I think he was talking more to himself than to me. "So, we'll add a siphon guard."

This is a device that changes the resistance of a shunt valve based on the patient's position. If the patient is upright, then gravity exerts a pull on the fluid and may act as a siphon. Draining too much fluid may cause a very classic headache; a patient is fine lying down but gets tremendous pain standing up. Chronic overdrainage may lead to "slit ventricle" syndrome, where all the fluid in the brain is sucked down the shunt. Thomas thought maybe Jocelyn's headaches were caused by overdrainage; therefore, adding this device might help.

"I can teach you a lot of things." Thomas sighed sadly. "But patient selection is not one of them."

The case started, and Thomas perked up. We gabbed about chess and the Boston Red Sox. He loved the Red Sox. This was prior to the comeback against the Yankees and World Series win, so I could respect his allegiance.[56]

We finished.

"Oh, let's get some coffee. Do you like coffee?" Thomas asked.

"Not really."

"Do you mind if I get some?"

---

[56] Unlike the catastrophically annoying rest of Poser Nation.

"No."

"Great."

We walked up to the little shop. Thomas ordered. He implored me to get a roll or something. I got a small Danish and munched away while he sipped his drink.

"I love coffee," he said. "I wish I could hook it up through an IV."

"Won't that keep you awake?" I asked.

"The only time coffee keeps me awake is if I fall asleep and my cup spills on me."

"Do you have any preference on what I give Jocelyn for postoperative pain?"

"Do they allow cyanide?"

"I don't think so."

"Well then, no. No preference. Although if you find some cyanide, bring it by my office. I'm expecting a phone call from my lawyer."

*   *   *   *

As expected, Jocelyn was a nightmare. The surgery required an incision about an inch long, but Jocelyn was *dying*.

Kendall looked at her medication sheet the next day.

"How is she even breathing?" he mused, seeing the narcotic doses.

We walked in as a group. Kelly took the lead. "Jocelyn, how are things? Let me see that bandage."

"Oh God, don't turn my head!" Jocelyn screamed, bracing herself. "The pain medication is *not working*! *I told Thomas I can only take Dilaudid!*"

"You're on it, honey," Kelly said.

"Well, it's not enough!"

"You're allergic to everything else."

Jocelyn began to weep large tears with deep sobs. "I have a high pain tolerance! I need more than other patients! I don't understand why you can't understand that I hurt so much!"

"You just had surgery." Kelly sighed, like a mother explaining to her three-year-old why she can't just eat cookies. "It's going to hurt a little."

"I need to speak to Thomas!"

"We'll call him," Kelly said without much conviction. "Make sure you get out of bed today."

We walked out of the room as Jocelyn kept wailing, "I can't get up! I'm in *too much pain.*"

Kendall sighed. "Bitch got issues."

"Bitch needs a punch in the face," Kelly muttered.

I was torn. Thomas had talked me into believing her. I kept an open mind. Each morning, we had the same dance. She would tell us that she got *no sleep* just after we woke her up. She *couldn't move* but somehow managed to get down to the smoking area about five times per day. We were all jerks or worse. Thomas was the only one who understood how much she suffered. She called him multiple times from the hospital bed.

"I don't care what Thomas says. She's out of here today!" Kelly exclaimed as we headed to her room four days later. "This isn't a hotel."

Jocelyn must have sensed we were coming.

"I can't move my legs! I'm paralyzed. Oh God, you paralyzed me!" she screamed.

Kendall rolled his eyes.

Jocelyn was sobbing loudly.

"You're going to have to quiet down, ma'am." Kelly groaned.

"Ican'tmovemylegs!"

Steve went to examine her.

"Can you feel this?" he asked, tickling her feet.

"No!"

"Wiggle your toes," Steve said.

"I can't! Oh God! I have a bad back. I know that's why! You guys don't care for me, and now my back went out and now I'm paralyzed! I'm going to sue everyone in this hospital!"

"You are going to have to calm down," Kelly said.

"I can't go home," Jocelyn cried.

We left the room discouraged.

Kendall offered some wisdom. "One of the things we have to check is whether or not she's abused. Some people act like crazy-asses because they are scared. But her husband has been here each day and we already called social work. Her home is fine."

"So?" I asked.

"So remember that next time you see this," Kendall said. "But this chick is crazy." He turned to Kelly. "Have them transfer her to a monitored bed with a camera."

The crying stopped as soon as we were out of what Jocelyn thought was earshot. Then she rang the nurse to get her pain meds. We transferred her, and she seemed happy that she was going to a higher-care bed.

The next morning, the situation was unchanged. Jocelyn was paralyzed and in catastrophic pain. Her husband screamed at us for neglecting his wife and threatened to sue everyone in the building. I began to entertain all sorts of diagnoses and presented them to Kendall at breakfast.

"Maybe she dissected her aorta?" I asked.

"Does she have distal pulses," Kendall asked, without looking up from his plate. He wolfed down a large forkful of hash browns. "Did you check them?"

"Uh …" I paused, knowing I hadn't.

Kendall knew I hadn't either.

"I did," he said. "They're fine."

"Transverse myelitis?"

"You want to do a lumbar puncture?"

"Sure."

Kendall laughed. "Let me show you something."

We walked up to the control room of the bed-monitoring station. Kendall rewound her videotape. There we were on rounds. There she was, wailing in pain and about her paralysis. There we go, uncaringly leaving her in squalor. Still crying. Now she's looking up. We're gone. Her husband goes to check.

Jocelyn then stops crying and spryly hops out of bed. She unfolds her wheelchair, sits down, and instructs her husband to wheel her down to the smoking area. After smoking, she comes back, folds up the chair, walks around for a bit, and then hops back into bed.

I was discouraged.

"No more tests," Kendall said.

We notified Thomas who said, "That's interesting."

We called the social worker. Jocelyn had already filed multiple complaints about us and how we weren't treating her pain. The social worker finally confronted her with the videotape. After watching herself walk perfectly fine and comfortably, Jocelyn said flatly, "That's not me. That's a different patient."

"No, that's you," the social worker said.

"No, I can't walk," Jocelyn said. Jocelyn was confronted by a hospital administrator. She still unequivocally denied that she was the woman on the videotape. The administrator called a meeting with the head of social work and the ethics team. They gathered, trying to figure out what to do with her.

The next day, only Kendall and Kelly went into the room. I could hear Jocelyn's pitiful wails from the hallway. They exited. Jocelyn was frantically listing a bunch of new complaints. We moved on, but Kelly stayed, partially hidden in a nearby nurse's room. As usual, Jocelyn continued crying until we were down the hall. Her husband came out to look around. Coast clear, soon Jocelyn emerged in her wheelchair, perfectly comfortable, heading down to smoke.

Kelly sprang.

"Oh, good to see you feeling better and out of bed!"

Jocelyn tried to speak and cry, but Kelly was too quick.

"Here's your discharge paperwork, already signed. Here's your prescription. Note that there are *no* refills. You'll have to get those from your primary care doctor."

"But I've been vomit—"

"Bye!" Kelly said sprightly, with a big grin, and then dashed away.

Jocelyn sat there stunned. She was the victim of a drive-by discharge. Sensing that she would get no support from the administration, Jocelyn begrudgingly left.

"That was *sweeeeeeeet!*" Kelly said, beaming over her coffee.

Kendall scooped a helping of eggs into his mouth.

"Listen," he said, motioning to me. "You've got to look for zebras in a patient like that. You need to look for things like dissection or other weird things. Those are the patients that get you in trouble. You assume they are lying, but sometimes they aren't."

He took a gulp of orange juice.

"But—and this is very important to learn—some people are just dirtbags."

*   *   *   *

I thought back to my hippie training in the first two years. I was taught (and I truly believed) that there were no *dirtbags*. Patients like Jocelyn just needed care, and eventually they would instinctively do what was right. I felt that believing differently led to the path of being one of those uncaring, unfeeling doctors. Thomas believed in the best in everyone. He believed Jocelyn's protests, no matter how ridiculous they became. Actually, I think he didn't believe her, but he was just too nice to refuse.

Kendall was right. Jocelyn was a drug-addicted dirtbag. She lied. She threatened to sue. She lied again. Jocelyn felt that it was her right to lie in bed, be waited on and fed, and get as much narcotic medication as she could stand. She was a flat-out bad person.

Dirtbags are a significant drain on the financial capital of medicine. Jocelyn probably cost the hospital and thus the taxpayers of the state upward of $200,000 for this visit. The most expensive hotel room in town is a hospital bed. Imagine how many vaccines, pap smears, or mammograms one could fund instead of this crazy, selfish lady's Dilaudid vacation.

I am thankful true dirtbags are rare. But they are common enough that they extract a significant emotional toll on doctors. Doctors at one time or another dream of going on a *House*-like litany of insults directed toward the malingerers, the cheats, and the abusers. Unfortunately, dirtbags are coddled in America. Lawyers salivate at the thought of a dirtbag who cried wolf too many times and the doctor subsequently missed a legitimate problem.

Dirtbags can be any sex, race, creed, or religion. Dirtbags can be rich or poor. A wealthy VIP who expects the royal treatment is just as big a dirtbag as the healthy young male seeking disability. Some rich people are dirtbags for inventing new ways to be sick for their own psychological benefit. There's a condition called *Munchausen syndrome*, in which patients will invent symptoms for various psychiatric reasons. These patients have a significant mental illness. This is subtly different from *malingering*, where patients blatantly fake symptoms for secondary gain, like drugs, litigation, or disability benefits. Jocelyn was a malingerer. Unfortunately, she's not alone.

Worse, there's a syndrome called *Munchausen-by-proxy*, where a parent will deliberately injure his or her child for their own benefit—financial gain, attention, or even pity. One patient at the Baby Hospital actually injected her own feces into the child's shunt, hoping to cause an infection. Psychiatric condition or not, people like this make me think the country should rethink any ban on the guillotine.

The common thread inherent to all dirtbags is a sense of entitlement. Maybe they feel entitled to attention. Maybe they feel entitled to disability payments or pain medications. Whatever the reason, dirtbags feel that they are owed a living.

It's hard to overestimate the emotional toll patients like Jocelyn take on a doctor. Seeing her name on the clinic schedule is a mental donkey punch to the groin. She's going to cry, she's going to take an hour, she's never going to be better, and eventually, the doctor is going to try to calculate how much narcotic he or she has to prescribe just to get her out of the office.

Jocelyn does not want to leave without more pain medicine, and she will do whatever it takes to get it. If a doctor confronts her about overuse of narcotics, she will act offended and complain to the hospital administration that she was insulted. Now, she may spread the word that the doctor "doesn't care about her pain." If that doesn't work, she'll quickly and loudly play whatever card is scariest—racism, homophobia, sexism ... Increasingly, patient satisfaction reviews are becoming important in determining reimbursement. While I've found most patients filling out a survey are honest and upstanding, there's a small but vocal minority who rate a doctor based on how much narcotics he or she will prescribe or how quickly they will sign a disability application. Some doctors try to help but realize it's a losing battle. Some doctors just give in. Some are just too nice to say no—like Thomas.

I've had patients cry, outright threaten, and try to blackmail me for drugs. I imagine any spine surgeon has had the same experience. One patient demanded a refill on Percocet. When my partner refused, she said she was going to sue because she needed to sell the drugs to pay her rent. When he refused again, she went out to the crowded waiting room and, loud as she could, yelled, "Me and my children are going to be homeless because of him!"

Most patients are decent enough. Most are good people with real problems. It only takes a few patients like Jocelyn to make a physician view any patient seeking pain medications with jaded suspicion. Clinic days with a patient like Jocelyn are about as fun as a Tabasco enema. There are definitely patients who are victims of abuse, discrimination, poor circumstance, bad genes, or just plain bad luck. But some people are just dirtbags.

*   *   *   *

"So, on-call tonight?" Steve asked me.

"Yep."

"Covering the Baby Hospital?"

Kendall snorted. "That place is whacked."

Steve laughed.

"When I was the resident there, I got called while I was scrubbed because the ER wanted me to come pronounce someone as brain dead," Kendall continued. "I felt bad, man. I told them I'd be down in a sec. Then the ER doc says, 'Can you hurry? The patient is requiring a lot of sedation to keep them still.' They wanted me say some kid who's fighting is dead? Are you kidding me?"

"Don't listen to him," Steve said. "You'll be fine. You just have to remember three rules."

"Okay."

"Number one, it's *always* the shunt," Steve began. "Number 2, *you can't fix Thomas.* Many have tried. I wish we could fix him, but we can't."

That one seemed strange. "And the third thing?" I asked.

"Nothing good happens at the Baby Hospital."

CHAPTER 11

Nights with Thomas

I settled into the call schedule and quickly became acclimated to neurologic trauma. My general surgery and ER training made this easy. I quickly learned how to place an intracranial pressure (ICP)[57] monitor and an external ventricular drain (EVD).[58]

During call, I was responsible for County, the U, and the Baby Hospital. It quickly became apparent that the Baby Hospital would require the most time. The resident on call for the Baby Hospital invariably develops a condition called *status pagicus,* a play on the words of *status epillepticus. Status epillepticus* is a life-threatening condition where a person has continuous seizures. *Status pagicus* means the pager won't stop going off. The Baby Hospital was notorious for this. The on-call resident got paged for everything, ranging from the critical to the mundane. This would seriously grate on the residents.

The pages came in waves from midnight to one in the morning.

---

[57] A pressure sensor inserted into the brain through a small hole in the skull. This will quickly give a reading of the *localized* pressure in the head.

[58] A catheter inserted through a small hole into the ventricle. This gives a more *global* reading of the intracranial pressure and allows drainage of spinal fluid. Drainage of spinal fluid is one of the most effective ways to treat elevated pressure in the head.

This was because the night crew settled down and went through the next day's medication lists.

Beeeeeeeeeeeep.

"This is five west. The dose of Kefzol ordered for Baby Smith is 275 milligrams. Pharmacy says it should be 280. Can we change it?"

Me: "And why couldn't this wait until morning rounds."

Nurse: "Because I'm thinking about it now."

Beeeeeeeeeeeeep.

Nurse: "The doctor wrote for a one-time suppository a week ago for little Sammy. But it was never given. Can we take the order off the chart?"

Me: "Again, why does this need to be addressed at midnight?"

Beeeeeeeeeeeeeep.

Nurse: "The doctor wrote for an order of Tylenol. Do you mind if we give it?"

Me: "You're asking me if it's okay to give the medication that is already ordered by the attending?"

Nurse without a hint of irony: "Yes."

I didn't make a single one of those pages up.

Tonight wasn't a particularly busy night. I cleaned up the few ER patients at County, rounded at the U, and then settled into the offices at the Baby Hospital. I answered all the absurd midnight pages and then propped open a textbook to begin studying. This was a blatant exercise in self-deception. Within minutes, I began searching the Internet for websites that *almost* but didn't quite trip the hospital security programs. I settled on online chess and began to play three-minute speed games with somebody from Latvia.

I could hear Thomas in the next office on the phone.

"I'm sorry you lost your prescription, but losing it three times in one week is a little much even for me ... Yes. I know the residents are mean. I'm glad you can walk again."

Oh no, it's Jocelyn!

"Well," Thomas continued. "If they keep breaking into your car to steal your prescriptions, I'd say you need to find another place to park ... No, I'm not calling any more in ... Yes, I do still care about you ... No, I'm not writing any more ... I've already written you three refills this week!"

[Histrionic sobs through the phone.]

"Come in tomorrow, and I'll dial up your valve a bit. Bye now!"

Thomas sighed deeply. Then his pager went off again. "Oh, I hope it's good news," he moaned. It wasn't. It was another adult patient. Same conversation. Then again. And again.

Thomas poked his head into my office.

"Anything I can help you with, boss?" I asked, without looking up from the screen.

"Ooooooooh, are you playing chess?"

"Yeah, I'm pretty good at the speed games—Damn it! He just took my bishop."

Thomas was fascinated.

"I do pretty well unless my concentration gets broken," I said honestly. I could tell Thomas felt a little guilty for talking to me during the game.

"Anything I can do for you?" I asked again, declining the rematch to the now-gloating Latvian whose mastery of the English language consisted of a truly impressive number of variations of the "f" word. I dashed off a few obscene words of my own in the chat box.

"You don't have a shotgun on you, do you?" Thomas asked.

"Sorry."

"I'd settle for a hand grenade. Or maybe some cyanide." Thomas laughed to himself. "That's a nice thought exercise. If you could place one hand grenade anywhere in the world, where would you place it?" Thomas stared off in the distance, pondering his answer.

I still wasn't that far removed from the military. "I'd say whatever cave Bin Laden is in."

Thomas seemed pleased with my answer. "Good one! I'd agree." He thought for a second. "Or my wife's lawyer's office!" He chuckled. "I'd be okay if she was or wasn't there at the time. Anyway, there's a kiddo coming in who I'll bet has a shunt malfunction."

Great. More shunts. Jocelyn part 2?

"The mother said he's been throwing up all day. I'll bet he's in the ER now."

"I didn't get paged?" I questioned.

"Oh, I told them just to page me. I thought you might be busy."

We walked down to the ER, and there was a small six-year-old child lying on the bed. He didn't react when the nurse patted him on the back. Thomas felt around on his head and then checked his CT scan.

"Vomiting all day?" he asked.

His mother looked very worried. She was not terribly educated, but she knew that something was wrong with her son. She nodded solemnly.

"Well, you certainly did the right thing bringing him in. I'll bet his shunt is plugged up. We should fix it tonight." Thomas's voice was calm and reassuring. I could tell Mom felt better. I think she appreciated that he said she did the right thing. "Let's take a look at the kiddo."

Thomas moved closer.

"Look, Timmy. Look who's here," his mother said, arousing the somnolent child.

He groggily woke up, fighting both the time of night and the pressure on his brain. He blinked a few times, trying to focus his eyes. He then glanced up at Thomas's smiling eyes and scraggly beard.

"Jesus?" the kid asked.

Thomas was a little startled. "No, not yet!" he said.

We shuttled him up to the operating room. There, I met the OR-Moms: Jill and Dana.

The OR-Moms were a part group of incredibly dedicated nurses who assisted in all pediatric neurosurgery procedures at the Baby Hospital. They were extremely competent and had the patience of Job. I didn't appreciate how wonderful they were until I began to operate at different hospitals. Dana was scrubbed and setting out the instruments while the Jill acted as the circulator, the nurse who handles all the stuff outside the sterile field.

"Hi, Thomas. Fancy seeing you here!"

"I'm using my block time." Thomas laughed. *Block time* is the scheduled time where a surgeon performs elective cases. Thomas was joking that all his surgeries happened at midnight.

We got to work. Thomas opened his old incision and exposed the shunt. He disconnected it at the valve and noted that there was no flow of spinal fluid coming from the catheter entering the child's head.

"Proximal occlusion." He took a small instrument designed to cauterize blood vessels and stuck it down the catheter. In a few second, spinal fluid came shooting out. "Okay, it's loose. Ready?"

The catheter had become stuck in the choroid plexus. Thomas had cauterized it to burn it back and free the catheter. If one pulls the catheter out before it's free, the child may bleed internally. I had a new catheter, ready to pass down the hole when he pulled out the old one.

"Ready."

Thomas pulled the catheter out, and I quickly stuck the new one in. Spinal fluid shot out under very high pressure.

"Whoa!"

Thomas fiddled with the length and then tested the valve and the distal system. Finding it satisfactory, he hooked up the new catheter.

"I hope he likes it."

"I'm sure he will, Thomas," Dana said.

We closed, and I had the mental image of Jocelyn sitting at the U, faking symptoms to get pain medications. What would this little kid do?

We wandered back to the office. Thomas kept getting pages. He got more pages than I did. I felt guilty about this for some reason. One of the pages came from a family member.

"Oh, that kid of mine ..."

"A handful?" I asked.

"Oh God, yes. He's a good kid, but his mouth gets him in trouble. You know, kids are like farts; they seem less obnoxious if they're your own."

Bad da bump!

He got paged to the ER again.

"Ugh!" I heard him exclaim. "Come look at this."

I left the resident office and walked over to his. He had an x-ray displaying on his computer. It showed the abdomen of another child with a shunt. The abdominal part of the shunt tubing dropped down toward the pelvis and then turned to the patient's right, up, left, down, right, and down again, forming a square shape. It was a shape that tracked perfectly with his colon.

"Do you think ..." I started.

We went back to the ER again. The baby had abdominal pain and fever. We examined the kid, and sure enough, when Thomas spread the legs, we could see the shunt tubing protruding out the anus.

"We've got shunts coming out of our asses!" Thomas said.

We took that kid to the OR also.

Finally, the dark early-morning hours brought us some relief from the incessant pager chirping. We settled back to the offices and sat down in sticky exhaustion.

"Want to play chess?" Thomas asked.

"Sure!"

He grabbed a ketchup packet, peeled it, squeezed it on his finger, and ate it like a lollipop. "Dinner."

I wrinkled my nose in disgust. Thomas found this funny.

I sat down in the resident office and logged on to my chess account. Thomas did the same. We met up in cyberspace. I had no prayer of beating Thomas in a game without a time limit. But I had a puncher's chance in speed chess. I was pretty good, unless something broke my concentration. Plus, I could move the pieces faster than he could. We started, and things were going my way.

Beeeeeeeeeeeeep.

Damn it. Oh well, I'm sure whatever it is can wait three minutes.

Beeeeeeeeeeeeep.

Ah crap! Just a few more moves. I've got him!

Beeeeeeeeeeeeep.

Dang it! He just took my rook.

Beeeeeeeeeeeeep.

Great. He's got me. Might as well answer the pages.

I checked. All four pages were from his office.

"Dirty pool, old man!" I shouted.

I could hear naughty laugher from the next room.

Thomas appeared in the door, grinning under that scraggly beard. We shared a laugh and then headed out to check on the first little kid.

I was amazed. After my experience with Jocelyn, I expected him to be curled up sobbing. No. He was playing, giggling, and acting a little goofy from the residual anesthesia.

"Hey, buddy," Thomas said.

"*Hi-fi!*" the little kid shouted gleefully, holding up his hand.

Mom chuckled.

"Hi-fi! Hi-fi! Hi-fi!"

Thomas looked puzzled.

"He wants you to give him a high five," Mom explained.

"Okay!" Thomas held up his hand, and the little kid enthusiastically slapped it.

He began singing to himself and playing with some small plastic toys that the nurses provided.

"He looks better," Thomas said. "I'll bet you can go home in the morning."

"Thank you!" Mom gave Thomas a warm, grateful handshake. "Thank you! Thank you for giving me my son back!"

We headed back to the office.

"Those patients are extremely gratifying to care for. I mean they are *extremely* gratifying," Thomas said. "They feel so much better."

"Different than adults?" I asked.

"Well, it depends on the adult. Kids aren't so much into pain medications and disability forms."

Thomas slumped into his office chair, seeming both happy and exhaustedly sad. He got paged again. I got paged again.

I took the phone call.

"Hey," said, "there's a patient coming in."

"Oh," Thomas said. "I'm happy to hear about it. I mean I'm *happy* to help. But I'm not on call."

CHAPTER 12

Trauma at Mos Eisley

County was a dilapidated old hospital, crawling with ghosts and roaches and filled with outdated, often broken equipment. If the U was the suburbs, County was the part of the ghetto the gangbangers avoided. County was the lair of the Professor. County was a "Level 1" trauma center, meaning it theoretically had the capability of treating the worst of the worst trauma.

One night when I was on call during my first year in neurosurgery, a bloody young man was whisked into the trauma bay, surrounded by hurried and stressed medics. A crowd of people descended on the room. The chief general surgery trauma resident began barking out orders. Lines were started. The patient was intubated. I was the neurosurgeon, damn it, so I muscled my way up to the front. His face was covered in blood. I pried open his eyes. One pupil was normal sized. The other was grossly dilated.

"He's bradying!" a nurse yelled, noting that his heart rate was dropping like a stone.

Conversely, my heart rate was rising—rapidly.

We shuttled him quickly to the CT scanner connected to the room. He was placed on the gurney, and the machine moved him through the spiral CT tube. Images began to come up. I saw a large crack in the bone and then a lens-shaped bright area.

"He's got an epidural!" the trauma resident shouted.

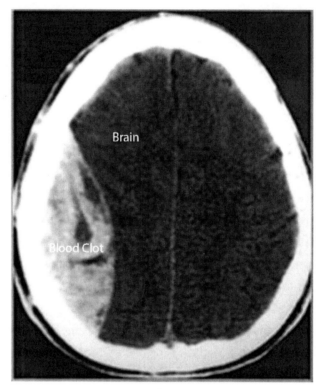

This.

The brain is surrounded by three layers of a protective covering. The outer layer is the *dura mater,* literally "tough mother." "Epidural" means between this dura and the inside of the skull. Our patient had a sizeable hematoma, a blood clot, in this space. It was compressing other parts of his brain and would kill him shortly if we did not act.

Steve arrived.

"Well, that's no good," he said curtly. "GCS?" he asked me.

"Uh, 6T?"

Steve nodded. I couldn't tell if I was correct; I was so flustered that I just guessed.

"Call the OR. Tell them we're coming."

I got on the phone and began stammering like a noob. "Uh, we've got a trauma victim, and ... we'd, uh, like to bring him to the OR. Umm, he needs a surgery."

Pause.

The nurse on the other end of the line kind of groaned.

"Okay, we'll call you when the room is ready."

"Thank you," I mewed meekly. *Wait! Did I just thank someone for doing nothing?* I relayed the message to Steve. I then noticed that he was removing all the IVs from the poles and putting them on the patient's chest, unlocking the bed, and rounding up a team to start pushing the patient out of the room.

"I didn't say *ask* them if we could come; I said, *'Tell them we're coming.'*"

I was still on the phone. The nurse on the other end said simply, "I heard."

For this patient, time was essential. He was moments from death. His heart rate was dropping because of something we call the Cushing's reflex, named for Harvey Cushing, the father of neurosurgery and winner of most namesake brain conditions. The Cushing's reflex is a marker for herniation, or rapid pressure on the brainstem. Patients have pupillary changes, a low heart rate (bradycardia), and high blood pressure (hypertension). It is caused by anything pressuring the brainstem hard enough to push it out (herniate) of the skull. Untreated, this situation is rapidly fatal.

We sprinted the patient down toward the OR. I tried valiantly to appear cool, suave even, despite my brain going: *"Ohgodohgodohgodohgodohgod!"* I was sweating.

"Relax," Steve said. Clearly my attempt to maintain a cool exterior had failed miserably. Steve didn't seem nervous in the least. For him, things were simple. The patient had a huge blood clot ("that's no good") that was about to kill him. All we needed to do was take it out and stop the bleeding. Simple. I was feeling sick.

Steve had asked me about the patient's GCS score. The GCS stands for Glasgow Coma Score, a reproducible scale that stratifies head-injured patients into the "mild," "moderate," or "severe" categories. The scale is easy and accepted. The patient is assigned a point score in three categories: eye opening, voice, and motor movement. You get one point automatically for each category and have a maximum score of fifteen. A GCS of three is on the verge of death, and fifteen is normal. The GCS scale has stood up remarkably well to large studies and scientific rigor. But there are caveats. An intubated patient cannot speak, so they get one point with the letter "T" for tube. The GCS is only valid after a patient has been resuscitated and stabilized. If, for example, the patient's blood pressure is too low, the patient will have an inaccurately low GCS. If doctors improve the blood pressure and stabilize the patient, the GCS may improve.

In the midst of all the chaos, Steve expected me to precisely evaluate the three categories and calculate the score. I was lucky in my guess. But I remembered the point; even though I was panicked, I was expected to be able to rationally assess the situation and function.

County was a dive, but it was the best hospital in the city for trauma. Everyone (besides me) knew exactly what they were doing. The medics, nurses, and Steve did this every day. Things happened automatically. One nurse knew it was her job to hook up the blood pressure cuff, another person rushed to start an IV, the trauma chief intubated the patient, and someone else recorded all the vital signs. It was a process.

Years ago, trauma and neurosurgeons decided to form a set of "guidelines" to manage head trauma. The goal of this effort was to organize medical treatment in a logical, science-based manner. There was nothing magical in the guidelines. They were simply a rational way of organizing what people already did. Practices were evaluated by science. Treatments that didn't hold up to scrutiny were abandoned. An unexpected benefit was discovered. Overall care improved simply by providing an organized plan. Steps weren't missed. Everybody was on the same page. Simply by doing things the same way every time, patient mortality dropped by *50 percent*.[59]

We arrived at the room in a burst of chaos. Steve seemed somewhat amused by the OR staff scrambling to open instruments. There's no subtlety in trauma. The patient was briskly shaved and soap was slopped onto his head. Steve squirted some alcohol on his hands and then donned his gloves. The incision was made before I completed the draping. The bone was drilled off in minutes. Three days later, the patient walked out of the hospital.

* * * *

Those guidelines are part of a growing movement of evidence-based medicine or EBM. The goal is to guide practices based on research and logic. EBM is all the rage with both medical and government bigwigs. Unfortunately, in real life the *E* of EBM often stands for something other than evidence. For example,

- *Eminence*-based medicine—Do something in a certain way because someone important says so. *I must stand in line for hours to get the next phone Steve Jobs told me to buy because the case is mauve!*

---

[59] Let me stress the significance of this value. If someone dropped the heart attack rate by 50 percent, they'd take home a Nobel Prize.

- *Eloquence*-based medicine—Do something a certain way because a speaker really convinced you. *Well, your argument and virtuoso use of ALL CAPS on my Facebook page has convinced me to change all my political beliefs!*
- *Experience*-based medicine—Do things that worked for you in the past. *I'm not sure why, but this seemed to work last time.* This is the way most medicine is practiced.
- *Evidence*-based medicine: Do things that are supported by research. This is ideally the way most medicine should be practiced.

Let's suppose you have high blood pressure. Let's suppose your doctor recommends you go on blood pressure medication. Why? You don't feel bad right now. Many blood pressure medications make you feel worse—run-down, tired, or dizzy. Well, your doctor knows that in a *large group*, the risk of having a future heart attack or stroke is much higher than normal in people with uncontrolled blood pressure.

The doctor may prescribe a drug to lower blood pressure. Which one? Suppose a doctor wants to decide between drug A or drug B. How to choose?[60] Ideally a large group of people is given drug A and an equally large group is given drug B. Researchers are blinded; they do not know which drug a given patient took. This prevents any bias. An objective finding (blood pressure) is then measured. Multiple hospitals are involved.

All of that is the gold-standard of research—a randomized (patients got either drug A or drug B), multicenter, double-blinded (neither the doctors nor the patients knew which drug they took) trial. A study like this takes a tremendous amount of time, effort, and money. It can be done.

---

[60] Besides the relative attractiveness of the vendor?

Just not in surgery.

How are we going to make a comparative study involving surgery? How can we blind patients to whether or not they had surgery? Seems like they'd notice the scar. Can we do *sham* surgery? In other words, can we put people to sleep, make an incision, do nothing else, and then close them up again? Well, no. At least not outside of Tijuana.

Let's say someone hits his or her head, cracks the skull, and develops an epidural hematoma. Some people have survived this. Some died. Some died despite surgery. How can we prove that surgery helps? Are we really going to randomize people?

We also know that some people in history have fallen out of an airplane and survived. We know that some people have died parachuting. How do we prove that a parachute is necessary for someone with the monumental stupidity to jump out of a perfectly good airplane? Should we run a study with one thousand people jumping out without a parachute and one thousand people with and compare results? This wouldn't make any ethical or logical sense.[61]

The upshot is that the *guidelines* are really just organized suggestions. However, patients benefit tremendously from these guidelines. Doctors have an organized, rational plan. The plan is modified as new research is added. Consistency prevents mistakes of omission.

In this case, the guidelines are clear. Take out the clot.

*　　*　　*　　*

What goes around comes around. Four years later, I was the chief. My junior resident called me about a patient with an epidural hematoma.

"Go!" I yelled to the junior. I raced from the call room to meet him in the OR. I arrived at the exact same time that the patient's team

---

[61] Unless the group without parachutes was all lawyers.

crashed through the door. We were greeted by the anesthesia resident. He was a friend of mine and was very, very good. We moved the patient to the operating table and quickly began to prep and drape. The anesthesia resident smoothly slid in an IV and then an intra-arterial line.

As I put on my gloves, a stern nurse bellowed out to the room, "*Stop!*" I looked around, concerned that there was some safety issue or that the patient was crashing. I saw nothing but a confused look on the anesthesia resident.

"You can't start!" she declared firmly.

"Uh, what?" I asked, decidedly *not* stopping.

She rolled her eyes, wondering why she had to explain the new policy to me. At midnight. "You can't start until the attending is in the room." Case closed. Too bad she didn't have a mic to throw down.

Right ...

I glanced at the anesthesia resident. I could tell he was grinning under his mask. We were thinking the same thing. *Just try and stop us, lady—this guy is going to die unless this clot comes out right now.*

"I *said*, you can't start until the attending is here!" *Probably followed by "all residents could use a good caning."*

"I heard you," I said, grabbing the knife.

She seemed befuddled that I was blatantly ignoring her obviously essential dedication to the policy cooked up in some boardroom.

"I *said*—"

"The attending is on his way," I interrupted. It was a half-truth. Assuming "half" means no truth at all. Maybe the junior resident paged the attending. I know I didn't. Oh well.

She was furious.

"I'm *reporting* you!"

The anesthesia resident made the motion with his hands behind the drapes that a third-grader would do while saying, "Uuuuummmmm, you're in troooooouuuublllllle."

"Spell my name correctly," I said, firing up the drill.

"I'm calling your attending! Who is it?" she demanded. *This* was getting noted in her log. I glanced at the junior. I had no idea who the attending on call was.

"It's the Professor," the junior said meekly, obviously worried that we were going to get in trouble and get a time-out or spanked or something.

She paged him.

No response.

She paged him again. And again.

By this time, the bone flap was off, and we were removing the clot. It was red and black and looked a little like afterbirth.

The phone rang. I could imagine a groggy Professor on the other end.

She smiled smugly. I was about to get censured. In a way, way too arrogant manner, she declared that she was putting the Professor on speakerphone for all to hear.

"Hello?" he asked sleepily.

"Do you know that *your resident* is starting a case?" she sneered derisively.

Pause.

Her smile vanished.

"And?" the Professor asked.

She tried again. Clearly she hadn't emphasized the critical breach of protocol that I was brazenly committing.

"He *started* a surgery!"

"Finished, actually." She didn't like my help.

"Policy states that surgery—"

"*Who's the resident?*" he angrily demanded.

Ah, she thought. Now we're communicating. Now we're getting to the punishment.

"Uh ..." She realized she didn't know my name. I helped.

"*Fulkerson!*" I yelled across the room.

"*And what's he doing?*" I could tell the Professor was fully awake and really, really mad.

"A crani ... crani ..." she began.

"Craniotomy," I said helpfully. "For an epidural."

"Craniostomy for epidural," she said into the phone.

Pause.

Here it comes, I'm sure she thought.

"You let him do whatever the f—— he wants and don't *ever* call me again!" Slam![62]

The anesthesia resident laughed. The nurse was mortified. The patient was saved.

---

[62] One tragedy of cell phones is the lack of ability to slam them down. No such lack here.

CHAPTER 13

M&M

Surgery requires introspection and self-evaluation. Answers and decisions are rarely crystal clear. The old axiom of "learn from your mistakes" rings true in medicine more than anything. People die from a surgeon's mistakes. Recognition of the need for quality medical treatment inspired construction of accepted guidelines previously mentioned. Another tradition in quality evaluation is honest retrospection of one's own performance. The M&M conference is an old tradition where the group gathers to review mistakes, errors, or unexpectedly bad outcomes. M&M stands for "morbidity" (injury) and "mortality" (death). Ideally, the conference is a gathering where both the experienced and the neophyte can learn and try to do better next time.

One of the greatest neurosurgeons in history was a chap named Charles Drake. Drake helped pioneer modern vascular surgery and, by all accounts, was a perfect gentleman. Toward his later years, his presentations at national meetings always included his complications. He was asked why he, such a noted and respected surgeon, would publicize his poor outcomes. His response was that he wanted younger surgeons to know that even the most experienced surgeons encounter problems. Ideally, M&M would be like that—colleagues sharing experiences to improve everyone's overall performance and knowledge.

Unfortunately, asking a group of egotistical sociopaths like us to share mistakes rarely creates a collegial environment. M&M often degenerated into animalistic savagery.

[Read in the voice of Marlon Perkins][63]: "Note the grace of peacocks as they file toward the watering hole. The most aggressive peacocks hurry to the front of the line to show off their colors to prospective mates."

The chief resident usually presented the cases. Steve had become the chief. Everybody could tell if the chief thought the attending really screwed up by the way the case was described. The chief may present it in such a way that we would all console the attending for bad luck with words like "You did all you could" and "That could happen to anybody."

"And the ritual has begun. Here we see a large, beautifully plumaged peacock strutting about the watering hole. A smaller peacock takes an aggressive posture. The larger peacock looks at him quizzically. And the dance begins."

Steve cleared his voice and braced himself for battle. "The patient is a ninety-four-year-old bed-bound demented nursing home patient who is a DNR.[64] Oh, and also thrombocytopenic."[65]

"Unexpectedly, the smaller peacock takes aim at the one with the largest plumage. With a quick flick of the foot, a large collection of poop is flung into the larger peacock's face."

Ouch. That sentence could have very well been changed to "This

---

[63] And if you don't know who Marlon Perkins is, go find old copies of *Wild Kingdom* and watch a few. I'll wait.

[64] DNR – do not resuscitate. This is an order from a living will that means the patient doesn't want aggressive measures to keep them alive.

[65] This means the patient didn't have enough platelets, the small cells that allow one to clot blood.

is a patient no sane person in his or her right mind would ever consider for surgery."

Steve: "She had a meningioma,[66] which you can see by the MRI, obviously had been there for years if not decades."

"The larger peacock tries to recover from the first blow, but the smaller one mercilessly strikes him with another clump of poo …"

The attending sat up to fire back.

Attending: "Nobody would help this patient." It was a weak argument.

"The larger peacock rights himself, but, by now, the crowd has sided with the smaller one."

The chief detailed the surgery and, to the surprise of absolutely no one, began to detail the complication. The patient suffered a large hemorrhage into her surgery site. For all her trouble, she went from being a bed-bound nursing home patient to a bed-bound nursing home patient with a scar.

"But wait, another peacock—an older one—has joined the fray."

Dr. Montgomery: "So, did you go back to the OR to take out the blood clot?"

First attending: "No."

Dr. Montgomery: "But the blood clot was bigger than the tumor."

"Victory complete, the smaller peacock begins to pick at the bones of his now dead foe."

Sometimes surgeons' eyes are bigger than their stomachs. I don't fault anyone for taking a long shot on a surgery, provided it's done for the right reasons. At the end of the game, sometimes the "Hail Mary" is the only shot. But a long shot for hubris or (worse) money is not respectable.

M&M is also the altar where surgeons go to confess their sins.

---

[66] A type of brain tumor that is often benign and grows extremely slowly.

There's a reason surgeons go over potential complications prior to a surgery. Every complication the surgeon describes at some point *has happened.* We've become remarkably cavalier about the risks of procedures that were almost uniformly fatal two generations ago. Surgeons all have the nagging feeling that disaster is just around the corner.

Good surgeons are honest and learn from their mistakes. However, confessing that you screwed up is hard—really hard—especially in front of your peers or your bosses. Some surgeons, despite all evidence to the contrary, simply refuse to believe that anything was their fault.

"The silverback gorillas are an impressive sight ..."

Steve began to describe another case. Uh-oh, he dared to present a case of Johnny Spine.

"The male silverback rises to his full height and puffs out his enormous chest as a warning to all who would dare question his power."

Clearly uncomfortable, Steve quickly detailed the history. A sick lady with multiple medical issues. Bad arthritis. Couldn't walk. Images are shown.

Johnny: "I really didn't want to operate on this lady. But she was getting worse." He glared at Steve, clearly threatening to put him in a body bag.

In a sick, brittle patient, most people will do the bare minimum surgery ...

Johnny: "So I did (the largest spine procedure you could think of)."

"The male silverback lets out a huge scream, practically daring anybody to challenge him."

Grandpa P.: "You did *what*? Why wouldn't you do a simple laminectomy?"

"The male silverback sizes up his older challenger. He growls menacingly at any potential question to his stature."

Johnny hissed, "Will you let me talk?" Johnny stared down

Grandpa P. for an uncomfortably long period of time. "As I said, I didn't want to operate, but I decided to fix all the problems."

"The other gorillas murmur uncomfortably …"

Johnny stopped and scowled.

"The male silverback then begins to scream and growl, with a series of unintelligible grunts, whistles, and bellows. This continues for what seems like hours. The other silverbacks begin to lose interest and start playing with their phones."

Johnny lays out the next three months of the poor lady's hospitalization. Complications. Infections. Intensive care unit. More major surgeries. I tuned out after he verbally smacked Grandpa P.

Johnny: "And so now, after all that, she's in a nursing home and—in some ways—she's better off."

Wait. What?

Grandpa P.: "What?"

The Professor: "What?"

"The male silverback stares at the pack, daring any lesser to question his power. The elder, wiser silverback shakes his head and mutters to himself."

Glowering silence. Johnny Spine stared ahead, comfortable in his own infallibility and peeved that anyone would question his judgment.

Sometimes nature shows reveal shocking brutality.

And sometimes nature provides high comedy. The next case belonged to Doloris, one of Thomas's partners at the Baby Hospital. She was an impressively trained hummingbird of a surgeon who flirted with five feet in height. She was brought up in a quite religious home and was a little unfamiliar with the seedy ways of the rest of the world.

She had performed a brain surgery in a child with autism. The child always carried his favorite toy—a stuffed monkey. He would alternately throw the monkey at the wall or smack himself with it. Unfortunately, he smacked himself in the head at his surgery site and split open the wound.

Doloris began to describe the scene.

"It's weird, but he's got this monkey. All day long he slaps and spanks it."

The Professor interrupted. "He does *what*?"

"Well," Doloris continued, now pantomiming the child's actions, "he likes to slap his monkey."

The Professor giggled.

"So all day long, all he wants to do is play with his monkey," she said, making slapping gestures in the air. There were a few more stifled sniggers. Doloris figured she was entertaining the crowd.

"Just spanking his monkey over and over again!" she yelled, her voice rising to climactic pitch. By now, the audience could contain itself no longer and everyone erupted in laughter. I guess except Johnny, who was still fuming and sulking.

We walked out of the conference. Doloris was beaming, happy that the audience had enjoyed her comments so much. Elizabeth, one of the other pediatric neurosurgeons, pulled her aside.

"Do you know why everyone was laughing?"

"Yeah, the picture of this little boy with his stuffed animal—"

Elizabeth shook her head. "No."

Then she explained the euphemism to the now-mortified Doloris.

"Next time, just say he was playing with his toys."

CHAPTER 14

Tales from County

The residents ran County, with the distant but ever-present gaze of the Professor. County was a dump. The equipment was outdated, except for the strangely expensive burn unit. Cockroaches outnumbered patients. I warned medical students not to eat anything from the cafeteria that wasn't prepackaged. The clientele was rough enough that there were armed guards and metal detectors at the entrance.

The ER and the ICUs were outstanding. The ward floors, however, were a different story. County was overcrowded and understaffed. More than once, patients called 911 from inside the hospital because they were afraid for their lives.

Jack was fast-tracked into the cardiology department. As a senior resident, he rounded on the medical wards at County. Every patient on the floor had the exact same vital signs: blood pressure 120/80, pulse 80, respirations 20. It was almost as if an overworked nurse just wrote down the same thing over and over.[67]

One day, he entered the room to check on a patient. He stared at the patient for a time, puzzled.

"May I see the chart?" Jack answered.

---

[67] It was exactly this.

Sure enough, the standard vital signs were recorded. A young nurse took back the chart, dutifully checked the IV, curtly smiled, and began to walk out.

"Any problems overnight?" Jack asked.

"No." She smiled sweetly, clearly incensed that he'd interrupted her exit.

He stopped her. "You know he's dead, right?" Jack said bluntly.

The patient had assumed room temperature hours earlier. But his vital signs were fine in the chart. The floors at County were a stress test for going back to the street. Unfortunately, this gentleman had failed.

The one ray of light in an otherwise dingy hospital was Vivian. She was the neurosurgery case manager. She attacked problems with a religious sense of purpose and duty. She found homes for the homeless. She found funding for the poor. She comforted when comfort was needed. At ~~government~~ poorly run hospitals, the entire system is geared to prevent doctors from performing good medicine. In these situations, a smart physician will try to find the one person in the hospital who can get things done. Kelly was that person at the U. Vivian was that person at County. Someday I hope to find that person at the VA.

Steve and I went to the ER to see a gentleman in his fifties with a severe headache and vomiting. His CT scan showed that he had a lot of blood in his head. The pattern of bleeding suggested that he had ruptured an aneurysm. His eyes were closed, and he insisted that the room stay dark.

"Do you smoke?" Steve asked.

"Umm-hmmm," he answered affirmatively. Smoking is clearly a risk factor for bleeding into the head.

"Drink?"

"Umm-hmmmm."

"Drugs?"

"Umm-hmmmm."

"What was going on when this happened? Did you fall?"

"Sex."

Steve shot me a quick glance. "I'm sorry; I didn't get that."

"You know, at the end of sex," the guy mumbled.

"Is your wife or girlfriend here?" Steve asked.

"No, Doc. I was flyin' solo."

An aneurysm develops from a weak spot in the arteries. Arteries in the brain are a little different from arteries everywhere else in the body. There are weak spots at junctions or branch points. The tissue here can be thinned by high blood pressure or smoking. Some people just get bad genes, and aneurysms run in the family. The thinned wall will pouch out like a water balloon. If it bursts, patients get a sudden onset of severe, nut-punching pain. Many describe this as a "bomb going off" in their head. About 15 percent just die on the spot. An aneurysm rupture is catastrophic—50 percent of the initial survivors either die or are severely disabled within one month.

Once an aneurysm rupture is diagnosed, our goal is to prevent it from bleeding again. Patients who make it to the ER bled initially, and then the open balloon clotted off. If it keeps bleeding, the patient dies before ever reaching the hospital. If it rebleeds, death is probable. We can try to prevent rebleeding by taking the patient to surgery and placing a metal clip across the neck of the balloon. A second way to prevent rebleeding is for the interventional radiologists to snake a catheter up through the vessels to fill the balloon with either glue or platinum coils. This "coiling" is becoming more and more refined and effective. In fact, for many aneurysms, it's *better* than surgery.

We operated on this chap. He recovered fairly well. Vivian patched things up with his estranged spouse, arranged his outpatient therapy, and then sternly scolded him to lay off the Internet porn.

*   *   *   *

Carmen was in her thirties, a former nurse, and obese. She had to quit work because of persistent, debilitating headaches that didn't respond well to medicine. She was eventually diagnosed with *pseudotumor cerebri*, or *idiopathic intracranial hypertension* (IIH), a condition where there is a chronic buildup of pressure in the head. Unfortunately, it's a disease that doctors don't fully understand. Patients have normal MRI scans. Their symptoms are pretty nonspecific at first. Untreated, the syndrome can cause blindness.

Most of the patients with pseudotumor cerebri are obese. Losing weight will, in a majority of patients, fix the problem. In fact, people may only have to lose 5 to 10 percent of their body weight to have a positive effect. Many patients have a congenital narrowing of the veins leading out of the brain. The cause of pseudotumor cerebri, therefore, is likely from the combination of many factors—weight, venous anatomy, hormones,[68] certain medications, vitamin problems, and probably many others. These patients can be very frustrating to deal with and, unfortunately, are often written off as "crazy" or "depressed" by a busy surgeon.

Carmen was all of these things. Plus, she was extremely angry. She had been chewed up and spit out by the medical system. I got the pleasure of seeing her in clinic. The clinic at County ran with the smooth clockwork efficiency I'd come to expect from a government system.

Here's how it worked. Let's say Carmen has a 9:00 a.m. appointment. At 9:00 a.m., the bowels of bureaucracy would begin the "check-in" process. For reasons unknown to me, this would take an hour and wouldn't start a minute sooner. Whenever I asked the staffers why this took so long, I got a heavy dose of "It's not my job."

---

[68] The condition is much more common in women.

After this process, Carmen is sent to our clinic where, remarkably, she's checked-in *again*. Finally, she hits the room. I see her immediately after she gets into the room, but now it is 10:30. She's passed the bowels of bureaucracy only to be crapped on me.

Carmen had a lumber-peritoneal shunt placed about two years prior. This is like the ventriculoperitoneal shunt described earlier, only it goes from the CSF space in the lower back to the linings around the guts. It didn't help. All the doctors who saw her took this as a sign that she was nuts. She was angry and frustrated. The residents before me did what most residents would do in this situation; they came up with some other test to run and asked her to come back in three months. Conveniently, three months was when the rotation would end and another resident would have to deal with it. I did this plenty of times. I sometimes surprised myself with my ingenuity at passing the buck.

Carmen was fit to bite nails. She waltzed into the clinic, proclaiming that she was going to sue everyone. Nothing confers "dirtbag status" with the Professor faster than complaining about service in a free clinic and threatening to sue. The Professor, louder than she, barked out, "Get her out of here, never to be seen again under any circumstance!"

Our clinic wasn't very big. I'm sure she heard him. I'm sure the west end of the hospital heard him.

I trudged toward the room. In front of me, an angry dragon. Behind, my angrier boss. Evisceration was inevitable.

The most valuable thing I learned in the ER in the military was how to talk to people. Some doctors are gifted in their intelligence, wisdom, or dexterity. My only gift was a preternatural talent for bullshitting. I could talk to people. You learn surgery by performing the procedures over and over. You learn to talk to people in the same way.

I entered the room and did what is always my first move. I sat down. Patients appreciate this. It's a nonverbal message that says, "I'm not trying to escape; I'm here to really listen to you."

Carmen and I talked for a while. We gradually got to the exam, and I did my second move, putting a hand on her shoulder. I find that it is very important to touch a patient, however briefly. This is especially true in examining children.[69] There is therapeutic value in touch. No matter how sophisticated computers get, they will never recreate this.

We finished the exam. It was normal. Carmen's initial fury had subsided, and we talked some more. I left the room with the impression that we should operate on her shunt. The Professor was seething. He had told me to get rid of her, and I had spent a good deal of time in the room. I hadn't gotten rid of her. I walked back to the office to discuss the case. There was a small but definite chance that he would kill me.

I sat down with the Professor and Steve.

"What took you so long?" the Professor hissed.

"I think we should explore the shunt."

Steve burst out laughing and had to leave the room.

The Professor's face looked like I had just struck him with a two-by-four. He was furious. Words failed him. He just sat there, sort of quivering. I'm not sure what stunned him most—the fact that I wanted to operate on this presumed dirtbag or the fact that I would tell him.

"Fine," he said.

We scheduled the surgery.

One of the best things about the Professor was he let us make our own decisions. And he also didn't stay mad very long. After all, I hadn't really screwed up. At least not yet.

---

[69] Or dogs.

Pretty soon, his normally jovial mood returned. We began to eat our traditional horrifically bad Chinese food lunch, and he was prattling off all Golden U's offensive deficiencies. I normally like Chinese food, but the carryout place that serviced County was absolutely terrible. Beyond terrible. The Professor ordered it every single clinic day. I'm positive he did it to spite me.

The day of surgery came. We placed Carmen on her side and opened up her back. After wading through the back fat, we found the valve of the shunt. Carmen had a particular type of shunt that incorporated an "HV" valve. This is a horizontal-vertical valve, which means it has a different resistance based on the patient's position. The particulars aren't important, other than the valve has to be oriented correctly to work.

"It's upside down!" Steve exclaimed.

This was manna from heaven for me. There was an actual, plain-as-day problem with the shunt. It had been stitched in when it was originally placed, but the lower stitch had broken. The valve had flipped. We checked the catheters, realigned the valve, and closed the wound.

When she awoke from anesthesia, she was smiling. Her headache was gone. When we saw her in clinic in follow-up, she had returned to work. Her symptoms were still gone. I happened to run into her in an elevator about two years later. She was headache free and back to work.

*   *   *   *

I'm not sure where the thought that people only "use" 10 percent of their brain came from. Science fiction stories love to toy with the idea that if we used *all* of our brain, we'd be able to communicate telepathically or lift cars with our minds.[70] I suppose this idea comes from the

---

[70] Maybe the writers of the Scarlett Johansson movie *Lucy* could use that extra brainpower to come up with a coherent plot.

fact that parts—sometimes large parts—of the brain can be removed without an obvious change in the patient.

Your brain has a right and a left side. One of those sides is dominant, in that it controls language function. For virtually all right-handed people (and most left-handed people), the left side of the brain is dominant. A surgeon can remove a large part of the nondominant right side of the brain, and the patient can still perform most normal daily functions.

This is not to say that the right side of the brain is unimportant. It's just that there is so much overlap, so many redundant programs, that the brain can make up for the part that is removed. However, detailed neurological and psychological tests will find a difference after surgery. More important, family members will notice a difference.

Perhaps the single most famous neurosurgical case in history belongs to Phineas Gage. Poor mister Gage was working on the railroad in 1848 when an accident shot a large metal spike through the front of his head. Amazingly, he survived. But Phineas was never the same. He changed from a jovial, well-liked person to a moody, lower-functioning chap. He could walk, talk, and function. But he was noticeably *different*. Incidentally, Phineas's actual skull and the metal bar are on display at the medical museum of Brigham and Women's Hospital in Boston.

What made Phineas "Phineas"? Phineas kept his functional abilities. But his personality and his life dramatically changed. He became "frontal-lobish" in neurosurgical terminology. There are parts of the frontal lobe of the brain that govern socially acceptable behavior. We try to hide when we have to burp, fart, or pick our noses.[71] We all do it. Nose-picking can feel pretty good, but we don't want anyone else to see it. We may feel a heroic sense of accomplishment after a

---

[71] Well, except the Professor, who may take a few minutes to draw an audience.

particularly satisfying bowel movement, but we prefer to do it in the privacy of a bathroom, not the middle of the street.

Why?

Maybe we've calculated the repercussions of a night in a New Orleans jail. There's a part of the brain that keeps us polite—or at least a step or two above cannibalism. Phineas lost this part of his brain in the accident, and he was never the same.

Amber was a teenage vixen. She was attractive in a stripper sort of way. She was a wild child and a rebel. Amber was always looking for the next thrill and the next fix. So it's not surprising that one day she was cruising along on the back of a motorcycle without a helmet when she and her boyfriend crashed.

Amber had a severe, life-threatening head injury. She had multiple skull fractures and a growing hematoma that was compressing an ever-swelling brain. We raced her to the OR and removed half of her skull. We sucked out the blood clot and then put the large skull piece in the refrigerator.

The skull in an adult is like a fixed box. There are really only three things in this box: brain, spinal fluid, and blood. If any of these things increases (like that big epidural blood clot), or if there is a fourth thing (like a tumor), the other things get squashed. The brain can tolerate this for a while. It can tolerate this to an amazing degree if the time course is slow; people can have a slow-growing tumor fill half their skull without having more than occasional headaches. However, if this process occurs quickly, the pressure rises in the skull and the brain starts to die. One of the main jobs of a neurosurgeon is to control this pressure. We can do this with medicines, control of breathing, and drainage of spinal fluid. In extreme cases, we can "pop the top" off the box—remove a large part of the skull.

We popped the top off Amber. We removed a large portion of

her skull, let the brain swell out instead of in, and, after a long and roller-coaster clinical course, she recovered.

Months later, we replaced the bone that we had removed. Unfortunately, the bone became infected and we had to remove it again. We eventually replaced it with a mesh of titanium.

On the surface, Amber seemed like any other rebellious teenager. But Amber had severe damage to her frontal lobe and had lost all the parts of the social checking of the brain. She became hypersexual. She took a liking to one of the surgical residents in the hospital and exposed herself to him at every occasion.

Amber's incision broke down again. We saw her in clinic, and part of the metal plating was sticking out like a metal warning siren. We scheduled her for surgery to try to repair it, but she disappeared.

As mentioned, the emergency room at County had a jail. It looked a lot like the Cantina in *Star Wars*, only with scarier, weirder inhabitants. Steve, Vivian, and I got a call that Amber was there, now about nine months after we unsuccessfully tried to schedule her for surgery.

Once we passed the security guard, we saw two very scared fourteen-year-olds who had been busted for underage drinking. They were huddled together, eyes wide with terror. Next to them was a filthy homeless bum, puking his guts out and swearing after every wretch. Talk about scared straight. I'm guessing the girls remained sober at the next party. Vivian gave them a stern mom lecture and arranged for their release.

There was another young man, who was driving drunk, crashed, and was flung down a hill into a patch of rosebushes. Amazingly, he was fine except for thorny scratches all over his arms and face.

"I look like I tried to jack off a bobcat through a barb-wire fence!" He laughed in a bouncy country accent. "Do I need surgery?"

"Nope. You've got a crack in a bone in your neck, but it should heal. You'll just have to wear that collar for a while."

"Super! Hey, can you bust me outta this jail?"

"No."

"Can't blame a guy for askin'." He laughed. Clearly, this was not his first time in this situation.

It was also not our first time treating a patient with a broken neck in the County jail. One ingenious gentleman broke his neck in a gang-related melee. He had a particularly dangerous fracture of the second bone in his neck. We thought this would heal without surgery, but only if he kept it perfectly still. We placed him in a *halo*, a large vest device with four poles and a ring that screws into the skull, much like that old-timey biopsy frame. It's an impressively medieval device. This chap was struck by a hankerin' to rob a gas station, so he had a buddy unscrew the halo, pull the pins out of the skull, and then find matching ski masks for the job. Unfortunately, they weren't very good at the criminal part, and soon the cops and the cop dogs were chasing him down the street.

He was screaming as he ran, "I've got a broken neck! I've got a broken neck!"

The police dogs tackled him, and their human friends beat the ever living snot out of him, as he kept crying, "I've got a broken neck!" Miraculously, he survived, and even more miraculously, his spinal cord was fine.

"What did you learn?" Steve asked.

We took him to surgery the next day.

*   *   *   *

We reached Amber.

The guards in the County jail were inundated a constant flow of human depravity and suffering. I doubt they would be surprised by anything. I also was pretty sure they didn't care about anything, other than sweet silence. Outside of Amber's room was a female police officer of about fifty, reading the paper.

"I've gotta *pee!*" Amber shouted.

Without looking up from the paper, she answered, "Go ahead, honey."

"I've gotta *pee!*"

"Go *ahead*. There's a towel there."

We walked into the room. Amber was chained to the bed, pants around her ankles, with a towel stuffed around her crotch.

"I've gotta *pee!*"

Sigh. "Honey, I'm reading the entertainment section ..."

"Amber?" Steve said.

"I need to see the Professor!" she shouted.

"He's not here."

"Then I want to see Dr. Scott!"

"That's me," said Steve. It was close enough to his name to call it good. "What are you in here for?"

"I got another DUI—*la di daa* ..."

The metal piece was still sticking out of her head, and miraculously, it did not look infected.

"I've gotta *pee!*"

"We'll get it scheduled once you get to jail, Amber," Vivian said. "At least we know you'll show up."

We took care of the state's prisoners at County. With Amber in jail, we didn't have to worry about her skipping an appointment. The female officer didn't look up from her paper as she pressed the button to buzz us through the security door. Such is life at County.

CHAPTER 15

Golfing with the Bosses

"He wants to do what?" Kendall asked incredulously.

"He wants to do the surgery on the Fourth of July," Kelly said.

"On a damn holiday? No way. I'm going to be sitting on my porch in flip-flops, drinking beer and eatin' meat. Steve?"

"Sorry," Steve answered. "I've got family coming."

Bryce glared. "No way."

"Super," I said, knowing it fell to me.

Grandpa P. wanted to perform a complex spine surgery on a VIP. He wanted to do it in conjunction with one of the orthopedic surgeons, and the holiday was the only day that the three of them would all be free.

I got the patient ready for surgery, escorted him to the OR, and positioned him on the table. The OR staff was not happy about working on the holiday, but soon Grandpa P. came, told a few jokes, thanked everyone profusely, and put everyone at ease. We headed out to scrub. He splashed about furiously. We walked into the room, Grandpa P. grinning and me dripping. I'm sure he did that on purpose. The scrub nurse handed us each towels, scanned me up and down, and gave me a knowing smile.

"Nice shower," she said.

Surgery went well. Grandpa P. did his part, and then one of the noted orthopedic surgeons in town took over. I helped him place a number of screws to stabilize the spine. I checked on the patient, made sure his legs moved well, and went to report to Grandpa P.

"He's doing great. Full strength."

"Super!" Grandpa P. exclaimed. "Hey, what are you doing tomorrow?"

As it happened, the holiday was on a Friday. I had the weekend free. "Nothing much."

"Show up to the Club around nine. I'll take you golfing as a reward for helping me."

The *club* was the nicest golf course in the state. It had hosted major professional golf championships. It was the gathering place of the town's high rollers. Everything about the club smelled of leather and money. The range balls were nicer than what I had in my bag. Playing the club was a rare, exotic treat for a commoner like me.

I felt sheepish pulling my Pontiac into a lot filled with Mercedes, Porsches, and an occasional Ferrari. Two uniformed lads sprinted to meet me, wearing plastic smiles. "Take your bag, sir?" they asked, looking me up and down. What they were really asking was "You sure you are in the right place?"

"I'm meeting Grandpa P.," I said.

Their aggressive demeanor changed. The smiles became warm.

"Excellent, sir! He's up at the clubhouse. Let me show you the way."

I parked in the most hidden spot in the lot and walked up to the clubhouse. Grandpa P. greeted me with a huge smile and hearty handshake. "Glad you could make it. Come on; we'll hit a few."

We warmed up and then headed for the first tee, where the Old Man greeted us.

"Eh, eh. I don't hit them quite as far as I used to," he muttered.

He leaned forward to tee up the ball. I half thought he was going to fall over and held my hands out like a spotter. He quivered, shook, and tremored, but eventually placed the ball on the tee. Then with bones creaking, he hit a shot that scooted along the ground and came to rest about thirty yards from the tee. "Nope, don't hit them as far as I used to."

Grandpa P. was next. He sized up the shot and then unleashed a short pop-gun burst of a swing, solidly striking the ball and sending it arrow straight about 240 yards down the fairway.

I was last. Shaking, I teed up the ball and silently prayed, *Don't duff it. Don't duff it. Don't duff* … Smack! By the grace of the Almighty, I hit a good one, with the ball coming to rest just beside Grandpa P.'s. I could tell Grandpa P. breathed a sigh of relief. There was an allotment for the Old Man. He'd been a member of the club from a time when the caddies carried spears to chase off the mastodons. The skeptical starter and the other wealthy onlookers had no such tolerance for me. They all nodded approvingly, satisfied that I wasn't going to hack up their course too badly.

The attendings golfed like they operated. Grandpa P.'s golf swing was short, precise, and conserved motion to the point that little could go wrong. He swung the club just like he'd done a thousand times before. He operated the same way. Every move was precise. Every move was scripted. And the results were always the same—technically good surgery, drive right down the middle of the fairway.

The Professor had a golf swing that Charles Barkley would find *turrible*. He had at least three hitches, twisted his head, and ended with a handsy flurry. Watching him swing the club, I thought, *There's no way that can possibly work*. Yet somehow, beyond logic and reason, the ball tended to go where he wanted. He operated the same way. I would skeptically review his plans and cringe at what appeared to be brutal, uncontrolled surgical moves. But his patients uniformly did very well when he operated. He was *blessed*. And he was creative on both the golf course and in the operating room. He had a knack for getting out of trouble.

We left the tee box. I tried to help the Old Man find his ball. It usually wasn't hard. He was having none of that. We began to race to his ball. I was determined to help my elder; he was determined to prove he could still golf independently.

At the end of the academic year, the department hosted a golf tournament, pitting the residents against the staff. There was a trophy—a brain with a golf ball stuck in it—and everything. Everybody looked forward to it. Grandpa P. sought me out just before the tournament, angling for a side bet. I accepted. His standard bet was a milkshake.

Grandpa P. was nice and cuddly everywhere but the golf course. Here, for some reason, he became a ruthless killer. I played with and against him many times. He was all business until he invariably built a commanding lead. Then the congenial side came back out. I trusted Grandpa P. completely, but on the course, I always double-checked the scorecard.

Grandpa P. had a notorious run-in with the most famous and beloved citizen of our fair city. As I said, the club was the nicest golf course in the state and thus attracted a quite upscale clientele. This clientele included the starting quarterback of the local football club.[72]

Grandpa P. and one of his buddies were scheduled to play against the QB and another NFL player in a club best ball tournament. Things started out well, but the competitive side of Grandpa P. took over. He was ruthless, and the friendly match turned a little snippy. At one point, Grandpa P.'s buddy mistakenly thought he heard one of the football players give him a four-foot putt. Grandpa P.'s buddy was in his sixties, so a fault in hearing cannot be totally dismissed. But

---

[72] And future Hall-of-Fame NFL star with a laser, rocket arm and penchant for pizza. I forget his name.

the football players were furious. The match turned from snippy to downright hostile. Grandpa P. stormed off the course, victorious but seething. It took him years to finally smile when an incorrigible smart aleck[73] kept reminding him of the fact that he alienated the best professional athlete in the state's history.

The resident faculty golf tournament (named in honor of the Old Man) wasn't quite so hostile, but it was competitive and fun. Grandpa P. teamed with the Old Man and two other beginners. As a scratch golfer, he tended to win the long-drive and near-pin contests. He would always write someone else's name on the card.

At the end of the day, the awards were announced. "Long-drive winner … the Old Man!"

"Eh, eh. I must have hit it pretty good. Too bad I don't remember." He smacked me on the back surprisingly hard before accepting his ill-gotten award.

Grandpa P.'s team beat mine, although we gave it a great effort. The tournament is held on the same day as the graduation for the chief resident. Kendall was graduating and moving on. To celebrate, the department gathered at the club for a dinner and speeches. I went early and stopped at a local ice cream shop. I ordered three chocolate milkshakes. I then scoured the menu for the biggest, most obnoxious thing I could order: the "King Kong" sundae—a ridiculously over-the-top orgy of twenty scoops of various ice cream, chocolate, strawberries, bananas, and nuts. It was meant to be eaten by five to ten people. I took the ice cream to the kitchen and asked the staff to bring it out for dessert. We finished the dinner, and the club personnel delivered the booty. Milkshakes for Grandpa P. and his two other partners, and the King Kong was set in front of the Old Man.

---

[73] Me.

"Eh, eh. It's not big enough." He muttered, to the delight of everyone at the table.

The Professor loved golf. At a later tournament, he and his partner were dueling Steve and me. It was close right to the end. We teed off on the seventeenth hole; the match was even. The hole was a par 5, with a creek to the left and out-of-bounds to the right. I laced my best drive of the day, setting up a possible approach shot to the green. The Professor's drive was average. The other two found water. The Professor laid up and then put a wedge on the back of the green. I hit a solid approach, nestling just short of the bunkered Promised Land. We walked up to the green. I had a routine uphill chip, then—I hoped—a putt for the winning birdie. Chipping has never been my strong suit, and I left myself about a six-foot putt.

The Professor faced a thirty-foot downhill putt, with a green that broke toward the creek. *No way*, I thought, *does he keep this within ten feet of the hole.*

"Ten to one says you don't make it," I said cockily.

He didn't hesitate. "Okaaaaay," he muttered softly.

Wham! He hit the ball so hard, I was sure it wasn't going to hold the green. It began to pick up speed going down the hill, and I became sure it was going into the water—that is, until it struck the back of the hole with fury and bounced straight up, then into the cup.

"Aaaahahaha*hahahaha*! The Old Man comes through again!" he yelled, high-fiving his partner, my partner, and then the air itself. "I putt *like a god*!" he screamed, in defiant blasphemy of the heavens and the laws of physics. I was so unnerved I missed my putt. "*Hehehehehehehe* ... You can't beat the *Professor.*"

The next year for the tournament, the Professor was paired with all three of the Old Dogs. I saw the team rosters before he did. I knew this was my chance to take advantage and made a pretty aggressive side bet.

"I got you this year, boss," I told him.

"Dr. Fulkerson, you know you can't beat the Professor." He began to mime his backswing. *What part of that swing is worth practicing?*

"I beat my brother. I'm putting like a god. I can't be beat. *Hehehehehe.*" He giggled and moseyed out of the room.

I continued to goad him right up to the first tee. His group was right in front of mine. When he saw his team, his face fell. The Old Man approached. He wobbled, teeing up his ball. *That's it*, I thought. *He's going to fall face-first and break his neck. Or hip. Or something.* But he made it, took his backswing, and rolled the tee shot about twelve feet.

"Eh, eh, I don't hit them as far as I used to."

The crowd was respectfully supportive.

"Good shot, Doctor!"

"Eh, eh. Really? Where did it go?"

Dr. King and Dr. Mason didn't have much success. The Professor hit a pretty good drive.

"Play fast," I said. "I'll be hitting into you all day."

He scowled and sped off in the cart but not before veering uncomfortably close to hitting me.

My team won. Beers were drunk. Grandpa P. won the near pin and the overall match. The Old Dogs had a good time, and by some miracle of fate, no one broke a hip.

"Eh, eh. How didja hit 'em?" the Old Man asked, smacking me on the back.

"Long and straight, just like you taught me," I said.

"Good, good. I don't hit 'em as far as I used to."

Later that night, the Lovely Wife and I drove to the club for the graduation dinner. The Professor was standing in front of the door, pacing furiously. As we approached, he dashed toward me.

"The bet's off. You had me playing with *three octogenarians!*"

"I didn't make the teams. What do you want me to do?"

"Their combined age was 250!"

"What can I say, boss? They aren't residents; they *have* to be on the staff team."

He grumbled something under his breath and headed for the bar.

*   *   *   *

Grandpa P. did all his business deals on the golf course. I suspect that's normal in some circles. It's been said that one can learn a lot about a person by playing eighteen holes of golf with him. Golf was part of our residency culture at the time. Golf may have shaped the future of Handsome Dan.

Handsome Dan was of Korean descent but born and raised in the American Heartland. He initially became a lawyer. Somewhere on the way, he realized he had a soul, left the law cartel, and went to medical school. I liked him right away. At the time, I was an upper-level resident and he was a student interested in neurosurgery.

Handsome Dan was very smart, deeply religious, and overly polite. He was so polite, in fact, that he rarely spoke unless someone directly asked him a question. Medical students have to find that fine line of being noticed without being annoying. Handsome Dan was the opposite of annoying. I was worried that he was too soft-spoken to be noticed.

One day, he joined me in surgery with Grandpa P. He assumed the solemn medical student vigil, standing perfectly still, as Grandpa P. and I worked. By then, I had perfected the Grandpa P. dance that Rich had demonstrated years before. I bobbed and weaved, trying to get some sort of view of the operative field through Grandpa P.'s ever-present giant head. Handsome Dan's view must have been similar to the one I had all those years ago as a student.

Grandpa P. and I gabbed throughout the case about the current news, football, and the case. Handsome Dan stood motionless and silent. I needed to break the ice.

"This is Handsome Dan, our student."

"Hello," Grandpa P. said, without looking up.

"He's doing a great job."

"Mmmm-hmmmmm. Hey, cut right here."

We operated a little. I knew it was time to step it up a notch.

"And he's a really good golfer."

The operation stopped. Grandpa P. stood straight up. I seized the opportunity to actually see what I was doing and began working feverishly to finish the surgery.

"Really?" Grandpa P. asked, his face lighting up.

I knew Handsome Dan would be quiet so I shot him a sideways look that said, "Talk! Damn it!"

Handsome Dan then began to recount the courses he'd played, his average score, and his golf ball brand of choice. I wasn't exaggerating; he really was a good golfer. Within seconds, Grandpa P. knew he was genuine and the two gabbed for the rest of the case. By the end, Grandpa P. had invited him to play in the year-end tournament.

Handsome Dan played in one of the last groups. The teams that had finished gathered around the green at the last hole to shout encouragement or jeers to the finishing team.

My team finished, and I was watching the Professor with a team that included some people below eighty. He was lining up about a fifteen-foot putt.

"No way do you hit that!" I shouted.

"Didn't you learn your lesson? I putt *like a god*!"

No way he does it twice, I thought.

The Professor lined it up, took a huge swing, and smacked the ball with obscene fury—right into the cup.

"*Yeaaaaah!*" he exalted, pointing at me. "I can't be beat!"

Grandpa P. laughed and greeted the Professor with a hearty shake and back slap. The Old Man said, "Eh, eh. That's how I used to do it."

Everybody was in a great mood. One resident group to go. They were about 240 yards from the green. Three people hit three bad shots. Then Handsome Dan stepped up. He launched a three wood so high that we all gasped. It soared beautifully. Grandpa P.'s eyes widened. The ball then gently plopped onto the green about four feet from the hole.

The gallery erupted in applause and shouting.

"*Beautiful!*" Grandpa P. shouted.

Handsome Dan had excellent grades and top scores on national tests. It would be selling him short to say that he was selected to the neurosurgery program because of that golf shot. But he was selected to the neurosurgery program because of that golf shot.

CHAPTER 16

The Blessed and the Cursed

Some surgeons are *blessed*. No matter what they do, things seem to work out. I'm not saying they luck into things; it's just that decisions that would get other people in trouble don't seem to affect them. Unfortunately, other surgeons are *cursed*. No matter what they do, things turn sour. Most surgeons are neither. Very few are either truly blessed or cursed.

The Professor was blessed. Like his golf swing, his operating style was aggressive and looked hideously uncoordinated. But things turned out the way he wanted. Things seemed to turn out well, even when there was a surgical mistake.

One day, as chief resident at the U, I was walking to the OR when I encountered the Professor quickly pacing up and down the hallway cursing.

"Darn! Fudge! Heck! Cow farting trucking poopies!"[74]

As chief, I knew this couldn't be good and that I would have to be involved. "Sir?"

He stopped, looked at me, didn't say anything for a while, and then began quivering in the way he did when he was burning mad.

---

[74] This is a family show.

After an uncomfortably long time, he said, "Dr. Kruger is not having a good day."

He usually called the residents by their first names. When he used the last name, I knew Dr. Kruger was in trouble. Apparently, they were doing a spine surgery when things started to go wrong. They planned to place a plate to stabilize the spine on a particular anatomic section. Dr. Kruger had inadvertently broken this part of the bone. A series of events later, spinal fluid was pouring out of the wound, one of the nerves had been severed, and they had to MacGyver another plan of the instrumentation.

I joined Dr. Montgomery for a brain tumor case. Dr. Montgomery was a full, tenured professor and a senior surgeon. Dr. Montgomery was cursed. We worked on a tumor and meticulously spent hours closing the wound. We couldn't have been more careful.

The next day, I rounded with the team. The Professor's patient was pain free, happy, had inexplicably full strength, and was ready to go home. Dr. Montgomery's patient was leaking spinal fluid from her wound, febrile, and looked like she was about to die. One surgeon was blessed, the other cursed.

*   *   *   *

The pager went off. We had a trauma patient currently en route to County. I was the chief, running the trauma service with my junior resident Vin. The message was terse: "Nail gun to the head."

Vin was antsy and excited. We had some time, so I outlined the strategy. We'd evaluate the patient, make sure he had appropriate IV access for a blood transfusion, make sure his vital signs were stable, and then take him to the scanner to get a CT angiogram, a study that traced out all the blood vessels of the brain. Then, we'd take him to the operating room where we could remove the nail. Carefully. Our approach would depend on what (if any) underlying blood vessels were involved. Something like this requires great caution. The nail may have lacerated a blood vessel but may be holding the blood at bay like a finger in the dike. So, never *ever* just pull it out. Ever.

I poked my head into the Professor's office to let him know. Vin called the operating room and put them on alert.

The Professor was excited. "A *nailhead*? When does he get here?"

"Not sure, boss. I'll let you know."

Vin and I continued on our routine. We headed to the floor to tie up some business. A few minutes later, we sauntered back into the office.

"Nailhead here yet?" the Professor asked.

"Not yet. I'll let you know."

Indistinct muttering …

Page from the ICU. We wandered over there to take care of whatever it was needed taking care of. The Professor arrived a few minutes later.

"Nailhead here yet?"

"Not yet."

The boss sauntered away, giggling to himself. "Nailhead, hehehehehe …"

"Is he always like this?" Vin asked.

"Only when he's excited."

"He's excited about a nail gun to the head?"

"Seems like it."

Finally, we got the call. Five minutes out. Vin and I went to the ER. There was kind of a buzz. ER residents milled around the ambulance bay to see what was going on. The patient—a young Hispanic worker—was wheeled out of the ambulance and taken into a trauma bay. I could tell a few things right away: he was conscious (always a good sign), and the nail was in his right frontal region. It was set at an angle that it probably missed the major veins located in the center of the head. The transfer took a few hours. If the nail had lacerated those veins, he never would have made it to us. We could also see that he was moving everything and following commands. So he likely didn't do major damage to the brain's arteries. So far, so good. The CT angiogram confirmed this.

Vin examined him and then we plotted our strategy. We'd use a drill to cut out a space of bone around the nail. This would give us access to the underlying brain and dura. We'd have the cautery ready and then gently elevate—

"Is Nailhead here?"

Uh-oh.

The ER people greeted the Professor like a local celebrity. "Hi, Doctor! How are you?"

"I am faaaaabulous!"

Please tell me those aren't pliers ...

The Professor parted the throng and made his way to the bed. I hesitated for a moment. He had a huge grin on his face. He held up a set of pliers he must have gotten from maintenance. His grin grew bigger. *Oh no ...*

Remember, Vin—never ever just pull it out.

"Come 'ere, young man."

The Professor plopped him down flat, put his knee up on the side of the guy's head for leverage, grabbed the nail, and yanked. It all happened instantaneously. I'm not sure the guy even had a chance to process what was going on. He yelped. The Professor grunted and yanked. It popped out.

"There! You can go home!"

The Professor held it up to me, grinning from ear to ear. "I just saved you four hours! *Hehehehehehe!*" He handed the nail to a nurse. "Send this to pathology. Tell them we want a frozen section. *Hehehehehehehe*!"

She looked stunned.

"Vin, how much should I charge for that?"

Vin looked baffled.

"A million dollars! Bye!"

In a flash, he was gone.

Ai yi yi.

Vin was wide-eyed and stunned. The guy looked around with a "Was that it?" look on his face.

I sighed. I guessed we should check another scan. No bleeding. The Professor is blessed.

CHAPTER 17

Bob the Fellow

I began my resident rotation at the Baby Hospital nervous but hopeful. I'd gotten to know Thomas pretty well by then. The day started early. I arrived around five thirty, looked up all the pertinent data, readied the day's surgical patients, rounded on the patients, and was ready to report to the staff by seven.

"I've consented your patient for the resection of the dermal sinus tract, boss," I said to Thomas. "Sacral dimples" are extremely common and are often totally harmless. As a general rule, a dimple at the tip of the tailbone, within the gluteal crease (butt crack), is benign. Rarely, dimples may represent a *dermal sinus tract*, or a communication tract that goes from the skin into the spinal canal. This requires surgery, as there's a direct pathway between the germy outside world and the spinal cord. Dermal sinus tract dimples are higher, above (but near) the butt crack, and generally surrounded by abnormally colored skin. This was Thomas's first case. His second case was a shunt revision.

"Then a shunt revision?" I asked. "Then another dermal tract near the butt?"

"Yes, my day is just odds and ends."

Rimshot.

"They are a patient of the urology service. You want me to call them?" I asked.

"Pediatric urology. They take care of the little squirts."

Rimshot.

"You're going to have to stop that now."

Doloris entered. She specialized in seizure patients and possessed a disturbingly boundless store of energy, especially for one who eschewed caffeine. She seemed to need but an hour or two of sleep per week. Steve had warned me, "She's like the Energizer Bunny."

I discussed all of Doloris's patients with her, and she scurried off to her office. The third attending entered. Elizabeth was an ICU nurse for many years before going to medical school, then the tortuously long neurosurgery residency, then a year of fellowship. Despite being relatively new, she'd been around the block a few times.

Doloris reemerged. She and Elizabeth began to argue about something. Each one talked a mile a minute, and each didn't pause long enough to let the other speak. So they each got louder and louder, both trying to overtalk the other. Thomas motioned for me to abscond to his office.

"Let's say you're trapped in an elevator with those two arguing. You have a gun with one bullet. Who do you kill?" he asked.

I didn't want to answer.

"Yourself!" Thomas smiled and chuckled to himself. "I never know what their opinion will be about something, but I do know it will be strong. They aren't always sure, but they're never in doubt."

He chuckled again, and then he stared off into space and sighed.

"You okay, boss?" I asked.

"Oh yeah. Oh yeah. Just ... well, I keep hearing about a big change in the business and this lawsuit. Well, no matter." He brightened up again. "I hear the new fellow gets here today! I hope he likes it."

"What's all this?" I asked, pointing to a pile of partially shredded paper on his desk.

"Oh, well, the office staff mistakenly shredded about twenty-five of my clinic lists."

"Can't you just print out more?"

"Well, these had some notes on them. Plus I only use the original notes …" His voice trailed off, and he sighed. The notes were put through a shredder. He had convinced maintenance to open the shredder, and he was now meticulously trying to tape all of them back together. I'm not sure he could stop if he wanted. Obsessive compulsion is a bitch. I left him to his task.

The office manager trickled in. She had been running the office for years and was always putting out fires. "Dan, we've got a new fellow starting today. Can you show him around?"

"Sure."

Later, a gentleman who looked suspiciously like Austin Powers tapped me on the shoulder. "Hi, I'm Bob the Fellow."[75]

*   *   *   *

Bob the Fellow and I settled into our daily routine, rounding in the morning and dividing up the cases during the day. Nothing bothered Bob the Fellow at the beginning. He worked hard. He stayed late. He insisted on being called for any emergencies at night. He worked weekends. Thomas sat him down and warned him to slow down.

"You'll burn out."

Bob the Fellow didn't believe it.

I accompanied Thomas on afternoon rounds. Doloris was working on an especially difficult case that was running well into the evening. Thomas wanted to check up on their progress.

---

[75] Followed by *Groovy, baby—Yeah!* in my head.

As we approached the room, we heard the unmistakable sounds of "Silver Bells."

Thomas was nonplussed. "Oh man, the Christmas music again."

"She has more than twelve hours' worth of 'Chestnuts Roasting on an Open Fire.' Twelve hours of different versions of the same song. No repeats," I said.

"How do you know that?"

I gave him a resigned look.

"Oh. How long have they been working?"

"Case started at seven thirty this morning," I said.

Thomas checked the clock. "Twelve hours. Think she's got that much 'Silver Bells'?"

"It's Christmas tiiiiiiiiiiiimmmmme in the city ..."

We walked into the OR to see Doloris diligently working under the microscope and Bob the Fellow sitting awkwardly on a stool, contorting his body to see into the second viewer's eyepieces.

"How's it going?" Thomas said softly.

Bob the Fellow looked up passively, as if we just woke him from a deep hibernation. He stared at us, as if trying to remember where he'd seen animals of our species before. Without a word, he turned and slowly walked to the back table. Dana watched him go and then gave us a curt nod that was a signal that they had a long way to go.

Dana was unfailingly polite and, despite being a karate black belt, was the nicest person one could ever meet. The second OR-Mom, Jill, was a *paesano*, a cancer survivor and had a bit of an edge and more than a bit of a mouth. I always worked to stay on her good side for the remote but completely plausible chance that she could have me whacked. Even she was quiet, trying to conserve energy for what was likely going to be a long night.

Bob the Fellow was fiddling around with something on the back table. He finished whatever he was doing and then began to walk slowly toward us.

He had found a sterile marking pen, used to draw the proposed incision on the skin. He had also found a towel. On the towel, he'd drawn a ridiculously detailed six-shooter. He slowly held the towel up to his head, pointing his cartoon gun at his temple.

"Ohhh-kaaaay," Thomas said, slowly backing out of the room. We exited. He looked at me and said, "I think Bob the Fellow is about to hit the wall."

The case lasted all night. I went home, slept, and came back for our morning rounds. Bob the Fellow was nowhere to be seen. The case was just wrapping up, now twenty-four hours later. I don't think Doloris even took a bathroom break.

I finished the morning duties and then saw a shell-shocked Bob appear in the hallway. He had a thousand-yard stare. He didn't make eye contact.

"Bob, why don't you go home?" I said. "I'll handle things today."

Bob the Fellow nodded slowly.

He slowly walked past me, not bothering to get his coat. He stopped and paused. He looked back at me.

"I'm never f———ing listening to Christmas music again as long as I live."

*   *   *   *

The holidays are a bittersweet time around the Baby Hospital. The hospital gets all decked out in tinsel and toys. People wear Santa hats. Doloris's surgical suite echoes with one Christmas song after another. People are festive and nice, but there's still the nagging worry that some poor child with some horrible disease is about to walk through the door. It seems disturbingly regular that a child with a new brain tumor will come in on Christmas.

Being a devout Jew, the Professor naturally loved Christmas. We had a department party, and he showed up dressed as Santa.

"Ho ho ho! What do you want, little boy?" he asked me at the party. "How about a better golf swing! *Hehehehehehehehe*!" He was beside himself. Grandpa P. worked the room, shaking hands, hugging people, bringing residents in for some close-talking praise. The Old Dog was following him.

Grandpa P. grabbed Steve. "This guy, *this guy*! Only resident to go through his entire first year without causing a spinal fluid leak." Steve looked sheepish. Grandpa P. bounded on, eager to greet another guest. I was impressed. The Old Man was not.

"Eh, eh. Steve, that just means you aren't operating aggressively enough."

Steve smiled.

"Did you really go the whole year without a durotomy?"[76] I asked. It's pretty easy to tear this covering of the spinal fluid water balloon. A durotomy occurs in about 3 percent of spine surgeries. When it happens and spinal fluid comes spewing out, the clear operating view is muddled; there's a much higher risk of nerve damage. The leak must be stopped, as it can set the patient up for a dangerous infection (meningitis). All and all, a durotomy is a problem that all spine surgeons will encounter and must learn to fix.

"Of course not," Steve said. "I caused just as many as everyone else. Except maybe him," he said, motioning to Bryce.

Bryce gave him an annoyed, tight-lipped smile and moved on.

I was on call Christmas Day. I was called to County to see a drug abuser with a serious infection in his spine. Infections such as these

---

[76] A *durotomy* is a hole in the dura.

can quickly and permanently paralyze someone. We had to take him to surgery immediately. I called the Professor to let him know. He was in a remarkably good mood. "Santa will be there presently!"

We took him to surgery, opened a long incision, dissected to the bone, took a drill and removed two of the lamina, and encountered a satisfying pocket of foul-smelling pus.

"Oh, that's horrible!" the Professor exclaimed, mock holding his nose. "The only thing that stinks worse than that"—pause for effect—"*is your golf swing! Hehehehehehehehe!*"

"Thanks, Professor."

"*Hehehehehehehehe!*"

We washed out all the pus and sewed him back up, leaving two big drains to siphon out any residual infection.

The Professor disappeared for the evening. The next day, I made rounds. I reviewed our patient's chart and found the Professor's note. This was still in the days of handwritten charts. The note read as follows: "In the true spirit of Christmas, a Jewish craftsman came in to save this dirtbag from the evils of infection. Maybe he'll repent and stop taking drugs!"

He then signed it: "Professor Jesus, the official rabbi of County Hospital."

This wasn't the first time the Professor had left something, well, *questionable* in a patient's chart. Legend has it that young Professor was dictating an operative note when his buddy and assistant Dr. Smith walked by. "We cut through the fascia. And then Dr. Smith inserted his penis into the patient's anus in the standard surgical fashion."

The transcriber dutifully entered this into the patient's official chart. That little stunt earned a trip to the chief of surgery's office and a reprimand. Now it would probably mandate forty-six hours of sensitivity training.

*   *   *   *

Soon after Christmas, Bob the Fellow hit the wall with the ceremony and dignity of a bug splattering on a highway windshield. As I would discover later, a fellowship year is emotionally taxing. You've graduated by then, so the temptation to get a real job and make real money never leaves. Fellowship is like volunteering for extra push-ups at boot camp. I'm sure every fellow in history has, at some point, questioned the decision.

Surgical training is a marathon. In a real marathon, there's usually a pack of professional runners leading the pack. Do *not* try to keep up with the professionals. Sure, maybe one could run with them for a mile or two, but at some point, the amateur runner hits the wall. Bob started by running with the pros, and now he was in the uphill portion with miles to go.

I'm guessing the Christmas music pushed Bob the Fellow over the edge. He met me each morning, sipping his coffee and looking like he'd rather be anywhere but there. Bob began to take solace in tweaking everybody around him. Doloris became his favorite target. He loved paging her to various numbers around the city.

"Hello, I'm answering a page," Doloris said, annoyed, into the phone.

"Suicide hotline, can I help you?" the voice on the other end answered.

"I'm a doctor. I'm answering a page."

"Are you suicidal?"

"I'm answering a page!"

"Maybe we should send someone over."

Bob the Fellow struck randomly, which made him all the more dangerous.

One day, Doloris was working on another tumor. One of my

coresidents was her assistant. Often, once a surgeon uncovers a tumor, he or she cuts off a small piece to send to the pathologist. The pathologist does a *frozen section*, where he or she does a quick preparation of the specimen, examines it under the microscope, and then tries to give the surgeon some idea of the diagnosis. This information may be crucial to the surgical strategy. For example, one common pediatric brain tumor is called a *medulloblastoma*. We know that this highly aggressive tumor responds well to chemo- and radiation therapy. If the surgeon resects *almost* all of it, the child has the same survival chance as if the surgeon resected *all* of it. This knowledge is critically important if the tumor invades the brainstem. The surgeon knows that trying to resect tumor from the brainstem puts the child at a high risk for neurologic injury. Therefore, if the frozen section is characteristic for medulloblastoma, the surgeon may leave a little bit behind rather than risk a significant injury.

Contrast this with an *ependymoma*, another common brain tumor in kids. An ependymoma does not grow as fast as a medulloblastoma. While this may seem to be a good thing, children with ependymomas often do worse than those with medulloblastomas.[77] Chemotherapy and radiation work by killing dividing, growing cells. The fast-growing, fast-dividing medulloblastoma is exquisitely sensitive to these treatments. The slow-growing but relentless ependymoma doesn't respond nearly as well. Therefore, the only real chance at cure is complete resection. Then, the surgeon may need to be more aggressive at trying to get it all, even if it means risking an injury. Within reason, of course.

Doloris sent the frozen specimen and waited for the call back from the pathologist.

The phone rang.

---

[77] Thomas calls an incompletely resected ependymoma a "death sentence."

Jill answered.

"What? Who is this? What is it?"

Doloris looked up from the microscope.

Jill looked back and covered the mouthpiece. "I don't know who it is. I couldn't understand him."

"Ask him what it is!" Doloris demanded.

Jill went back to the phone. "Okay, say that again. Uh-huh. I'm sorry. I just can't understand you!"

The voice on the other end had a thick, indistinguishable accent. Maybe it was Asian? Swedish? Eastern European? Borat?

Borat.

"Eeet isth naaahmal tesdickular teeeeshooo."

"*What?*"

"Naahmal tesdickular teeshooo."

"Testicular tissue?" Jill screamed into the phone.

"*What!*" Doloris yelled. "Itcan'tbethattheymusthavemixedupthe specimenscallthemback ..."

Jill tuned out the now relentless yelling stream emanating from the surgeon and went back to the phone. She took a deep breath and tried again.

"Can you spell that?"

"Yes."

"Okay, spell it so I know what you are saying."

"G."

"Okay, G, got it."

"O."

"Uh-huh."

"T."

"Yes."

"C. H. A."

"Okay, *G-O-T-C-H-A.* Wait a minute!"

Bob the Fellow giggled and hung up the phone. Jill was furious, and Doloris was still chattering about why the specimen couldn't have possibly been testicular tissue.

Bob the Fellow got a scolding and a talk about professionalism. It didn't take.

A few days later, Doloris was doing a cranial reconstruction case with the senior plastic surgeon in the department. The plastic surgeon, a large man with surprisingly deft hands, was world-renowned. Surgeons from distant countries would travel to the Baby Hospital to spend time with him.

Jill was working the case.

She answered the ringing phone. The voice on the other end had a heavy accent.

"'Ello. Dis is Dr. Hansenfrueder."

"Dr. Hansenfrueder, huh. Look, Bob. This isn't funny! I've got work to do! Don't call back!"

"But—"

"You heard me, Bob!"

Slam!

The case went on. Eventually, the plastic surgeon looked up and checked the clock.

"I was expecting a visiting professor to come observe. Has anyone heard from Dr. Hansenfrueder?"

Jill's stomach fell. "Uh, well, I thought ... Oh crap." She didn't talk to Bob for a month.

* * * *

"Do you have any interest in pediatrics?" Grandpa P. asked me.

"I like the kids, but the Baby Hospital is kind of rough," I said.

"I'm worried about Thomas. Last night, he was driving home. He stopped at a traffic light and fell asleep. A policeman had to bang on his door to wake him up. I don't even think he was on call."

I felt a little numb.

"The Professor and I agreed that we need to start covering his adult patients. I just don't think he has enough time to cover both the adults and the kids. He just can't say no to anybody, and some of the adults take advantage of him."

"Oh, I'm well aware of that."

"Anyway, I think he needs some help. Think about it. I'll do whatever it takes to get you to stay there."

"Well, thanks, boss," I said, feeling genuinely happy that Grandpa P. wanted to hire me after training. My happiness was mixed with a small, gnawing sense of dread about Thomas.

CHAPTER 18

Chicken Wings

The technical length of pregnancy is forty weeks. If a child is born before thirty-six weeks estimated gestational age (EGA), he or she is considered *premature*. Babies born very early (in the twenty weeks EGA) are extremely premature and have significant problems. Their lungs are not developed. Their immune system is not developed. They can get eye problems that may lead to blindness. They have a high risk of developing cerebral palsy.

About 25 to 50 percent of children born prematurely develop bleeding into the brain. The cause of this is unknown, but low oxygen levels and immature blood vessel walls probably contribute. The bleeding occurs in a part of the brain called the *germinal matrix*, an area near the ventricles that plays a part in the developing brain. The bleeding may fill the ventricles. This is called intraventricular hemorrhage (IVH). Approximately 57 to 85 percent of premature babies with IVH will develop hydrocephalus and will need a shunt.

Shunting these children is fraught with risk. Their skin is tissue-paper thin; getting the incision to heal is not a trivial matter. Their immune system is immature so they have a higher risk of infection. A shunt infection in a neonate is tremendously damaging to the child, with severe, lifelong consequences.

I was consulted on two NICU babies (Jason and Harvey) who were born within a week of each other. Both were born at around twenty-six weeks gestational age. Both had IVH, and both developed hydrocephalus. In addition, both had a particularly devastating abdominal condition called *necrotizing enterocolitis* (NEC). It's well known that we have a significant amount of bacteria in our guts. They even make commercials about this with surprisingly upbeat women prattling on about their bowel movements. The adult gut is made to handle these bacteria. In fact, our relationship with the bacteria is essential. We need these bacteria for a number of reasons, including, apparently, to make Jamie Lee Curtis regular.

The premature baby's gut walls are very thin. Bacteria can escape through the walls of the intestines, causing infection, inflammation, and eventual perforation. This can be fatal. These babies may need parts of their intestines resected. In both Jason and Harvey, the NEC infections were so severe that the general surgeons could not get the skin closed. They stayed on their back, cooking in their incubators, with only a carefully packed plug of gauze keeping their intestines from spilling out of their filleted bellies.

Normally, we place the distal end of the shunt into the belly. We can't do this if the abdomen is open. So usually the next option is to put the shunt into the right atrium of the heart. This does make physiologic sense, as the spinal fluid is normally reabsorbed into the bloodstream.

Different people have different ideas; however, I believe that placing a shunt in the most premature babies is a bad idea. The infection rate is too high. I'm fairly dogmatic that the child has to be at least thirty-six weeks gestational age before shunting is safe.[78] So what do we do in the baby who is twenty-three weeks old?

---

[78] Others wait until the baby attains a certain weight.

We temporize the hydrocephalus. We can stick a needle directly through the skin, through the brain, into the ventricles and draw out spinal fluid. While this is generally safe, I don't like doing it more than once or twice. Another option is to place a small reservoir. This is a piece of tubing that sort of looks like the house on *The Jetsons*.[79] We can then easily stick a needle in this and draw out spinal fluid. This is my preferred temporizing method.

Jason and Harvey had the same problems. Both had NEC. Both had severe hemorrhage and developed hydrocephalus. Both got a reservoir and eventually a shunt. Both started the same, but their outcomes couldn't have been more different.

Four years later, Harvey looked like a normal little boy. He was a bit behind his peers in his speaking ability, but not by much. He had some stiffness in his left leg, but he could run, jump, and play. He belonged to a single dad who was tremendously attentive. *Harvey*, I thought, *is going to have a good life.*

Jason, however, did terribly. He was blind. He never spoke. He had spastic quadriparesis, which means his arms and legs were too stiff to move. It was a minor miracle to get him to sit in a chair. He had continued lung problems. Jason was born to a teenage mom who couldn't handle him, so she farmed him off to his grandmother. Grandma dedicated everything she had to Jason. She ran his ventilator. She performed all of his feedings through the PEG tube. She was a woman of very little means, but Jason was always clean and well groomed when I would see him in clinic. Grandma loved him with all her heart. Could Jason love her back? I don't know. Jason died when he was four from breathing problems.

Why did one child do well? Why did Harvey recover when Jason didn't? I don't have the answer. And I don't know how to tell. If I

---

[79] Elevated, over the polluted and desolate world below. In hindsight, *The Jetsons* was surprisingly dark.

had a crystal ball when I first saw them and told Grandma that Jason would have three years of misery and then die, would she want any treatment? I don't know the answer to that either. There's no such thing as "fair" at the Baby Hospital.

The Baby Hospital forces one to ask the big questions. Unfortunately, it is loath to give back the big answers.

CHAPTER 19

A Jew, a Mormon, and a Black
Guy Walk into the Hospital ...

During medical school, there was a contingent of African-American students who sat in the middle of the front row for every lecture. They were always well dressed. They made the rest of us—clad in a T-shirt, flip-flops, and baseball cap covering unshowered hair—look bad. I became friends with one of them, a Godly man whose career goal was to treat AIDs patients. One day, I asked him why he always sat up front. He told me that the professor needed to know that he and the other African-American students were serious and were there because they were smart, not because of affirmative action.

I had never thought about this before. This was so foreign to me but so ingrained in him. I never thought someone would question why I was there. Well, except *me*, wondering why I didn't know any of those stupid amino acids. He didn't just have to worry about the test; he had to worry about the teacher questioning his right to be in the class.

Handsome Dan went to the same elementary school as Ryan White. In the early 1980s, AIDs was a scary mystery. It was a strange, terrifying disease that affected gay men, drug users, and TV evangelists.

Some dirtbags thought AIDs was "God's judgment" against homosexuals. I wonder of those same dirtbags think cystic fibrosis is God's judgment against white people. There was public hysteria. Doctors weren't really sure how it was transmitted or who was at risk. All people knew was that it affected people on the bottom or fringe of society.

All that changed with Ryan White. Ryan was born a hemophiliac, and he required regular blood transfusions. In 1984, he contracted AIDs after receiving a contaminated transfusion. His family sought treatment at the Baby Hospital. Ryan, as a small-town white kid, became an innocent, national face for AIDs. Celebrities like Elton John and Michael Jackson embraced him and made regular visits to the Baby Hospital. Ryan, along with other high-profile patients, including Magic Johnson and Arthur Ashe, helped bring AIDs into the mainstream consciousness.

In 1984, however, the mystery remained. Famously, the parents of other children at his elementary school wanted Ryan kicked out. When that wasn't going to happen, parents basically went on strike. They refused to send their kids to the school. Handsome Dan was part of that class.

"So," I asked him once, "did your parents send you to school?"

"Of course," he replied. "I'm Asian."

Handsome Dan and Handsome Dan's three-wood joined our residency program. He always downplayed and joked about his Korean heritage. I think this was his method of dealing with the shockingly large amount of casual racism directed his way. Racism is obviously a big problem in America. Unfortunately, it has also become big business, as inflammatory stories remain effective clickbait.[80]

Recently, the PC squad at the medical school asked us to fill out a survey on the racial background of all the physicians, looking for

---

[80] I'm looking at you, CNN.

the percentage of minorities. We listed our faculty from Asia, India, Pakistan, and Iran as "nonwhite minorities." We were told by the PC squad that, despite their skin color, didn't really count as "nonwhite." The only *true* minorities were African American, Native American, and Hispanic.[81]

White people are terrified of even the perception of racism toward black people. White people will go through often hilarious histrionics to avoid saying key words in the company of African Americans. I'm not even talking about *the* word, which can bring a professional to tears when pressed by Samuel M. F. Jackson.[82] I'm talking about innocent words in context such as *boy*, *brother*, and *watermelon*. Saying these words will cause white people to look around nervously and say, "Some of my best friends are black!"

It doesn't seem that people are nearly as worried about casually racist speech directed against people of Asian heritage. Racist stereotypes may even be cast as a joke by the mainstream, such as the regrettable headline "Chink in the Armor," published by a major sports media outlet discussing basketball player Jeremy Lin. Even in the racially charged 2016 Academy Awards ceremony, someone wrote and someone else approved a painfully awkward skit involving Asian children. This skit was played for comedy by a host who had just lambasted the voters for lack of black nominees. I guess not all racism is equal.

Handsome Dan finished examining a patient. The patient, presumably giving a backhanded compliment to his doctor of Korean heritage, said, "You speak English really well."

"Thank you," Handsome Dan said, without missing a beat. "So do you."

One time at County, we walked into the room of a dirtbag trauma

---

[81] Sadly, this is not a joke.
[82] https://www.youtube.com/watch?v=tYYBJ8XRdh4.

victim. As soon as we entered, he sized up my partner and bluntly blurted, "I'll bet you know karate!"

Handsome Dan smiled and said nothing.

Another colleague of mine of Korean heritage was in the process of trying to adopt a child. He and his wife were with a government-appointed social worker and a three-year-old child of Burmese descent. The child was inconsolably wailing, and the social worker was growing impatient.

"Can't you calm her down?" the social worker asked him. "Can't you find out what she's crying about?"

"How do you want me to do that?" he asked.

"Well, don't you speak *Asian*?"

"I'm from Texas."

Xiaofang was from China and first came to the United States as a graduate student. Her only knowledge of America came from watching reruns of *Friends* and *The X-Files*.[83] She arrived in America alone, speaking very little English. Within a few years, she learned English, earned a PhD and an MD, married, gave birth to two beautiful little girls, graduated medical school, began training to become a neurosurgeon, and picked up her Certified Badass trophy. Xiaofang had precious little tolerance for whining.

"What's the problem, ma'am?" I asked a disgruntled, entitled parent of a child with a shunt.

"Well, we called Thomas—"

Uh-oh, danger.

"And I told him that Susie was feeling sick."

Susie looked fine to me. At least as fine as any emo, pouting teenager can look. She looked up from her phone and glared out at me

---

[83] Not a joke.

behind an impressive amount of attention-seeking black makeup. She scowled and retreated back to her phone.

"Thomas told me we should tap her shunt."

A shunt tap is like a reservoir tap on the chicken wings. The shunt has a small *Jetsons'* bubble that one can feel. We stick a tiny needle into this to draw out spinal fluid. If we can't get any fluid out, usually it means the part of the shunt going into the head is plugged. If the fluid comes out at too high a pressure, it means the valve or the distal tubing is clogged. It takes a few minutes and hurts about as much as a tuberculosis test.

In this case, a shunt tap was a reasonable diagnostic maneuver.

"Now usually when Susie gets her shunt tapped, we take her to the procedure room and give her fentanyl[84] for pain control—"

Not reasonable.

I interrupted, "Fentanyl for a shunt tap?"

"Susie has a very high tolerance for pain," Mom continued, proving exactly the opposite of her point. "Anyway, that little *Oriental* girl just did it right here!" she yelled, emphasizing "oriental" to make it perfectly clear that she was offended that Xiaofang would touch her daughter.

"We never give fentanyl for a shunt tap," I said. "I've had babies sleep through that procedure."

Mom was not happy with my response.

"The good news is that the tap, CT scan, and examination are fine. I don't think her headaches are coming from a shunt problem. You can go home."

"But what about her headache?" Mom protested.

"The ER can give you some pain medications. Make sure you talk to your primary care doctor soon."

---

[84] A very powerful narcotic.

"The shunt tap never shows a problem, but *Thomas* always takes her to surgery anyway. And it always fixes things!" Now Mom was mad at me.

"How many surgeries has she had?" I asked.

"Thirty-two. And they *always work*!"

"If they worked, she would have had *one*," I said.

Mom didn't know how to process this information.

"Her shunt is fine," I said.

"The only thing that works for her headaches is fentanyl and Percocet," Mom challenged.

"Boy, that sucks. Well, good luck," I said with my body language conveying that I was not, under any circumstances, prescribing powerful narcotics to treat crazy.

"The rest of you just don't care as much as Thomas! I'm calling him. I'm calling before we come to make sure *he* sees us!" Mom shrieked.

Emo girl looked bored.

"You're planning your next emergency around Thomas's call schedule?" I asked sweetly.

Mom stormed out. However, she wasn't about to leave without her pound of flesh.

"I don't want to see that *Oriental* girl anymore!"

Xiaofang bristled. "I did everything correctly! Her shunt tap was fine. She's just a crazy teenager. Needs more discipline. Crazy mom."

"I know. Don't worry about it."

Xiaofang snarled. She had no patience for the wimpiness of Americans. When she was twelve, she had to have her tonsils removed. In America, this is generally done under general anesthesia. Kids (or George Costanza) may spend the night in a hospital and famously eat ice cream. Twelve-year-old Xiaofang was taken to an office, placed in a chair with a barbershop-type paper drape, leaned back, and then given anesthesia consisting of a combination of "suck it up" and "hold still." She had a little numbing medicine sprayed on the area. The surgeon pried open her mouth and removed the tonsils. The drape came off, and twelve-year-old Xiaofang was sent bleeding and crying from the office.

"It only cost twenty dollars, and I was home in twenty minutes!" she exclaimed proudly.

"Didn't it hurt?" I asked.

"Oh yes. My mom scolded me for crying. That crazy girl wants fentanyl for a tiny needle stick? She's sixteen! *This* is why your people won't put up a fight when China invades."[85] She clucked her tongue in disgust and stormed off. "I'll show her *Oriental* girl …"[86]

*   *   *   *

I can't say that all dirtbags are racist. But all racists are dirtbags.

One of the duties of County was to take care of the state's prisoners. A prisoner in the northern part of the state was quite offended that he was sent to see a local African-American doctor. He vehemently requested a transfer to us. At the time, the neurosurgery team at County consisted of Kendall (black), Steve (Mormon), and the Professor (Jewish).

Steve handled the call. *Of course we'd be glad to take him.*

The chap showed up covered from head to toe with swastikas and white power tats. Steve evaluated him and thought he needed back

---

[85] She was kidding. I think.

[86] Xiaofang also told me that in China, the police would line up condemned prisoners in public and then shoot them. The prisoner's family would be responsible for cleaning up the body. However, many families were embarrassed by the shame of the prisoner and refused. So medical schools quickly descended to harvest the bodies for cadaver studies. China sounds fun.

surgery. I guess since Steve was white, the dude trusted him. Kendall took one look from the door, muttered an obscenity, and moved on.

The day of surgery came. Kendall and Steve performed fairly large spine surgery. The Professor poked his head in. At this time, the prisoner was completely draped out, hiding his ink. The Professor checked the residents' work, made some smart-aleck comment, giggled to himself, and left. Patients usually do well from this type of surgery, but in the short term, it is really painful. We generally give high doses of intravenous narcotics for a few days, much to the chagrin of Xiaofang.

After the surgery, the Professor rounded with the team and got his first full look at the prisoner. He saw all the tats,[87] including the Mansonesque swastika on the forehead.

"Oh *god*," he muttered. "What the hell did you two sign up?" He surveyed the prisoner, growing progressively more disgusted. Finally he declared, "*No* pain medicine, Tylenol only," and stormed out.[88]

---

[87] A general rule for medicine: the amount of tattoos on a young male is inversely proportional to his ability to handle pain. Young men covered in hard-core tattoos are invariably whimpering pansies.

[88] No, Steve didn't cut off all his pain medications. Now, can the guy from the ACLU please stop calling the office and condescendingly whimpering into the darn phone?

CHAPTER 20

Life at the U

$\mathbf{M}$y favorite surgical case as a chief resident was called a mesial temporal lobectomy. This is a surgery that helps people with certain types of seizures. The temporal lobe, as the name suggests, lies just deep to your temple. If the brain looks like a boxing glove, the temporal lobe is the thumb. Patients with scarring, malformed brain, or a tumor in this area may have life-wrecking seizures. Seizures may keep a child out of school or an adult out of a job. Patients live in steady terror that they will seize in their church or at their child's wedding. Driving is out of the question. Children with regular seizures will struggle learning basic skills. Surgical resection of the abnormal area may provide a definitive, satisfying cure.

Plus the surgery is really fun. The surgeon gets a beautiful view of the elegant organ's anatomy. The seizure surgeon at the U was the Distinguished Gentleman. The DG was *smooth*. I never aspired to be the fastest surgeon in the world; I have known a bunch of fast, terrible surgeons. Poor surgeons try to be fast but are often slow. Great surgeons don't worry about speed but are fast. DG never looked like he was in a hurry (he wasn't). Yet every case moved efficiently from one step to the next.

On one particular surgery, junior resident Handsome Dan tagged along. DG sat by the computer as we positioned the patient. Handsome Dan and I proceeded to perform the exposure. First we made a curved incision, and then, careful to preserve the underlying arteries, stripped the temporalis muscle from the side of the skull. This is the "chewing" muscle, and eating is a little painful after this type of surgery. We placed two holes in the skull and then used a high-speed drill to remove a plate of bone. We could see the dura over the temporal lobe and the way it tucked over the boxing-glove thumb, outlining the fissure between the temporal and frontal lobe. We opened the dura and exposed the beautiful underlying brain. Trauma surgery is fast and brutal. In elective surgery, one gets to see the brain in lovely form, uncluttered with blood and bruising. The brain glistens and pulses gently. It is colorful, with red and blue vessels meandering through a rolling meadow of graiege.

DG scrubbed in, and Handsome Dan took a backseat. We proceeded to remove the front lateral part of the temporal lobe to gain access to the medial, defective part. This is high-rent territory, especially on the dominant left side. A too-aggressive resection may lead to significant difficulty talking. Too deep a resection risks violation of a spiderweb-thin membrane that separates the temporal lobe from the brainstem. Unknowingly wandering through this membrane could be disastrous or even fatal. A resection too far posteriorly may leave the patient with a large visual deficit. I sometimes catch myself taking surgery for granted. While everything was usually smooth with DG around, there was a part of me that knew that one lapse of judgment could seriously injure the patient.

DG would have fit well into Old England's gentry. He wore silk. He had a smoking jacket. He matched his pocket handkerchief to his tie. We talked about his primary passion: math. I tried to summon all the math knowledge I could remember from my engineering days at Golden U, but usually I was lost within a few minutes. We also talked about his somewhat incongruous enthusiasm for heavy metal music. We had many discussions about whether Iron Maiden's transformation from metal to storytelling prog rock was a positive.[89]

DG seemed satisfied with the resection. He instructed us to close, and he scrubbed out, eager to get on to something much more intellectually stimulating than brain surgery.

As this was one of Handsome Dan's first craniotomies, he wanted to make sure he got everything right. This included the postoperative orders.

"Do you want me to continue their current medications?" he asked DG.

DG was filling out the requisite paperwork and seemed a little annoyed to be asked. "Sure."

"How about pain medications?"

"Whatever you want."

"Antibiotics."

"Sure."

"What kind?"

DG sighed. "I don't know. Whatever you want."

Handsome Dan looked confused.

I said, "Kefzol."

"Do you want me to page you when the patient wakes up?"

"I don't carry a pager," DG said.

"Then how do I get ahold of you?" Handsome Dan asked, a little timidly.

"You *don't*," DG said, scurrying out the door, dashing to a class about knot theory.

*   *   *   *

---

[89] It was. *Empire of the Clouds* is a masterpiece.

Brittany, the young girl in surgery when I first met Thomas, was sweet as pie despite life making an impressive effort to repeatedly punch her in the face. She experienced every complication that one can experience with spina bifida. She suffered through over thirty surgeries involving her shunt, a Chiari malformation, and multiple procedures on her Judas spine. She was bound to a wheelchair and suffered from severe headaches. On top of all that, her dirtbag husband left her in the middle of treatment of breast cancer. She was thirty-one.

Thomas had saved her life on multiple occasions, and she loved him. As opposed to Jocelyn, she was an adult patient who was truly grateful for help. She never requested pain medications. She would get depressed, but really, who wouldn't? Despite all this, I always found her to be a ray of sunshine. She was infectiously upbeat and gratifyingly thankful. My experience with her in that first surgery wasn't unique; invariably, her first words upon waking up from anesthesia were "Thank you!" On her clinic days with Thomas, she would be dressed to the nines, belying her not-so-secret crush on him.

I had just returned from vacation during my chief resident year. I was driving to the U, smiling and humming along to the music—Rachmaninoff Op 23. No. 5.[90] I received a stat page from Handsome Dan.

"We've got this thirty-one-year-old adult spina bifida patient with an EVD. She's crashing. How soon until you get here?"

Ugh. All the stress I had lost on vacation flooded back.

"Is the drain working?"

"I'm not sure."

"How can you not be sure?"

"How soon until you get here?"

I parked and sprinted to the ICU. *Oh no ...*

---

[90] Editor's note: Taylor Swift's "Love Story." Please correct for honesty.

Brittany was lying motionless in the bed, a breathing tube sticking precariously out of her throat while the respiratory technician taped it down. The anesthesiologist had just emergently intubated her. I quickly assessed her, seeing that one of her pupils was dramatically larger than the other.

"What happened?"

"She just crashed. She'd been pretty sick, but she just crashed."

Handsome Dan recounted the recent events. Brittany began feeling sick at home. Then she began to run a high fever. She passed out, and her mother called 911. She was transferred to the U emergently with precarious vital signs. Her shunt was tapped, and the spinal fluid was infected. Her shunt was removed, and a temporary drain (EVD) was placed. Despite the correct treatment, she didn't improve. In fact, she was getting dangerously and expeditiously worse.

"Is the drain working?"

"I think so," Handsome Dan said quietly. "But it only drains fluid if we drop it well below her head.

"Scan this morning?"

"Her ventricles are bigger. The drain must be clogged. I think she's herniating!"

I examined the EVD/drain. It was a small orange catheter that entered the ventricle in her head, came out through the skin, and then ended in a collecting receptacle. The amount of spinal fluid that drained was dependent on the relative height of the receptacle compared to Brittany's ear. If we set the receptacle well above the ear, the fluid would have to overcome gravity to drain. If we set it below the ear, fluid would be siphoned out. Usually we set this about ten centimeters (about four inches) above the ear. Draining too much fluid may be dangerous or even fatal. I dropped the receptacle well below her ear and fluid dripped out easily.

"Her pupils are back to equal!" Handsome Dan exclaimed.

Well, that's a start.

Normally, Brittany's ventricles were extremely small or slit-like. In fact, they were tough to see on a CT scan. In the morning's scan, they were bloated and squishing the surrounding brain. Her rapid decline, coma, and asymmetric pupils suggested that the pressure in her head was too high and she was herniating. Untreated, Brittany would die.

"Drop it to the floor."

We drained off an aliquot of fluid. Her pupils returned to normal, but she remained comatose.

"The drain must be clogged. Her pressure must be really high, but I'm not sure why more fluid isn't coming out," I said.

Handsome Dan nodded.

"I just don't understand it. I don't understand why it comes so easily when we drop it. If it was clogged, wouldn't it just stop?"

I met with Dr. Montgomery, who was the attending in charge of Brittany.

"Any ideas?" he asked.

"Just one," I said. "Let's talk to Thomas."

"I'd love to, but the schedule shows he's on vacation. That's why I didn't call him this weekend."

"I'll bet I know where to find him."

Fortunately I knew Thomas's vacation spot. I dashed over to the Baby Hospital and, as expected, found him in his office among a pile of haphazardly scattered charts.

"That's interesting," he said after hearing the details of the case. "You know, I'll bet she has low-pressure hydrocephalus."

"What?"

"I'll bet your drain is fine, but her intracranial pressure is just way too low. This is why you can only drain it at a negative height."

"Wouldn't that make her ventricles smaller?" I asked, not quite buying his logic. "Her ventricles are clearly bigger."

"Normally. Yes, normally. But not in this case. Her brain compliance is off, so things may not behave like you'd expect. Sort of like my kids."

I was puzzled.

"Her brain doesn't react like normal," he continued. "Think of the brain as a sponge. A wet sponge is pliable and squishy and expands. A dry sponge is brittle and hard. The difference is the compliance and, really, the water content. You need to rehydrate the brain tissue. Then it will expand, like a wet sponge, and shrink the ventricles. Her symptoms aren't from a high pressure; they are from big ventricles."

"Aren't big ventricles a sign of high pressure?" I asked.

"Usually. Usually. But not in this case. You don't need to lower her pressure; you need to shrink her ventricles. Keep the EVD well below her head and wrap her neck."

"What?"

"Put an ACE wrap around her neck. Compress her jugular veins."

"Boss, usually I go along with your theories, but what the what?"

"Increase the venous pressure. This will reduce spinal fluid reabsorption in the veins. Water flows where it's easiest to go. If you make it hard to flow through the veins, it will preferentially flow through the drain. Her ventricles will shrink. Oh, and tell me how she does."

"I'll definitely tell you how she does."

"You know," he said, staring off into space, "I get calls from past residents all the time. Usually they are asking me about shunts. They always start by asking me about my life, you know, chitchat and so forth. I'd kind of rather they just get to the shunt problem, because it's probably less depressing than my life!" He chuckled and then stared at his computer. "Look at this new system. I already take too long on these stupid charts, and now each one takes twenty minutes longer." He sighed. "Well, let me know how Brittany feels."

I wandered back to the U, completely confused. However, my faith in the shunt guru was strong. We wrapped the neck. We dropped the drain. Dr. Montgomery looked at me quizzically. He was even more confused than I was. This whole plan made no sense.

Brittany's vital signs stabilized. Fairly quickly, her pupils returned to normal. She began breathing on her own the next day. She woke up three days later. We rechecked a CT scan; her ventricles were back to her normal.

"This is the part where you tell me, 'I told you so,'" I said to Thomas, the day after Brittany left the hospital, back to her normal self. She profusely thanked all of us, promised to pray for us, and gave me a giant, tear-filled hug.

Thomas smiled.

"I got lucky," he said.

"I don't buy that for a second."

"Hey, want to play a game of chess?"

"Maybe. Are you going to page me in the middle?"

"No promises ..."

*   *   *   *

Grandpa P. had two specialties: spine decompression and pituitary surgery.

The pituitary gland hangs from the brain like a tiny scrotum, just behind the eyes. Despite the small size, this gland plays a vital role in many major hormones of the body. A problem in the pituitary gland may cause either an excess or a deficit in these hormones. One of the major hormones controls growth. If a pituitary tumor secretes extra growth hormone at a young age, patients may be drafted into the brute squad. Sometimes a pituitary tumor secretes excess cortisol, a natural steroid. Excess cortisol from the pituitary causes Cushing's disease.[91]

Patients with Cushing's disease have characteristic findings, such as high blood pressure, excess weight gain, and round (moon) faces. The list of findings with Cushing's disease is quite long and tends to show up on every neurosurgical board examination. Patients with gigantism, acromegaly, or Cushing's disease die early. Thus, we may remove a tumor or, if need be, the whole gland. However, *lack* of cortisol is extremely dangerous or even fatal. If we remove all of the capacity to make this hormone, patients require medical supplementation for life. In fact, pituitary surgery was often fatal prior to effective hormonal supplements. We tend to resect tumors that secrete excess hormone with one exception. Sometimes a tumor secretes prolactin, a hormone important in lactation. Excess prolactin may prevent menstrual cycles and cause breast leakage. This tumor may grow frighteningly large. Thankfully, these tumors often shrink dramatically with medication.

The pituitary gland sits right below the eye nerves. A tumor that grows and pushes on these nerves may cause a characteristic loss of peripheral vision. The technical term is *bitemporal hemianopsia*. Patients have tunnel vision; they lose peripheral vision and can only see straight ahead. Rarely, patients may bleed into a fast-growing tumor. This may be a true, life-threatening emergency called *pituitary apoplexy*. Patients need an emergent infusion of steroids and usually go right to surgery.

Grandpa P. was a master of pituitary surgery. He was unapologetically old school in his methods. Younger surgeons often scoffed at

---

[91] Yep, there's that guy again.

his methods, right before they asked him to fix their complications. Grandpa P.'s patients rarely (if ever) had complications.

Pituitary surgery is generally done through the nose. There's a pathway that leads up the nose, to an air cavity in the base of the skull called the sphenoid sinus. The back wall of this is the lower wall of the sella turcica (literally, Turkish saddle). We chip through this, and there's the pituitary gland.

The surgery kind of looks a bit like Arnold pulling that tracking device out of his nose in *Total Recall*.[92] One would think that operating through the nose would introduce all kinds of complications. However, it's tolerated remarkably well. The inside of the nose has a very robust blood supply. Any parents dressing their nose-picking four-year-olds in Easter white can attest to the voracity of a nosebleed. Patients are stuffed up for a few days, but they tend to recover quickly. With improved technology, we can now expand the use of this technique to remove tumors that, a few decades ago, were unresectable.

The field of view for these surgeries is extremely limited. After all, the entire surgery is done through a nostril. It's a deep, uncomfortable reach in optimal conditions, but Grandpa P. made this even worse. He would stand between the resident and the patient, yet expect the resident to operate by reaching around his shoulder.

The ballet dance I perfected doing his spine surgery was kicked up to mosh pit expert levels for a pituitary case. We jockeyed for position. I began to elbow him out of the way. Grandpa P. was having none of that. We began griping at each other. We eventually completed the surgery, but he stormed out in a huff.

It was always a little disconcerting when Grandpa P. was mad. However, a chairman has to occasionally lay down the discipline.

---

[92] *Only Mah Brutahl*, https://www.youtube.com/watch?v=mSiFXhrxE3Y.

Bryce was usually the target. About once per month, he smarted off to the wrong person and got suspended.

As mentioned, positioning a spine patient can be tricky. The surgeries may last hours. Bryce had no patience for delay. One morning at the U, the anesthesia team was having a particularly difficult time getting a patient ready for surgery. Bryce began to become antsy as the seven-thirty surgery time stretched to eight thirty and then to nine. The patient was positioned facedown, but the team couldn't adequately breathe for him. The attending anesthesiologist dropped to the floor, flopped on his back, and scooted under the table much like a mechanic going under a car. He happened to be fairly portly.

"Look, kids," Bryce said to the surrounding medical students. "Ever seen a beached whale?" Unfortunately he said it a little too loudly,[93] and the anesthesiologist heard. This led to multiple angry phone calls, a trip to Grandpa P.'s office, and a suspension.

*   *   *   *

I got called into the principal's office once. I had walked into the preoperative area at the U to finish the paperwork on a surgical patient. This area was an open bay with multiple rooms spread out along the periphery. The entrance to each small pod was covered with a curtain. My patient also had a line of Scotch tape on the entrance floor and a small, handwritten note on the door.

Hospitals are justifiably afraid of the spread of disease from patient to patient. Patients with a communicable disease are quarantined, and the treating staff follows strict gowning, gloving, and handwashing protocols. These measures are necessary to protect both the hospital workers and other patients.

---

[93] Knowing Bryce, this may have been intentional.

Sometimes these protocols go a bit overboard. A person with a fully treated infection a decade earlier is still labeled as a contagion, even if any current danger is negligible. This was the case with my patient. I was expected to "gown-up" before pulling back the worn carpet and stepping across the tape.

"*Stop,*" a cranky nurse snapped.

"What?" I said.

"You didn't put on your yellow gown," she hissed.

"Oh." I noticed the sign. "Oops."

Apparently I didn't show enough remorse or contrition.

"I'm going to write you up!"

"For crossing the tape without a gown?"

"Yes!"

"Knock yourself out."

Apparently she didn't like this answer either. She searched for the appropriate forms and made a big flourish with her pens.

"So, can I ask you a question?" I asked to the grumpy nurse, still delightedly filling out her form.

"Sure!"

"How did you get the patient into that room?"

She seemed puzzled.

I gestured around. "Seems to me the only way that person could get into that room would be to walk through that crowded waiting room, past all the nurses eating at their station, then past all the other sick patients. So how did you get her to the room? Did you make everybody else wear a gown, or did you carelessly expose them to a potentially fatal infection? Also, do you believe that the tape will protect the patient in the next pod?"

She fumed. I was definitely getting written up.

Grandpa P. called me into the office and seemed disappointed that I got in trouble. Grandpa P. had a very distinct way of talking.

He would speak quickly, then usually snicker a little, then take a deep hissing inhale. He would sort of squint his eyes at you while he was thinking. Occasionally, he would go into the *Grandpa stare.* He would lean back in his chair and take a big inhaled breath, and then time would stop. He wouldn't move. He wouldn't exhale. He wouldn't speak. His eyes would fix on you, unblinking. It was really disconcerting the first time one experienced it. The first time I saw the Grandpa stare, I thought he was having a seizure. The residents knew that the proper protocol was just to wait it out. There was no point speaking, because anything said would be lost in that rift of the space-time continuum that he was currently occupying. After a pregnant moment, he would return and exhale, and the conversation would pick up exactly where he stopped. He scolded me, told me to respect the nurses, and bid me to go.

"Tape?" he asked as I left the room. "That's pretty stupid."

*   *   *   *

Bryce's smart mouth led to trouble many times, including the time he mocked the accent of a foreign-born resident in a particularly offensive way. Bryce was extremely gifted at impersonations and could quickly mimic the speech and walking patterns of virtually anybody. He was particularly adept at impersonating all the attendings.

At one national meeting, a large group of the faculty and residents gathered for dinner in a fancy New Orleans restaurant. Cam, long since graduated, showed up. Tall and now ferociously bald, he regaled us with old stories of the Professor and DG.

"You know there's a surgical move named after you?" Bryce said.

"What?" Cam queried.

"DG tells us about the 'Cam' maneuver."

A vagal nerve stimulator is a device placed in the neck that may reduce seizures in some patients. Delicate little electrodes are wrapped around the vagal nerve and connected to a battery that's implanted in the wall of the chest. It's kind of like the DBS, except no one has any idea how it actually works on the brain. DG was the expert at this procedure. It's a safe surgery, but wrapping the electrodes around the nerve is a frustrating hassle, especially if one is late for math class. Apparently, Cam had spent a good deal of time getting things exactly right, only to accidentally rip it all apart when he removed the skin retractors. DG dubbed this gaffe the *Cam-maneuver*.

This was the first time Cam had actually heard that his name had been sullied to the future generations. He became twitchier than usual.

"F—— DG. F—— that guy!" he shouted.

As a general rule, a resident does not want a surgical move named after him or her.

Cam then told a funny, disparaging story of the prim and proper Dr. Montgomery, a favorite lampooning target of Bryce. Bryce was now a few drinks to the night and broke into full standup comedy mode. Sensing the comedic possibilities, I immediately began playing the straight man.

He began to mimic Thomas in conversation with Jocelyn.

Thomas's voice: "So, you say you need more Percocet? I'll prescribe you two hundred if you promise to take them all at once!"

The Professor chimed in.

"Hehehehehe! I'll bet you guys imitate Thomas more than anybody else!"

Again, epiphanies are not always pleasant.

Bryce immediately jumped into full Eeyore-Professor voice, lurching around with the boss's characteristic stoop. Every resident instinctively develops an impression of the Professor, but Bryce's was the standard.

"How are you doing, Professor?" I asked, setting him up.

"Oh, I am *faaaaaaaabulous*!" Bryce shouted to the roar of the now growing crowd. "I'm putting like a *god*." He pantomimed a herky-jerky golf swing.

The Professor, initially stung that he would be a source of ridicule, soon began to laugh along with the increasingly drunken table. Soon, people were shouting requests. Someone shouted, "Do Grandpa P.!"

Bryce took a deep, hissing inhale and stared off into space. "It's the stare!" the Professor shouted. He moved on to DG and then to his android-like partner. I fed him questions while he gave me the robot stare.

"So do the impression!" the Professor exalted.

Bryce stared blankly at him.

"He *is* doing the impression," I said, pointing out the android's stereotyped mannerisms. The Professor got the joke and laughed.

Bryce rebooted himself and then broke into his closer: a stinging barrage of Dr. Montgomery. His finale was *Inception*-like: an impression of the Professor doing an impression of Dr. Montgomery. This brought down the house.

Suddenly, someone from the raucous crowd shouted, "Do Johnny!"

I had forgotten that Johnny Spine was there. We looked down to the end of the table to see Johnny's angry glower. The laughing slowed uncomfortably.

Bryce caught his fuming eye, paused, and in a rare recognition of limits, said, "Noooooooo."

Johnny grumbled something to himself[94] and went back to his dinner.

I'm not sure what made Johnny so angry that day. Maybe it was the way the bosses were bonding with Bryce. Maybe he felt left out.

---

[94] I'm pretty sure it was "sweep the leg."

Maybe he realized that Bryce imitated and mocked him behind his back (he did *a lot*). Maybe bullies don't like to be mocked. Whatever the reason, Johnny finished his dinner and stormed out in a silent huff.

CHAPTER 21

When It Hits Close to Home

I give our residents a thought experiment: if *you* needed surgery, who would you want to do it?

I straightened up after sitting in an awkward position for a particularly long surgery when I was struck with severe, searing, tearing pain in my back, shooting down my leg. It was horrible. I could barely catch my breath. I stumbled to the office to rest, only to realize that I couldn't go upstairs. I had fairly profound weakness in my left quadriceps.

These are the classic symptoms of a herniated lumbar disc. With the amount of weakness, I am sure doctor me would have told patient me to get an MRI and surgery. I may have recommended urgent surgery, given the amount of weakness in my leg. Dana urged me to get treatment, but doctors rarely listen to anybody. I delayed seeking an MRI, more out of laziness than anything. I also had the nagging thought that there was *no way* I was going to consent to surgery. Eventually, I got better. Over 70 percent of patients with a herniated disc will get better with time. It's remarkable how many spine surgeons I would recommend to any given patient. It's even more remarkable how short the list became of who I would even consider letting operate on *me*.

The residents usually list one or two surgeons. I challenge them to aspire to be the surgeon that a future resident will name with the same question.

Dr. King was getting frail. He had heart problems and a stroke. His wife, also an octogenarian, was in poor health. He walked with a cane but recently couldn't even do that.

"I saw my MRI," he told me flatly, a few years after I had become an attending surgeon. "I've got lumbar spondylosis. I think most of the problem is the ligament."

I couldn't argue with the founder of pediatric neurosurgery at the Baby Hospital.

He sucked air through his lips. One side of his mouth drooped.

"I want you to decompress me."

I nodded. "Okay."

"And I want to do it under local anesthesia."

"Nope."

"We used to do these under local all the time."

"You also used to directly put a needle in the carotid artery while the patient was in a ward bed. At the VA no less.[95] I'm not a fan of that either," I said.

He smiled.

"You need a two-level laminectomy. I can do this through a one-inch incision, but you're going to be prone and under general anesthesia."

He scrutinized me, like a disapproving grandfather would when the grandchild told him how he was going to make it big in punk rock. "Fine."

---

[95] Prior to CT scans, x-rays were the only way to image the head. Surgeons of Dr. King's generation would directly puncture the carotid artery, forcefully inject dye, and then snap an x-ray to track the blood vessels in the head. Just saying that gives me the willies. That generation had guts.

I learned from my ER days that one of the biggest mistakes physicians make is to treat fellow doctors differently than other patients. While we make some professional allowances, I try to talk to another doctor exactly as I would talk to any other patient. The Lovely Wife and I went to see an obstetrician about a pregnancy-related complication. The OB doctor, realizing I was a neurosurgeon, began talking to me strictly in professional jargon. I had no idea what he was talking about.

I finally stopped him. "Let's just say I only got a pass in OB. Talk to me like I sell insurance."

The day for the surgery arrived. There he was, the dean emeritus of the Baby Hospital, unceremoniously clothed in a gown that didn't close in the back. He was sitting with his wife and the Old Man. The Old Man pulled me aside to discuss strategy.

This was a case that I had performed hundreds of times, but I was shocked by how nervous I felt. A spinal decompression in a patient pushing ninety has a pretty high risk of complications. The complications tend to be minor and annoying but still. The dura is often paper thin—like aged parchment skin. It tears easily. It's often stuck to the grummus accumulated from years of walking upright. I took a few deep breaths and began.

A few hours later, I went to talk to the Old Man in the waiting room. The patient's wife had gone home.

"Eh, eh. So, how'd it go?" he asked.

"Smooth as silk," I said, borrowing a phrase and voice inflection from the Professor.

"Did you get a durotomy?" he asked.

"You must be thinking of the Professor's cases. I don't get those."

He appreciated my joke and laughed. "He gets a lot of durotomies?"

"They call his OR the champagne suite," I said.

He laughed again.

Sometimes surgeons appreciate a little bravado. Overconfidence is dangerous. But underconfidence is just as bad. If you need a brain surgery, do you want a surgeon who seems nervous?

The Professor famously operated on a world champion professional cyclist. The athlete required brain surgery. He asked the Professor if he was the right guy to do the job.

"Young man," the Professor said without a trace of hesitation, "as good as you are on a bike, I'm better at brain surgery."

I definitely *was* nervous operating on Dr. King. But I wasn't about to divulge this to the patient or the OR staff.

The surgery went perfectly, and he did as well as a sickly eighty-nine-year-old could do. I should have felt happy when I got home, but all I could think about was getting a stiff drink.

*   *   *   *

I was the resident on the vascular service when we got the call that an aneurysm patient was about to hit the ER. He had been intubated by the medics and was in critical condition. The vascular fellow Pete and I wandered to the ER.

We waited. They were "five minutes" away. We waited some more. We chatted nonchalantly. We thought about getting a sandwich. Nothing. All we heard were the mundane sounds of the ER—doctors and residents shuffling papers, somebody asking for pain medications, the phone ringing … We were getting bored.

"Where are they? I thought you said they were five minutes away?" Pete half screamed at the receptionist.

She rolled her eyes and shrugged. Pete stomped back to our chairs and plopped down.

"So anyway," he said, "I was checking out this Audi." He fiddled around to bring up a picture on the computer. "Pretty sweet, eh?"

I know next to nothing about cars. It looked nice.

"Sure."

We talked about nothing for a few more minutes, and then we saw a few of the ER docs scramble toward the door. This was the unmistakable first snowball of the avalanche. Suddenly a small army of people burst through the door, pulling along a gurney with the patient. They were rushed and noisy, shattering the drone of the surroundings. The senior ER doc began barking out orders, and the patient was flung almost violently from the gurney to the hospital bed.

"Raise his head!" Pete yelled.

We had to elbow our way through the throng to get to the patient.

"Blood pressure is 240!"

"Shit," Pete said. "He's blown his pupil. We need mannitol! Go ahead and blow him down. Let's get to the scanner."

We were in the trauma bay less than five minutes before we headed off to the adjacent CT scanner—just long enough to begin medications and confirm the breathing tube placement. Nurses were scrambling to start IVs as we moved. One of the senior ER residents broke open a kit to start a large central line.

"Any history?" I yelled.

No one answered.

I tried again. "Any history?"

"He collapsed at work," one of the medics yelled. "No problems, then he collapsed. We're contacting his wife."

"Where does he work?" I shouted back.

"I think at County. He may be a doc."

Pete and I looked at each other. *Oh shit*. When patients arrive, it's tough to really look at *them*. We look at the endotracheal tube to make sure it is in the right place. We look at the lines and catheters. We look at the blood pressure. We look at the monitors. But we don't really look at the patient.

"You know him?" Pete asked.

He looked familiar, but I couldn't quite place it. I shook my head. "Let's get the scan."

We did. It showed Death.

He had a giant aneurysm with an even more giant blood clot. His brain was swollen and squished.

"We're going straight to the OR!" Pete ordered.

I called.

The OR was hurriedly getting ready. We pulled him out of the scanner and sprinted to the elevator. We rode up to the OR suite where we met the attending vascular surgeon.

"Can you guys hit the ventricle?" he said briskly.

"Yep," I said.

"Is there a chance?" Pete asked.

We had the scan pulled up on the computer screen.

The attending nodded grimly. "He's a doctor?"

"We think so," I said.

"I heard he was a surgeon," one of the nurses said.

"*Is* a surgeon," the attending corrected sternly.

He nodded to Pete and me again. We knew what this meant. We were going for broke. The three of us knew the patient had little to no chance of meaningful survival. There's an unwritten rule about the medical family. You aggressively care for your family. Surgeons who deal in trauma commonly work with police, medics, first responders, and firefighters. They are family. A cop with a gunshot wound may go to surgery, despite the fact that we know that he or she will likely die. A criminal with the same injury probably will not. Judge all you want. This patient was a surgeon. We didn't know him, but he was our brother. Deep in our hearts, we knew there was no chance. But we weren't in the mood to debate.

Pete and I rapidly positioned him. I took a hand drill and drilled a hole in the skull. I then estimated the position of the now shifted ventricle, stabbed a hole in the dura covering the brain, and passed a drainage catheter. Spinal fluid shot out under sickeningly high pressure. While I was doing this, Pete and the attending scrubbed. I secured the catheter, rapidly shaved half of the head, positioned and prepped the patient, and then headed to the sink to scrub.

The attending vascular surgeon was one of the best and fastest technical surgeons in the country. The skin was opened, and the bone flap was off within a few short minutes. He was greeted with a dura bulging out, under pressure from the underlying blood clot.

"Open the drain!" he ordered. The anesthesiologist drained spinal fluid, which provided disappointingly little brain relaxation.

He sliced open the dura, and a mixture of brain and blood came pouring out.

"Damn it. *Suck*!"

Pete grabbed the biggest sucker and desperately tried to clear a path for the attending to see. I grabbed a second sucker to help. All we could see was a torrent of dark-red slurry of clot and brain. The attending plowed forward and somehow found the bleeding aneurysm in all that mess. It was huge, with calcified, stiff walls. He placed a clamp, more on intuition and feel than exposure, and the bleeding slowed.

"We've got to get proximal control!" he shouted, quickly dissecting through the fissure between the frontal and temporal lobes. This is a challenging endeavor, even in the best of circumstances. He was doing it with a swollen, bleeding brain obscuring every visual cue. Calling on years of training and experience, he found the correct path and the feeding main branch of the internal carotid artery. He placed a temporary clip on this. This stopped most of the bleeding, but it was also shutting off the main artery to half of the brain. We could not leave this clip on very long.

Without a wasted motion, he began to separate the base of the aneurysm from the angry brain. The goal was to find the neck of the aneurysm. We found it, but it was small comfort. The aneurysm was what we would call *giant* and *fusiform*. "Giant" is self-explanatory. "Fusiform" meant it was not a discrete water balloon, but rather a broad outpouching of an abnormally shaped vessel. The walls were also filled with calcium and thus bone stiff.

The attending grunted and cursed.

When a temporary clip is placed on a vital artery, one of the scrub nurses starts a timer. After more than a few minutes, the patient will have a stroke. The nurse calls out the time.

"Five minutes."

We tried a clip. It didn't close. The walls were too stiff.

"Seven minutes."

We tried another one. It slid off. Then another. It slid off too. He tried various combinations. He tried multiple clips. He tried to clip one half and then the other half.

"Twenty minutes."

"Shit."

The aneurysm would not yield. It was like trying to get a paper clip to block half of a racquetball.

"Only one option," he said, mostly to himself. He was right. He permanently clipped the middle cerebral artery leading to the aneurysm and the artery leading out of the aneurysm. This would stop the bleeding. This would guarantee a catastrophic stroke.

He looked at me and Pete. "No choice."

We nodded.

"Close, leave the bone flap off."

We did. It wasn't easy. The brain was already swelling. Despite the large cavity created by removing the side of the skull, we had difficulty pulling the skin over the mushrooming brain. We laid a piece of plastic over the brain, and then I stretched the skin while Pete quickly placed skin staples. By the end, I was basically leaning on the brain trying to keep it in the head.

All three of us felt defeated. The patient was wheeled to the ICU. The operating room, so noisy just moments before, was now dark and silent.

"We get any information about him?" the attending asked the anesthesiologist.

"Surgeon at County. Uh. I think you guys know his wife," he said dejectedly.

"Who?" I demanded.

"She's your case manager."

My heart fell. I stood there, unable to move, feeling like I was about to throw up. Vivian? The one light at County? *No ...*

Pete elbowed me. "You know her?"

"Yeah."

The attending looked dejected. "Let's go talk to her."

Pete accompanied the patient to the ICU. I went with the attending to the quiet rooms. We opened the door. I hoped beyond hope that our information was incorrect.

Vivian saw me first. We locked eyes. She knew instantly.

"Oh *God*," she muttered.

Tears began to flow, but she tried for a second not to make a noise. Then she shook briefly in a crying spasm. She got up and wobbled over to me. We hugged tightly, and she sobbed violently for a few seconds. Then, ever the rock, she straightened herself up, wiped her eyes, composed herself, and held out her hand to introduce herself to the attending. He explained the gravity of the situation and what happened at surgery.

For the next few days, Vivian held vigil over her husband. She sat calmly by his side in the ICU. I would round early. I would check the vital signs and the blood work. I would make sure the drain was putting out CSF. I would check the pupils, now grossly dilated and misshapen. He was in a drug-induced coma, so there was little else to check. Even the coma could not mask the unmistakable presence of Death.

Vivian didn't say much. She just held his limp hand. I would pat her on the shoulder, and she would say, "Thank you," as I left.

I stopped by to round on the day we planned to remove the ventilator. We had performed the very strict protocol to declare brain death.

"Vivian," I started, "I don't know what to say. You've heard me give this speech a thousand times." I felt like I was letting her down. She'd been with me many times when I told a family that their loved one was dead. I felt horrible that I was garbling the words.

She grabbed my hand. She tried to comfort me. "I know you did all you could."

Somehow this made me feel worse. I should be the one trying to soothe her.

"The first time I saw him in this room ..." she said, looking around. She paused and took a deep breath. "The first time ..." She let out a short, involuntary sob. She seemed a little frustrated that her voice had cracked. "The first time I saw him in this room ... I knew he was gone. I've been sitting here, but I knew he was gone." Her voice grew in strength. "I knew he wasn't in pain. I knew he wasn't here." She smiled sadly.

Then she looked back at me.

"I believe in a loving God. My husband is with him now. I know that to the very bottom of my heart." She began to cry, but her eyes remained locked with mine. "I know that to the bottom of my heart. I'll never stop missing him. I'll never stop loving him. He's a good man. He really is. You'd like him." She looked wistfully at her husband. "I'll

230

be with him again someday. I have no doubt. I believe he is with God. He's God-fearing and strong in his faith. I know he's with God now."

She sat down and held his hand.

"Is the protocol over?"

"Almost."

She smiled with the awkward splash of irony in the face of tragedy. "I don't know what to do. I've always been on the other side of this. Do I stay here? Do I need to sign something?"

To be honest, I didn't know. I knew I didn't want her in the room when he was disconnected.

"We've got a chaplain in the quiet room. Why don't I take you there? The nurses will come get you in a little bit."

The nurses had gathered outside the room. Most of them had dried tears on their face. Nurses have a bond also. Vivian was part of their family, even if they had never met. They took her hand and escorted her to the quiet room.

I had to sit down for a short time.

I was on the vascular service. We would see aneurysm patients every day. We would see *this* every day. I wouldn't fumble the words with any other patient. I would know how to dispassionately do my job. I would be comforting but would have the necessary professional detachment. I couldn't detach from one of my own. I felt beat up and helpless. I felt somewhat emasculated that we couldn't do a single damn thing to help Vivian's husband.

I sat alone with him in his room for a few minutes, digging my fists into my eyes.

Well, enough of this. I have work to do.

I got up and finished rounds.

*   *   *   *

Hadley was six and had been vomiting for about two weeks. Her parents became concerned when she started to get sleepier and wasn't interested in playing with her toys. They took her to see her pediatrician, who checked some blood tests, recommended hydration, and gave her some stool softeners, thinking that she might be constipated. She continued to worsen, becoming listless and refusing to eat.

This is a very common story for children with brain tumors. It's also a very common story for children without brain tumors. I must have seen hundreds of children exactly like this during my four-year paid vacation to Japan. Looking back, none of them had a brain tumor. All the kids got better with tender lovin' care and time. But Hadley didn't. She kept getting worse. Her parents took her back to an emergency room where a CT scan showed a large brain tumor. She was transferred to the Baby Hospital.

I went to see her in the emergency room. She was lying on the bed, huddled under her blanket. All I could see was a tuft of blond hair sticking straight up, with a tiny fist clutching her woobie. The parents were hovering, nervous, with wide eyes of disbelief and terror. I've seen that look many times. I talked to the parents, got the history, and then began to peel back the blanket from the protesting kid.

My God, she looks exactly like my youngest daughter!

I was startled for a second. She had the same blond hair that laughed at combing attempts. She had the same fair skin covering a doll face and knobby knees. Her skin was peaked from the vomiting, and her nail beds were too light. She needed more hydration. I felt the urge to pick her up. Everything about her looked familiar, as if I was staring at my daughter in the living room. Even their birthdays were similar.

"We'll admit her to the intensive care unit, give her some medication that will help her feel better, then check an MRI," I said, somewhat lost in the disturbing thought of what if this really had been my daughter?

The MRI confirmed the diagnosis of a brain tumor. We took her to surgery. Once she was asleep, we flipped her facedown on the operating-room bed. I then squeezed the medieval head clamp, with its three pointed spikes, into her skull, affixing her in position. I had placed a head holder thousands of times. This one hurt me. I felt like I was hurting my kid.

There's a necessary disconnection during surgery. Once the drapes are on, we often forget that we're working on a real flesh-and-blood person, much less someone's little girl. We only see skin, bone, brain ... We see the relevant anatomy and do our job. I suppose this is good; if we got too caught up in the magnitude of our job, perhaps we wouldn't have the guts to stick in the knife. I've seen medical students faint at the end of surgery, when all the bleeding is done but when the drapes come off. Then the interesting anatomy becomes a person and what just happened seems more like Freddy Krueger than Harvey Cushing.

I was having trouble disconnecting myself with this one; the resemblance was so striking! But training took over, and soon the resident and I were starting the case. We started by placing an EVD to drain the spinal fluid. We opened the back of the skull, saw the back of the tumor, and went to work. The resident sucked and irrigated while I cut and dissected. The tumor was a dark grayish-purple and extremely bloody. I was thankful there was a nice plane of separation between it and surrounding brain.

I get a burst of adrenaline when operating on a tumor. It is almost like getting pumped up before a basketball game. I should know, as I was a veritable high school phenom—basically a bigger, stronger LeBron James.[96] But I digress. Thomas likens surgery to playing

---

[96] Editor's note: The author scored a grand total of thirteen points in two years of high school basketball. The team had a play called "anybody shoot but Fulkerson." Just thought you should know.

baseball. A new player on the field is probably thinking, *Please don't hit it to me!* An experienced player is probably thinking, *Hit it to me!* I feel a rush of adrenaline, especially in a tumor that will require quick work. The only way to stop a malignant tumor from bleeding is to take the bugger out.

I inspected the tumor bed. It was dry. We didn't see the bleeding mess anymore. We saw glistening white brain tracts and the undisturbed gentle floor of the fourth ventricle. We could look up at the undersurface of the cerebral aqueduct, smiling at us like a tiny toilet. We irrigated. No bleeding. We scouted around with the intraoperative ultrasound machine. No tumor. We irrigated again. Still clean.

At this point, we both took a deep breath. The resident began to sew things back up, and I began to relax. There's a wonderfully exhausted victorious feeling that comes with the removal of a brain tumor.

Hadley woke up fussy but well. We checked an MRI, and we were happy. The tumor was gone. A day later, she was out of the ICU. Three days later, she was in the play room as if nothing had happened.

My youngest daughter is in kindergarten, and she's a brat. She's sassy and bossy and never stops flitting from place to place like a tiny sprite figuring out the world. She doesn't so much play with dolls as she attacks them. For her, Barbie is not one who dresses in stupid clothes. Barbie fights dinosaurs. Sometimes she'll disappear in her room and, not realizing that sound travels, will *roooooaaaar* viciously as Barbie and Rex from *Toy Story* battle it out. This is the way six-year-olds should be. While I see it every day, I still can't imagine what it would be like to put my little girl through all that.

I see Hadley now once every six months. She still strikes me as my little girl's long lost sister. Hadley has no idea who I am, other than she has to see me after she gets an MRI. Four years later, no tumor. Hadley is perfect. Mom wondered about her coordination. At first, I was worried, until Hadley grabbed one of her feet with her opposite hand and then pogoed around the room on the other leg.

"I think she's fine."

*   *   *   *

Merlin was one of the first residents trained by the Old Man. He was intelligent and facile. Like many of the surgeons of his generation, he could expertly treat whatever came through the door. Today, in the age of specialization, the number of neurosurgeons who excel at both brain and spine surgery is shockingly small. In his prime, Merlin could do it all.

He was short, hunched, bald, and wise. He had a neatly trimmed goatee and professorial round glasses and spoke with quick precision, often punctuating his sentences with a brief guffaw. As his clinical career wound down, he spent more time with his second passion: teaching. He loved having students and residents around. In fact, his love of teaching was so strong that he began a program to help neurosurgeons across the country study for the final board examination.

The process of becoming a board-certified neurosurgeon is this: graduate college (four years) and get accepted to medical school, graduate medical school (four years) and get accepted to residency, graduate residency (seven years) and pass a written test, practice for a few years and collect data on surgical patients for at least three to six months, and then apply to sit for the oral boards. So this process takes about eighteen years. The oral boards are the cumulative exam, and there is a fairly robust fail rate. A group of the most noted neurosurgeons in the country will meet with the applicant in a small room and basically grill him or her under a hot light like an old-timey detective movie.

It's remarkably stressful. The applicants have completed residency and been in practice for at least a few years, yet some will break down like an intern quivering before the dean. Merlin knew this, and he started a review course. In the course, he would pull each person up to the hot seat, a chair in front of all of his or her peers, and ask questions. This was nerve-rattling, but it was much better to fumble in practice than in the real examination. Merlin's course quickly became recognized as quintessential training for the real thing. Now, over 90 percent of all neurosurgeons in America attend the course bearing his name.

Merlin could turn any topic into a teaching lesson. He was a surgical Yoda. I loved it. One year, he took me to his course as a resident. Technically, the course was closed to residents, but Merlin was never above flouting the rules. After all, it was *his* course. As luck would happen, the governing body of neurosurgery decided to name the course after him that year with a ceremony. My job was to distract him for about thirty minutes, while others hung up a banner and brought in a cake. Distracting Merlin was ludicrously easy. We returned after chatting about nothing, to see some of the neurosurgery royalty standing in front of a banner bearing his name. He was mortified, emotional, and grateful. It really was a tremendous national honor.

Merlin and I were working on a research project when he began to have trouble. I would give him a draft of a manuscript; he would scribble suggestions in the margin and then ask me to do it again. I noticed his suggestions began to make less and less sense. Some were illegible. *Oh well*, I thought, *he's just distracted. He's very busy. It happens*. Merlin was extremely active, even though he'd long stopped operating. He was involved in many administrative positions and had a significant number of humanitarian projects. He traveled all over the world. He was single and without kids; neurosurgery was his life.

One day, Merlin got lost on the way to work, taking the route he had traveled thousands of times before. He had trouble finding the right words to say. He was quite disturbed and a little scared. He confided in one of his older partners who took him to the office to do a full neurological examination. Merlin was worried that he was getting Alzheimer's disease and was deathly afraid of losing his remarkable mind.

"Let's see if we can get a CT scan."

They went down to the scanner and got the radiologist to do the unscheduled test. The three of them went to the computer to check the results. As the scan came up slowly, they all recognized the unmistakable pattern of a malignant brain tumor.

"At least I'm not getting Alzheimer's," Merlin said with a nervous guffaw.

The other two were silent in shock. Merlin sighed, looked at his shocked colleagues, and said defiantly, "No surgery."

His partners talked him into a biopsy to confirm the diagnosis. He relented but under protest. This confirmed the worst: glioblastoma multiforme (GBM). This is the most common primary brain tumor in adults. It is also the deadliest. Many smart people have worked very hard to cure this tumor, but our ability to treat it today is only marginally better than it was fifty years ago. With no treatment, the tumor is fatal within a few weeks. With maximal surgical, radiation, and chemotherapy treatment, people survive about one year. Merlin knew this. He refused treatment. He passed within two months.

Other authors have noted how differently doctors view end-of-life questions compared to the general public.[97] Doctors have experienced the horrors of the hospital, where patients are flogged incessantly in some false hope that death can be averted. In fact, internal medicine

---

[97] A terrific read, http://www.zocalopublicsquare.org/2011/11/30/how-doctors-die/ideas/nexus/.

specialists are often given the derogatory nickname of "fleas," because fleas are the last things to leave a dead body.

I'm not sure why we've evolved to view death in such an antagonistic way. Why is there a stern effort to try to wring every last grim second out of an elderly person's life? It's a fool's errand. Americans spend a ridiculous amount of money on futile care in the last month of a person's life. On one hand, it sounds cruel to withhold treatment (including feeding). On the other hand, doctors often think it's cruel to condemn someone to perpetual torture in a hospital.

It's one thing to save a life. It's another thing to prolong a death. Extending someone's life is valuable; extending someone's death is not. It's almost selfish.

Death and medicine have entered the political arena, and like always, reason and intelligence have been sacrificed. Politicians work for political gain, scaring the populace with tales of "death panels" and the like. Other politicians view end-of-life questions under the lens of how their position will score with the illogically rabid abortion lobbies.[98] It's a shame really, because this is one topic where we should have a meaningful discussion.

Am I a part of a death panel? Maybe. Believe me; there are times I want to just flat out tell a family that they don't want Grandma to survive her injury. I want to tell them to let her go, take her home, and let her die with dignity in her own house. I want to tell them that if we save her life, she will never again be able to talk, interact, feed herself, or wipe her own butt. Please, take Grandma home and never bring her back to the hospital for any reason.

Families have a hard time with this. Some may feel guilt. For the elderly, there's often one family member who is the caregiver. Usually that person will agree to withhold aggressive therapy. Then someone

---

[98] See Schiavo, Terry.

else shows up who usually has had little to no contact with the patient for years, but he or she will viciously insist on every last medical option. His or her view may be predicated on guilt or mistrust. In a time where a family should come together, conversations degenerate into arguments. Some families view any doctor giving bad news with suspicion, convinced we're trying to bump off Grandma for selfish, financial, or racial reasons.

Some governmental idiots[99] think that doctors have an investment in keeping people sick. Hospitals can be financially punished if the family, despite all reason, keeps bringing the ninety-six-year-old grandma back to the ER. No doctor sees this scenario and thinks, *"Score!"* Every single one will groan and comment how he or she would never do the same thing to their mother. This misconception is total, unadulterated lunacy.

Doctors die at home. Merlin knew the consequences of withholding treatment. He knew these more than anyone, as he was a specialist in treating this exact sort of tumor. He knew he would die. He was happy he didn't have Alzheimer's. He didn't want to lose his mind and memories in a protracted spiral to the end. He died quickly, quietly, and peacefully. We should all be so lucky.

I want to die at home, in my jammies, watching bad TV.

No way in hell do I want to die in a hospital.

*　　*　　*　　*

"Did you think about coming back to the Baby Hospital?" Grandpa P. asked.

I'd thought about it a lot.

"Nothing good happens at the Baby Hospital, boss," I said.

---

[99] Editor's note: redundant.

"Thomas fell asleep in the clinic. Patients could see him. Some were pissed off. The nurses told them that he was meditating. I just don't know how long we can keep this up," Grandpa P. said, looking at the floor. "I'm worried."

"I think we all are," I said.

Grandpa P. sighed and fell into his stare. A few minutes later, he looked at me and said, "I need you at the Baby Hospital."

* * * *

"You can't do this!" Handsome Dan said. Handsome Dan had blossomed into a superior resident and all-around good guy. I trusted him like family. "You can't do this. The Baby Hospital will chew you up. Look what it's doing to Thomas."

Thomas was ragged. For his own health, Grandpa P. asked the other attendings to take over Thomas's adult patients. Jocelyn got pawned off to the Professor, who saw her once and told her she was crazy and that she'd never get a single pain pill from anyone in the department ever again. Jocelyn protested angrily and tried all her emotional blackmail tricks but to no avail. The Professor was not a man who suffered dirtbags. We never saw her again.

I had spent that day in the clinic with Thomas. He seemed depressed at the start. He was worried about some business merger and some lawsuit. He struggled with the new computer charting system, repeatedly asking the staff how to enter orders.

Soon the patients arrived, and Thomas brightened. He saw a few of his adult patients, including Brittany, who was all decked out in her Sunday best. She was bubbly, grateful, and unflinchingly positive. I was happy she had survived her time at the U. She left, quite sure that I didn't catch her flirting with Thomas.

Most of Thomas's adult patients were like Brittany. Life had kicked them in the groin, but they had kicked back. There were a few like Jocelyn. Thomas patiently consoled them, while I sat in silence, stewed, and wished I could effectively perform the *Avada Kedavra*.

On this day, most of the patients were children. Truly, these were the least of our brothers and sisters. We saw children from foster care, children who had been abused, children who were blind and deaf, and children who were twisted from cerebral palsy into a macabre pretzel.

One of Thomas's specialties was *spasticity*. Children with cerebral palsy or brain injury may develop devastating tightness in their arms and legs. This hinders basic movements like sitting or bathing. Thomas was a specialist in a number of techniques to help these speechless, invalid, weak children. The children would file in, pushed in their chairs by a grateful mother or grandmother. Thomas would speak to them, and for that fifteen minutes, the world would be a beautiful place. Children, blind, deaf, and mute, would smile when the king of the Island of Lost Toys walked into the room.

"Thomas has taken care of my daughter since she was born," a mother told me. Her child had spina bifida. "He fixed her back and placed her shunt. We've been through a few shunt surgeries." She looked around the waiting room. One of the features of the Baby Hospital is the constant reminder that no matter how bad you perceive your situation, someone else is going through something worse. She saw the devastated children around her and then looked at her own daughter—in a wheelchair but doing well at school. Happy. "But I guess we have it pretty good. Anyway, a couple of years ago, she was in a bad car accident. The ambulance brought her here, but she was unresponsive. The doctors pinched and yelled at her, but she wouldn't respond. They called Thomas. As soon as he walked in the room, she opened her eyes and said, 'Hey, buddy!' Right then, I knew she was going to be all right."

Hail to the king, baby.

"Well, we reviewed her CAT scan. Thomas thinks her shunt is fine. He wants to see her back in about six months," I said, handing her the discharge paperwork. She smiled.

"I'm not sure what we'd do without him," she said.

I walked back to the office. Thomas was passed out next to a half-eaten salad.

*   *   *   *

"I mean, I'm worried that he's going to *die*," Handsome Dan continued, talking about Thomas.

"I know. I am too."

"Not figuratively, I'm mean literally *stop breathing* die."

"I know."

"He doesn't eat. He doesn't go home. This is what the Baby Hospital does to you. I mean, you like your kids, right?"

I guess so. At any given time, I liked three out of the five. Which three changed daily.

"Yeah," I said.

"You can't do this. You'll be dumped on until you die; then you'll be thrown out to pasture. You know the business is changing. In the grand food chain, pediatric neurosurgeons are the bottom."

He was right.

The world of medicine was (is) changing, and it's not going well. Neurosurgeons are the proverbial canary in the medical mineshaft. We have relatively small numbers,[100] so any environmental change affects us first. Thomas was concerned about the impending merger of the two major neurosurgical groups in town: one based at the

---

[100] There are approximately 3,500 practicing neurosurgeons in the United States, and the number is dropping every year. Of these, there are about 170 who are fully board-certified pediatric neurosurgeons.

Mothership hospital and the other at the U. Two competing groups were joining together to resist the crush of various government and hospital entities. In the business of medicine, like in the jungle, only the lions survive. Thomas was a sickly antelope.

*   *   *   *

"Have you thought about it?" Grandpa P. asked again.

"I've thought quite a bit."

"And?"

Loyalty means something to me. I never forgot the time when Grandpa P. somehow was able to call me in Nowhere, Japan. I remembered all the support and help he'd provided for me over the years. I remembered the guidance, the mentoring, the golfing, and the fun he had provided. It meant something to me that Grandpa P. could name every one of my kids. It meant something to me that he prioritized family life and that he treated his residents like family. If Grandpa P. needed me, well …

"Let's do this," I said.

Grandpa P. smiled. I felt like I did when I showed my parents my first good report card. I left for fellowship, determined to learn enough to help Thomas and the kids at the Baby Hospital—even the bratty ones who made their Barbie fight dinosaurs.

CHAPTER 22

It's the Little Things

Each day is stressful for a neurosurgeon. Even the technically simplest case can quickly morph into a disaster. It's amazing how simple things can be the difference between a day full of positives or negatives.

Positive: Music

Your surgeon may be rockin' out during your operation. Does that disturb you? You listen to music at work, right? Surgeons do the same thing. Surgery may take hours and, despite the fact that the surgeon may be working in the brain, can get kind of tedious. Many surgeons like background music.

Orthopedic doctors tend to like house music, presumably so they can pump their fists and towel-snap each other's rears while yelling "You da man, dog!" Older surgeons prefer classical music. Doloris listens to Christmas music. I have partners who are Beliebers and others who prefer Rage Against the Machine.[101]

---

[101] Perhaps recapturing their childhood angst caused by being driven to soccer practice in Mom's minivan.

Me? I'm particular to eighties music and Iron Maiden.[102] Don't judge me.

The Professor likes Air Supply.

Negative: Screensavers

There was a time when the hippest, coolest, cutting-edge technology was a program that made toasters float across a computer screen. This totally blew our minds in 1991.

Screensavers have evolved. Initially, they were necessary to prevent damage to phosphor or plasma computer screens. Now they are primarily a source of security.

Computer security is a hot-button issue in hospitals today, both for criminal and privacy concerns. Accidentally leaving a patient's chart open on a computer can lead to embarrassing (and illegal) circumstances. So the IT department makes sure a computer doesn't sit idle for long. In fact, if one leaves it alone for a minute or so, it will convert to the screen saver.

In the operating room, the computer allows us to project high-resolution images of the patient's MRI or CT scan. This is remarkably helpful. We can zoom, rotate, and manipulate images to highlight exactly what we want to see. It's wonderful to perform a delicate operation to get deep in the brain, reach the tumor, look up to check the position of that critical blood vessel, and—

Dang it to bloody hell!

Instead of the exact picture I wanted, I see the dancing, mocking logo of the hospital. The screen is locked up. I'm scrubbed into surgery and can't log in to the computer. The circulating nurse has to navigate the system and find the exact picture I want to see.

---

[102] I took Handsome Dan to an Iron Maiden concert. This was an experience that I'm sure he'll never forget, despite years of intense therapy. Word of advice—a pressed pastel polo shirt and golf cap are a little out of place at a concert like this.

Ugh. Every time. There's no way to stop it!

We've tried to talk to the IT department. We've tried to argue logically that there are no casual bystanders or crooks in the OR. They've promised me that they'll consider our request. They then all had a good laugh and went to lunch.

Speaking of lunch ...

Negative: Lunch

I'm not sure who negotiates nursing benefits with the administration. The nurses certainly don't seem to be paid enough, have enough protection, have enough staff, or have enough time off. However, they do have one thing: lunch.

OR nurses are downright militant about lunch. Around eleven o'clock, the shifts begin to change and a lunch crew goes around to spell your team for forty-five to sixty minutes. This sounds pretty innocent. But when a new person comes into the field, everything stops. There are safety measures—everything is counted, the procedure is reviewed, and a safe handoff is attained.

All is well and good. But from my point of view, the surgery comes to a grinding halt, often in a critical part of the operation. Invariably, the lunch crew does not know the case or the procedure as well as the primary team. This can be a real problem if we're in dangerous territory.

The OR crews at County had lunch down to a science. Something always delayed the start of the case. Then there was the slow play for setting up the equipment. Finally the operation started when—*lunch*! The substitutes came in and watched the clock for an hour with zero interest in anything else but getting to their own lunch.

One of the former aneurysm surgeons used to ban his nurses from taking lunch. In his view, if you started the case, you finished the case. His reasoning (sound) was that no one gave *him* lunch. He also did not want a substitute, possibly from another specialty, now helping him when the patient's life was at stake. The nurses hated, hated, hated him.

Somehow, it's even worse at night. The surgeons are tired and bitter that they are operating at midnight. Usually, they are just trying to finish when, somewhere around one in the morning, everything stops for lunch. I'm not sure the nurses kept dental coverage in their last negotiations with management, but they sure as heck kept lunch.

*   *   *   *

Surgery does things to a person. The world looks different. One begins to notice buffoonery all around. I began to realize how stupid television and movies really can be. I'm willing to suspend realism for a chance at escape. In fact, if a movie doesn't have hobbits, robots, aliens, or giant space lasers, I'm really not interested. I don't need to see movies about "real life." I've got enough of that in my daily job. However, if the medical buffoonery reaches critical levels, I lose it, for example:

1. A person without a heartbeat needs CPR, not a "shock."[103] This only works on Baywatch.[104]

2. Spinal cord injuries cannot be overcome by sheer will. Believe me; I wish they could.

3. People in a coma look and smell bad. Even Beatrix Kiddo wouldn't look sexy in a coma.

---

[103] Complete disregard for cardiac protocols is a total hot-button issue with Jack. It ruined the 2014 version of *Godzilla* for him. He was okay with the genius plan to lure giant monsters to a heavily populated area instead of, well, *anywhere* else, but he couldn't get by a character using an improper cardiac medication.

[104] Hasselhoff can jump-start my heart anytime.

A few years ago, the Lovely Wife asked me to watch *Grey's Anatomy* apparently because I needed to be punished. I began to watch the show and enjoyed the antics of this particular group of supermodels having sex with each other.[105] Apparently the hero of the early seasons was a neurosurgeon, played by Patrick Dempsey and Patrick Dempsey's dreamy eyes. I'll admit; it was disconcerting to see my identical twin on the screen.[106]

In this particular episode, he was planning a stereotactic biopsy. Like with the young girl Rich and I biopsied, McDreamy used a sophisticated procedure to insert a probe into the patient's brain. They then talked about sex or the meaning of life or something else with dialogue straight out of a sixth-grader's diary.

The procedure began as planned. The needle was inserted. Then— horrors! The computer went down. The poor patient has a huge needle stuck in his brain, and the computer went down! The neurosurgeon began screaming at the equipment vendor, who just happened to be a nubile young coed on her first day. So she opened the computer box, hardwired something, adjusted the flux capacitor, and jettisoned the warp core, all to the sound of tense music that they surprisingly were piping into the OR. She fixed it! The patient was saved! Patrick Dempsey was getting some vendor nookie later that night! Disaster was averted, and the Lovely Wife was relieved.

"Vendors are marketing majors," I said flatly. "Asking one of them to muck around inside a computer is stupid." I congratulated myself on providing insight that would further the Lovely Wife's enjoyment of the show.

"Further, the needle was *already in the head*. This is the hard part. All he has to do is pull it out."

---

[105] Aside from this, it wasn't a realistic depiction of a typical hospital.
[106] Editor's note: You wish.

Lovely Wife: "Go away and never watch *Grey's Anatomy* with me again."

I guess we both ended up winners.

*   *   *   *

The closest I ever came to that scenario was when I was working on a particularly delicate spinal operation in a young child. We were trying to place a screw into a deep section of bone that was about 3.5 millimeters (about 1/7 of an inch) wide. If we missed to the side, we could injure the vertebral artery and cause a catastrophic stroke. If we missed to the middle, we could damage the spinal cord. To be as precise as possible, we were using a portable CT scanner that allowed us to navigate screws with amazing precision. The scanner looks like a giant claw that then encircles the patient. On that day, the claw wouldn't close, apparently because one of the rotating wheels had fallen out of alignment.

The vendor, a beautiful young woman who happened to be eight months pregnant, called the tech support. They, in what I don't think was a practical joke, instructed her to smack the bottom of it with her fist as hard as she could. This scanner, by the way, costs upwards of $800,000 and tech support's instruction was to hit it Fonzie-style.

She valiantly gave it a go, dropping her gravid tummy to the ground and kicking, punching, and smacking the broken piece. It wouldn't budge, apparently because tech support left out the part where she was to check her hair in the mirror, not comb it, and say, "Aaaaaaaayyyyyyyyy!"

CHAPTER 23

Open My Eyes That I May
See Wonderful Things[107]

Caleb came into this world at an unexpected time in an unexpected place. He was born very early while his parents were in Jamaica. Caleb was hospitalized but seemed to thrive. He first presented to Elizabeth when he was about three months of age.

Medical records from other hospitals are sometimes difficult to procure. Medical records from other countries are nonexistent. Elizabeth had no idea what had happened, but she knew Caleb's head was way too large. An MRI showed multicystic hydrocephalus. The CSF spaces were too large, but instead of smoothly connecting, they were segmented by large cysts. This is a problem that occurs with hemorrhage or infection.

Elizabeth used an endoscope to try to open these cysts for a shunt. The shunt worked for about two months. It was revised. Then it was revised again. Keeping a shunt working in a child with multicystic hydrocephalus is a tremendous challenge. She tried again when Caleb was about seventeen months old. Then we didn't see the family for

---

[107] Psalm 119:18, New International Version.

a while. They missed appointments. They lived fairly far away, and travel was problematic.

Apparently Caleb was doing well until he began to vomit. His pediatrician saw him multiple times. Nothing worked. Caleb seemed fine between episodes. All manners of stomach treatments were prescribed but to no avail.

Caleb was finally seen in an emergency department where a CT scan of the head was performed. The ER doctor called the on-call surgeon and asked for a review of the films. The surgeon noted that the ventricles were smaller than the last image, now over a year earlier. The ER doctor took this as a sign that the shunt was working.

Over the next three weeks, Caleb got sicker. He kept vomiting. Mom bounced back and forth between doctors who saw the previous ER note and took the shunt out of consideration.

It's always the shunt ...

Mom was getting upset. The doctors were getting upset at Mom. Maybe she was crazy. After all, the kid generally looked fine in the ER. Maybe she was drug seeking. Maybe Caleb was being abused. All of these things are possible and *happen routinely*. But all were wrong. Finally, Mom planted herself at the pediatrician's office and wouldn't leave. They called me.

After the usual brief history, the doctor told me that Caleb was sleeping more. They had checked a CT scan, and it looked the same as when they had called the Baby Hospital a few weeks earlier.

"Send him," I said.

I turned to the resident on call with me that night—a big, burly chap named Brian. "I doubt it's the shunt. Sounds like a stomach problem. We'll check him out."

Brian gave me a skeptical look.

"If a person comes back to the ER three times, they get admitted, no matter how minor the concern. That's something I learned back in my military days," I said.

Caleb arrived. He was lying on the bed with his eyes closed. Mom looked blurry-eyed. I had heard that she was hostile, but she was quite pleasant to us. She explained that Caleb had been vomiting but then would seem fine. Every time they went to the ER, he was fine, but as soon as they went home, he would vomit again. Caleb woke up easily but was in no mood for interaction. He lay back down and closed his eyes. Caleb had yet to develop the ability to talk. He communicated with a few grunting noises and pointing.

We left the room to find a computer to evaluate his CT. Stable. The ventricles were smaller than a year ago, but they were so misshapen that it was hard to make heads or tails of it.

"What do you think?" I asked Brian.

"We should call GI."

"Why don't you go tap the shunt?"

Brian rolled his eyes.

Brian tried to tap the shunt, but Caleb cried and fought. He didn't get any CSF flow. He came back to where I was sitting.

"Nothing."

"Nothing as in the shunt has failed, or nothing as in you missed?" I asked.

"I'm not sure."

"Damn it."

My turn. I grabbed a few nurses and headed back to Caleb's room. Brian held his head with two powerful hands. I felt for the reservoir and, by magic or luck, popped the needle in. Brain shrugged.

Slowly, I could see CSF creeping up the tubing attached to the needle. Caleb was crying and fighting for all he was worth, but Brian had him pinned. The CSF crept up to a normal level and then stopped.

"We'll, I think the shunt is partially working," I told Mom. But I wasn't convinced it was perfect. "Let's see how he feels in an hour or two. We'll send this fluid to check for infection."

Brain and I walked out of the room.

"So, what did you think?" he asked.

"Well, something came out spontaneously. I guess it's not completely blocked. But he was fighting pretty hard. I'd expect more to come out."

The pressure in the head fluctuates. When people are quiet and sitting up, the pressure may be lower. If they are lying down, gravity may make it higher. If someone is screaming and fighting, it should be much higher. Caleb's was normal.

"I'll bet he's got a partial proximal obstruction."

Caleb didn't feel better. We checked on him again. He was lying in the bed, crying, with his eyes closed. He heard us come into the room and cried a little harder.

"It's okay, kid; I'd cry if I saw this guy coming too," I said, winking and pointing at Brian. "Well, no infection. But he doesn't look any better. We can either wait and see if he perks up or take him to surgery."

Mom had a thick Jamaican accent. "He's *not* getting better."

Decision made.

We made the arrangements, and Caleb was brought to the operating room. He was put to sleep and prepped. I opened the incision and exposed the valve. I disconnected the valve from the proximal catheter. Spinal fluid gently dripped out. *Well, so that's reasonable. Let's check the valve.*

I attached a manometer. This is a long tube with an inlet and an outlet. We fill the tube with a measureable amount of water and hook it up to the distal system. The water level should then drop to the valve pressure. In this case, nothing dropped. I tried to force fluid through the valve. Nothing.

Okay, we've got the problem. His valve isn't working. I removed the old one, checked the distal tubing (it was fine), and replaced the valve. I was all ready to hook the original proximal catheter back up when I decided to check it again. Clearly dripping. Consistently dripping. Gently.

Sometimes a problem in the valve can lead to occlusion of the proximal catheter and vice versa. So, probably stupidly, I decided to mess with a good thing. Replacing the catheter would introduce a risk of internal bleeding. I stuck a metal stylet into the catheter and zapped it with cautery.

Whoosh!

Spinal fluid came jetting out, squirting across the room. The pressure in his head was much, much higher than I had thought. "Wow!" I exclaimed to no one in particular. So I replaced the catheter, hooked it up, and left the operating room satisfied that Caleb would be fine.

Caleb was fine. He woke up. He stopped crying. He became much more alert. He was also stone blind. We didn't discover this until the next day.

"What?"

"I don't think he can see," Brian said over the phone.

"What do you mean he can't see?" I asked.

"Well, I shine my light and he doesn't react. He's reaching for things but not looking at them."

"Call the ophthalmologists. Have them see him now."

Caleb had atrophy of one of his optic nerves and severe papill-edema[108] in the other. Atrophy means that there was significant pressure on the nerve to his eye for a long period of time. Caleb's pressure

---

[108] Swelling around the optic nerve.

in his head had been dangerously high probably for weeks. We didn't notice any visual problems in the ER because his eyes were always closed and he couldn't talk to tell us.

I didn't correctly diagnose his catastrophic shunt malfunction based on CT. I didn't diagnose it with tapping the shunt—an invasive test. I didn't really diagnose it three-quarters of the way through surgery! Caleb had a life-threatening condition that was missed for weeks. It was only by the incredible resiliency of the three-year-old's body that he survived. In fact, he *really didn't even look that sick*. His heart rate was normal. He would awaken easily. Yet, now he was blind.

Three years old and blind.

I felt sick.

"What can we do?" I asked the ophthalmologist.

"Did you fix the shunt?"

"Yes."

"That's all we can do. The one eye is totally gone. We can hope the other eye gets better, but frankly, I think it's gone too."

I sighed. I had a long talk with now Dad, who had taken over hospital vigil.

"How come nobody picked this up?" he asked. Dad was a stout, muscular man with a tightly clipped beard and short afro. "How come nobody tapped the shunt?"

"Well, that's not something that is usually done outside of neurosurgery."

"They told us the shunt was okay. Now you're telling me my kid's blind?"

I felt horrible. I looked over at Caleb, who was happy, head cocked, listening to the TV. He felt around on his tray in front of him awkwardly. He located a prized French fry and jammed it into his mouth. Well, his vomiting was gone.

Dad did not strike me as a particularly educated man, but he seemed genuinely smart. A diagnosis was missed. A diagnosis with dire consequences was missed.

One of the biggest medical concerns, especially in surgery, is *safety*. A single, catastrophic flaw may cause dangerous situations. Many times, dangerous situations are the result of multiple minor, often innocent bad choices. The airline industry has been a leader and innovator in exploring risk management. Plane crashes are rarely caused by a single catastrophic event. More often, they are a culmination of many small events. The goal is to spot the smaller factors leading up to the disaster, while there's still time to intervene.

In this case, the small factors were as follows:

1. Neurosurgeon is asked a specific question about a scan. Neurosurgeon responds correctly but never actually examines the patient, as the child was in a different ER at the time. Neurosurgeon only comments on the scan.

2. ER doctor takes the neurosurgeon's evaluation that the scans were stable as proof that the shunt is okay.

3. Everyone else sees the ER note and assumes that the shunt has been adequately evaluated and is not the problem.

4. There's no other cause for the vomiting. All other tests are normal. Maybe Mom is the problem. She does seem difficult.

Taken step by step, each factor makes sense. Each is somewhat logical. But each is flawed. I'll start with the first one. A neurosurgeon *cannot* tell if a shunt is working just by looking at a scan. We can guess and with experience have a pretty good idea but cannot tell for sure. The neurosurgeon did *not* tell the ER doctor that the shunt was working; he just answered the specific question about the ventricle size. The neurosurgeon should have made it clear that if the ER wanted him to evaluate the patient (not the scan), then the patient needed to be transferred. One cannot tell if a shunt is working over the phone.

In this case, the shunt malfunction was not clear. The scans *were* stable, and the ventricles *were* smaller than over a year earlier. I examined the patient and didn't really have an understanding of the problem until almost the end of a surgery.

Caleb most likely had a near-complete clogging of the proximal tube. Very little fluid would go through. But then the pressure in his head would rise to dangerous levels. This is when he would vomit. The pressure would go even higher and force some fluid through the blocked catheter. Then he'd feel better. By the time he got to the ER, the vomiting was over, a little fluid drained, and he was better. Then the cycle would repeat. The blocked catheter led to fluid pooling in the valve but not flowing. Sediment would likely build, finally occluding this. That's what I think happened, anyway.

Didn't matter. Caleb was blind.

He was discharged, and I was deflated. I told Elizabeth what had happened. She was despondent. No one takes sick kids harder than Elizabeth.

*   *   *   *

Caleb returned to the clinic at his scheduled follow-up. I didn't recognize him. It's strange how different a well patient looks from a hospitalized patient.

When I was an intern, a skinny teenager got sucked Wile E. Coyote–style into two giant rollers of a large printing press. Somehow he survived and remarkably thought it was funny, despite breaking most of the bones in his body.

"Did it hurt?" I asked.

"Well, the second time through did."

"You went through it twice? Holy crap!"

"I think I did that too!"

In the hospital, all I saw was a skinny, jovial young man with casts on all his limbs. Months later, I saw him again. "Hey, Doc!" he said as he waved. I didn't recognize who he was at first. I was shocked to see he was about six feet eight inches tall.

Caleb was the same way. He wasn't the crying kid. He bounded into the room and hopped up on the bed. I glanced at my old notes and ...

Wait a second ...

"Caleb," I said. "High five?"

I held out my hand, a little away from Caleb's. He grinned, reared back, and smacked it.

Dad was smiling.

"Can he see again?" I asked incredulously.

"Yep! It's a miracle. I pray to God every day, and he can see!"

Amazing.

"How's he doing?" I asked Dad.

"He is fantastic. Happy and playful. Just the way a kid should be."

Yes, just the way a kid should be.

"Come here; I need you to talk to someone."

We walked out into the hall between clinics. "Caleb," I said, "go up and give that old lady a high five." Caleb grinned and bounded up to Elizabeth, who was quite perturbed that this moppet was interrupting her walk to the desk. She smiled curtly and then stared, trying to place his cherubic face. Suddenly it dawned. Caleb was staring up at her grinning.

"Caleb?" she asked.

He nodded vigorously. Her eyes watered once she realized that he had recognized her and run up to her without assistance. She scooped him up and hugged him like a mother. "I'm so glad to see you!" She carried him around for about ten minutes, happily introducing him to all the office staff. They greeted him with enthusiastic "Hi's," and he reveled in the attention.

"I pray to God," Dad repeated.

"Me too," I said.

Sometimes the good guys win.

CHAPTER 24

We Are Living in a Material World[109]

I walked into my first staff meeting as an attending with the combined feeling of excitement and trepidation that children get the first
time they are invited to the grown-ups' table. The Professor greeted
me. Thomas arrived in a late rush and promptly fell asleep. The other
surgeons filed in, flanked by Grandpa P. I sat across from Elizabeth,
who sat next to Johnny Spine.

There was a lot to talk about. The business merger was happening. A new structure was coming, and Grandpa P. didn't like it. The
program had always been run like a family business. Now, we were
going corporate.

We covered the basics of the program: what was going on with
the residents, who was doing what research, and when all the offices
would move. Everybody was stressed out and felt under siege.

Elizabeth voiced her worries about being overworked at the Baby
Hospital. Johnny Spine, who wanted to focus on finances, condescendingly dismissed her concerns. Thomas opined that he was count-
ing on winning the lottery. Even the normally wisecracking Professor
seemed tense.

---

[109] Indulge me for a chapter here. There's a point. Really.

During my training, every meeting I attended was for education about patient care, surgery, or science. Now, every meeting I attended was about legal issues, money, policy, and an ever-increasing steaming pile of regulations. The business side of medicine was much more complex, unforgiving, and brutal than I had ever imagined. The merger was a circling of the wagons, and the surgeons were under siege. I had the sickening realization that I was swimming in shark-infested waters. Worse yet, I was completely unprepared.

I thought back to all those hippie lessons in medical school that made so much sense at the time. A doctor should be above the Neanderthal concerns of business and money. I understand the nobility of this attitude. I respect it. I also think that way of thinking is dead wrong. Ignoring, trivializing, or belittling the real world is a setup for failure. Doctors are being sent to battle unarmed. My lack of knowledge of how the business side of medicine worked was not a triviality; it was dangerous.

Here are a few things you should know about this brave new world.

- **Medicine is a growth industry for everyone but doctors.**

The federal government spends $1.3 *trillion* on health care each year. It spends 60 percent more on health care than on the military. These kind of dollars attract CEOs, businesspeople, total slimeballs, and, at the risk of being redundant, lawyers. Someone's making a lot of money.

Without question, one of the biggest factors increasing medical costs in the United States is the exploding number of hospital administrators. In the United States, there are roughly ten administrators for every one doctor.[110] *Holy crap ...*

---

[110] http://www.healthline.com/health-news/policy-ten-administrators-for-every-one-us-doctor-092813.

Honestly, I have no idea what most of these people actually do. Whatever they do, I imagine it involves a lot of catered meetings. I guess they spend time creating policies designed to correct everything that's worked fine for decades. It seems like their solution to every problem is more management.

As bad as the bureaucracy is in the private sector, it's even worse in a government system. I guess this is not surprising coming from the same people who run the BMV. The quintessential bureaucratic breeding ground is the VA system, which is lousy with managers but very short on doctors.[111] The VA system made one brilliant decision that almost makes up for the thousands of decisions that can best be described as "baffling." The brilliant decision was to locate the major hospitals near a medical school, where they can be staffed by medical students and residents. Students will jump through any hoop to take care of their patient, as they are so invested in doing a good job. The smaller, community VA facilities are a different story. They have significant trouble hiring good doctors because of a combination of below-market pay and an overregulated environment that makes doctors feel like they are carrying around wet mattresses all day.

- **The vast hordes of administrators get paid.**
  A lot. And you're funding it.[112]

I'm just as incredulous as you are when I see what our administration makes. The CEO can't afford a summerhouse *and* a yacht by flitting away money. I've also found that administrators are not terribly excited about cutting their own pay. But they seem more than

---

[111] http://www.stripes.com/news/veterans/tens-of-thousands-more-medical-staff-needed-says-va-chief-1.302543.

[112] http://www.nytimes.com/2014/05/18/sunday-review/doctors-salaries-are-not-the-big-cost.html?_r=0.

happy to put the squeeze on doctors and nurses.[113] In fact, I think they rather enjoy it.

Around the time of the merger, a CEO of a local major hospital system told a business journal that doctors needed to "tighten their belts," despite the fact that the hospital system had turned in record profits the year before. There was a conspicuous absence of a belt-tightening plan for the executives. The same system sent a satisfaction survey to all the physicians. The "positive" response rate was a whopping 5 *percent*. This led to big changes—to the survey. The next year, the administrators announced that the executive bonuses would not be tied to the physician survey results.

If that's not tone deaf enough, there's a second, more evil cottage industry that is to doctors as worms are to dogs.

- **Doctors reallyreallyreallyreallyreally hate lawyers. Really.**

A lawyer gave a talk for the surgery department about malpractice and led by writing this on the board:[114]

$$You + dirt = \$\$\$\$$$

The law is a profit-driven business, which is wrong in all kinds of ways. Don't let anyone tell you it's about quaint, out-of-date concepts like justice and fairness. It's about money, money, and money. Hospital systems are *very* conscientious about this. Lawyers are much more apt to sue a hospital than, say, a first-year intern. The hospital has money; the intern does not. Lesson 2 in law school is "Never *ever* sue people who have no money." Lesson 1 involves pentagrams and

---

[113] Even in Canada, http://www.torontosun.com/2012/05/09/study-reveals-there-are-doctors-driving-cabs-in-toronto.

[114] Sadly, this is not a joke or even an exaggeration. *Double sigh.*

goat's blood.[115] So the loving hospital response in potential lawsuits is to look for any reason to hang a doctor out to dry.

As the entire system is based on money, it is flooded by people looking to cash in. The legal system coddles and may even create patients like Jocelyn, who would have no problem using any and all means to bleed money and drugs out of a physician. Even if innocent, the doctor is punished by a drain on time and resources. Word of advice: never, *ever* get involved with a lawyer. The legal profession is a state-sponsored old-timey Mafia shakedown.[116]

Don't get me wrong here. Doctors who are negligent, unethical, or liars *should* be punished. Very few things elevate a doctor's blood pressure like discovering negligence. Dirtbags in the medical profession make us all look bad and, (much) worse, *hurt* people. The medical community must police itself, as we are entrusted with such an immense responsibility.

Doctors may deal with incredibly sick people. Some surgeries carry a large inherent risk. A bad outcome or a complication is not necessarily indicative of negligence or substandard care. I know that, despite my best efforts, some patients *will* get surgical infections. Some patients *will* be injured in surgery. Some patients *may* die. The vast majority of patients understand this and are grateful for care. But a growing minority, fed by a predatory legal system, believe any mistake is a winning lottery ticket.

"Can you videotape the surgery?" a patient asked me as I considered him for an elective spine procedure.

"Interested in seeing how we do it?" I asked hopefully.

"Nope, just want evidence in case I sue."

---

[115] Well, that's what I heard.
[116] I had a lawyer charge me for an hour's work (over $500) for reading and responding to an email. A *three-line* email. Apparently he had to ponder it for fifty-nine minutes and thirty seconds.

"You don't need surgery."[117]

This constant threat leads some doctors to hide potential complications, which is exactly the opposite of what the medical system needs. This prevents rational analysis of safety measures and medical efficacy. A report quite famously stated that four hundred thousand people die from medical mistakes per year in the United States.[118] I can't possibly believe this. In twenty years of medicine, I can think of three times total that someone was killed from a flat-out mistake. But that's the point; we don't know the real data because doctors keep it hidden. And most doctors think reports such as this have an underlying political or business bias.

Doctors are increasingly practicing "defensive medicine," ordering unnecessary tests or procedures in hopes of avoiding a lawsuit. These tests are costly and drive up the bill for everybody. Some tests may even be a little dangerous. If one hundred patients roll through the ER with a bad headache, *maybe* one will have a life-threatening aneurysm. The doctor probably realizes the chance of a bad problem are low but will often order a CT scan "for the lawyers." This may lead to ninety-nine bills and ninety-nine unnecessary exposures to radiation. Many doctors practice medicine based on what *could* happen, not on what most likely will happen.

We published a research article examining the cost of transferring children with a crack in the skull to the Baby Hospital.[119] Over an eight-year period, hundreds of children were transferred based on the perceived risk that the child would decline and need surgery. None of the children declined or needed any treatment other than tender

---

[117] I didn't make this up.

[118] http://www.healthcareitnews.com/news/deaths-by-medical-mistakes-hit-records.

[119] I. K.White, E. Pestereva, K. A. Shaikh, D. H. Fulkerson, "Transfer of Children with Isolated Linear Skull Fractures: Is It Worth the Cost?" *J Neurosurg Pediatr* 17 no. 5 (2016): 602–6.

lovin' care. Despite that knowledge, children are still transferred routinely because the smaller hospital is deathly afraid of a lawsuit in the lightning-strike rare case of a problem.

Once a case heads to the courtroom, the doctor is guilty until proven innocent. The doctor's honor is laughably meaningless. The only information that matters is what is written down. This leads to a disturbing concept:

- **Your chart is more important than you are.**

There's a medical adage: "If it's not in the chart, it didn't happen." Medical people know it. We've all heard it. And it's garbage.

I once got paged "stat" for a patient of mine who was "coding." A "stat code" page is medical lingo for "Holycrapcomequicktheyregonnadie!" It's an emergency. People rush to the room.

This was at two thirty on a Saturday morning. I was in the hospital and literally hit the room less than two minutes after the page. As I headed to the room, I saw three nurses, looking extremely concerned—panicked even—*outside* the room furiously typing on the computer. They thought the patient was going to die, but charting needed to be done.

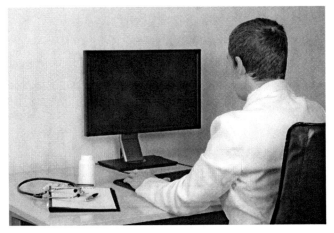

Pictured: Medicine.

In the room were the patient (who was fine) and the respiratory technician. That's it. The nurses were resuscitating the chart, not the patient. I was angry. I let them know.

In my e-mail box Monday: "You are required to attend a sensitivity training seminar."

Dang it all to bloody hell!

Charting is drilled into everyone's head for three reasons: (1) billing, (2) lawyers, and (3) lawyers a second time. Notice that patient care doesn't make that list.

So we chart and chart and work on the computer because that's good medicine. Since yacht prices keep going up, the CEO demands that doctors see more and more patients, which means more and more charting, which means more and more computer time, which means less and less patient time, which means—Ugh, I need a drink.

But, you say, don't computer records make things easier? It has to be easier than handwriting everything Thomas-style. Well ...

- **Electronic medical records (EMR) are designed for billing, not patient care.**

Theoretically, EMR is a good idea—no more paper charts that can get lost or misplaced, no more illegible handwriting, chart access from any computer terminal. In a perfect world, EMR makes your care better and my job easier. Unfortunately, an EMR system is expensive. The people who shell out the big bucks do so with three things in mind: (1) lawyers, (2) billing, and (3) billing a second time.

The charts generate reams of data that's clinically useless but needed to bill properly. Billing is based on a little book called the ~~Necronomicon Ex-Mortis~~ *ICD-10.*

That little beauty contains approximately *155,000* different codes that doctors need to record exactly correctly on each patient. The documentation in the chart must contain a variety of buzzwords and catch phrases invented by some army of tools to justify the bill.

Klaatu Barada Nikto.

Incorrectly entering a code or not providing enough charted buzzwords to justify the code is technically fraud. If this is done on a Medicare patient, this is fraud against the federal government.

Overcoding (and thus overbilling) can land a doctor in jail. Undercoding can land a doctor in jail.

By the way, here's how specific some of these codes are:[120]

- T63622A—suicide by jellyfish (Is … is this really a thing?)
- V9542XA—injury during forced landing of a spacecraft, initial encounter (Please, Lord, let me use this code just once in my life!)
- V9107XA—burn from water skis catching on fire (???)
- W56.01xA—bitten by dolphin
- W56.02xA—struck by dolphin
- W56.09xA—other contact by dolphin
- W56.09xD—other contact by dolphin, subsequent encounter

Apparently dolphins are bigger dicks than any of us realized. Here's the thing: it is *impossible* to get this correct every time. I've asked professional coders to tell me the correct coding on a particularly complex case. They never agree. People whose entire job is to figure out these codes can't agree. So you can imagine the odds of success for a dolt like me.

I recently had an eye appointment with a gentleman who looked like he was in his midsixties. I watched in sympathetic amusement as he fiddled with the EMR on his computer. He couldn't get the right screen to come up. Then something crashed. Under his breath, I'm pretty sure I heard some "Constarn' its," "dagnabits," and maybe even a "Get off my lawn." It pretty much went exactly like you would expect when your grandmother tries to program the DVR. I was amused, because the system looked very similar to the one I had to

---

[120] I didn't make any of these up.

use. He spent thirty seconds looking in my eyes and twenty minutes fidgeting with his computer.

Thomas practiced medicine for years with handwritten notes and his memory. He provided good medicine, and his patients loved him. But he struggled to adjust to taking time playing the nonsensical "guess the code" game. Geniuses are often set in their ways.

- **Patients are not happy.**

Patients are getting sick and tired of the doctor staring at the computer screen instead of looking at them.[121] Patients are getting sick of waiting months for an appointment, only to get a hurried doctor who is more concerned with the computer than with them. I absolutely and totally agree. That old eye doctor couldn't care one whit about his computer, but if he didn't do things correctly, he could be fired or, worse, *go to freakin' jail.*

*   *   *   *

I realize that no one wants to hear a doctor complain. We generate about as much sympathy as an NBA superstar.[122] But here's why this is a problem:

- Physician burnout is getting out of hand.[123]

Burnout is characterized by doctors feeling detached from their patients and their care. Physicians feel unsatisfied with life. Medicine becomes a grind, a slog, a chore. Doctors become depressed and stop caring. They view patients as work, not as people. Burnout is

---

[121] http://www.cnn.com/2014/03/09/opinion/greene-doctor-patient-computers/.

[122] Thanks for ruining it for all of us, 'Sheed.

[123] P. Klimo, Jr., M. DeCuypere, B. T. Ragel, S. McCartney, W. T. Couldwell, and F. A. Boop, "Career Satisfaction and Burnout among US Neurosurgeons: A Feasibility and Pilot Study," *World Neurosurg* 80: e59–68.

characterized by basically everything I was warned about in my first two years of medical school.

A number of studies on doctors have reported factors that predict burnout, including legal/malpractice accusations, uncertainty about future earnings, fear of further government intervention, poor work/life balance, too much work, and frustration with EMR. Stress is unavoidable in neurosurgery. Some stress may actually be beneficial. But soul-crushing additional stress from the vast administrative hordes and the spreading fungus of lawyers takes its toll.

This next part gets a little dark, so let's cleanse the palate with puppies:

Better? Better.

Every year, the number of physicians who commit suicide is roughly the same as a full graduating class from a major medical school. The suicide rate among male physicians is about three times that of the general population. It is four to five times higher among female doctors.[124],[125]

[124] E. Frank, H. Biola, and C.A. Burnett, "Mortality Rates and Causes among US Physicians," *Am J Prev Med* 19 (2000):155–159.

[125] S. Lindeman, E. Laara, H. Hakko, and J. Lonnqvist, "A Systematic Review on Gender Specific Suicide Mortality in Medical Doctors," *Br J Psychiatry* 168 (1996):274–279.

The suicide rate of medical students is well *below* the national average. On the whole, medical students are high-achieving, smart, athletic, well-adjusted people.[126] However, every mental health test score declines drastically each year after medical school. The number of major depressive episodes a doctor experiences increases exponentially within one short year of entering the workforce (from 3.9 episodes before internship to 26.1 episodes one year later).[127] Most of the studies examine residents. I argue that all the factors that lead to depression in residents are significantly *worse* after leaving residency.

Burnout is rampant, and creates exactly the same kind of monster I didn't want to be. Dissatisfied doctors are looking for reasons to leave medicine. Only about 55 percent of neurosurgeons would encourage their children to pursue a career in medicine. Doctors are heading for the hills at the same time that the American population is increasing and aging. Taken together, these factors lead to a projected shortfall of up to ninety thousand doctors by 2025.[128]

*   *   *   *

The U merged with the Mothership. Painful as it was, it was absolutely necessary to stave the tide of the vast hordes. But the merger had casualties. Dr. Montgomery was pushed into retirement. DG left medicine to teach math. Grandpa P. was a dinosaur. He was a throwback to the generation that valued family and people over the bottom line. But this was no longer his world. Grandpa P. was out.

Thomas spent his career giving everything to his patients. His patients were the poor and the downtrodden, and unfortunately, there's

---

[126] Well, except for Kevin in chapter 1. He was a douche.

[127] Sen et al., *Arch Gen Psych*, 2010.

[128] https://www.aamc.org/download/426260/data/physiciansupplyanddemand-through2025keyfindings.pdf.

no money in charity. Thomas was a liability on the business side. A huge liability. The vast hordes dumped more and more bureaucratic mattresses on his back—a new EMR system that he couldn't figure out; a new coding system that befuddled the most tech savvy, let alone a savant who was puzzled by the Disney pager; and an increasing population of narcotic-seeking patients.

Thomas was in danger.

This new environment seemed joyless and cruel. I didn't like it.

CHAPTER 25

Superman Does the Chicken Dance

It was a light day. Routine cases. No pending problems. Nice weather. It was not a day where I expected to meet Superman.

I was heading home when I got a stat page. Then another. Then another. That's never a good sign. All three from the Baby Hospital ER. I called the first number, and my resident Edward answered. Edward was outstanding. He was calm, unflappable, and extremely gifted at surgery despite being early in training. There was a very slight note of nerves in his voice as he succinctly outlined the situation.

"Five-year-old child. Gunshot wound to the head. The bullet entered the left eye and exited the right scalp. His hemoglobin is under three."

"Three?" I repeated. This meant the child had lost nearly *all* of his blood.

"Three. We've started the massive transfusion protocol. He's in the scanner now, on multiple pressors."

"Is he alive?" I asked.

A gunshot wound that travels from one side of the head to the other, especially through the base of the brain, is rarely survivable. Given the entry and exit point, this bullet must have traveled through his optic nerves, major blood vessels, and probably the hypothalamus.

"GCS 5. He moved a little."

That didn't sound like much.

"What do you want to do?" I asked.

"His scans are coming up. Significant damage to the right frontal lobe with a large subdural."

"Well, is there enough life there to go for it?"

Edward paused. "Yes, I think we should do it."

Okay. I had to trust my infantryman. Time was of the essence here.

"Take him straight from scanner. Don't wait for me."

I was still on the highway but broke into my best Steve McQueen, wheeled around a divider, and sped back to the Baby Hospital. I double-parked and sprinted in. I met Edward in the preop area and quickly perused the scan.

We looked at each other. "This looks like a losing battle," I said.

"I know. Still think we should do it."

In for a dime, in for a dollar …

I had beaten the kid to the OR. They were wheeling him down the hall; a gaggle of various medics, anesthesiologists, and nurses were blocking my view. One was furiously compressing his chest. Another was physically squeezing a bag of blood, trying to force it into the little red body hidden beneath the monitors. Superman was tiny and covered with blood.

The child's mom had arrived, and the nurses were hurriedly rushing her up to the preoperative area.

"Get going," I blandly told Edward, and then I intercepted Mom. I knew I had thirty seconds to carry out one-hour conversation. English was her second language.

I quickly introduced myself. "Your son was shot." *How else do you say that?*

Her face fell. She knew, but I think she was hoping this was all a big mistake. Maybe he wasn't shot but just hit his head?

"He's in critical condition. He may not survive. Right now, we're considering surgery to remove a blood clot. We'll take off part of his skull to give the brain room to swell. Our other option is to hold off on surgery."

Mom was understandably confused.

"The bullet did significant damage to very important parts of the brain. He may die even if surgery is successful. He may never wake up. Even if he survives, he will have significant disabilities, including, probably, he'll be blind. Do you want us to do the operation?"

"He'll die if you don't?" she said calmly, but her eyes were wide with fear.

"Yes."

How is this fair? I pride myself on doing a good job communicating with families. This conversation should be done in a quiet room, unrushed, with time to fully explain everything. Here we were in a noisy hallway in the wake of a bleeding, virtually dead little five-year-old. How could any parent grasp what I was saying? It was not possible. How could I explain adequately that if the thalamus and hypothalamus were damaged (they were) that he would probably never wake up? He would definitely be blind. He would definitely be paralyzed on one and maybe both sides. There was a very good chance that all I would do with surgery would be convert him into a vegetative nursing home patient, rotting away in a bed until an inevitable infection claimed his life. I wanted to explain to Mom that there are worse things than death. I wanted to project my feelings, my biases, and my experience to a young Hispanic woman whose son was just shot in the head.

No parent cares about those outcomes. All parents hear is that if I don't do something, their son—their hopes, their love, their dreams—will die. Who could possibly be expected to answer this question with any degree of understanding? I felt horrible, but if we were to have any chance, I needed to get into that OR right now, not five minutes from now. Right now.

"Then do it."

"I can't give you any guarantees."

"I know."

In retrospect, I can't express how remarkable Mom was in that instance. I knew it then, but my mind jumped quickly to the task at hand. Mom solidly digested the brief, inadequate explanation I had given, recognized the gravity of the situation, and made the decision that all parents would make. But she knew. She understood. Her life had changed in a second. Some stranger had come at her in a rush, told her that her kid would probably die, didn't hang around for questions, and then rushed away. But she understood. I guess she did the only thing left—she sat down and waited.

I burst into the OR where seemingly a hundred people were huddled around the little body. He was still getting CPR. Edward was quickly shaving the head while putting his hand over the bleeding wound. The scrub nurse was furiously setting up the equipment. Anesthesia was sticking him in a desperate attempt to cannulate collapsed veins.

No time to waste. We slapped some prep on the still-bleeding scalp, squirted some alcohol on our hands, and then hurriedly put on our gowns and gloves. We stapled some towels around his scalp and then put the drapes on halfway, so as not to cover the anesthesia team still working on resuscitating the child. The anesthesiologist looked up at me a little surprised that we were starting without waiting for the lines, but, well, we were starting without waiting for the lines.

Speed counts in trauma. Edward cut a quick reverse question

mark incision and held the scalp flap out of the way with some hooks. Brain and blood were oozing briskly out of the exit wound. In bullet wounds, the exit wound is usually larger than the entrance. The entrance was a pinhole just above his right eyeball; the exit was a gash that blew out a fair amount of his scalp. We took a high-speed drill, removed a big chunk of the skull, and then widely opened the rest of the dura.

A large blood clot squirted out. The brain was pulped. Worse than that, bright-red blood was squirting out at us in rhythm to the CPR. I grabbed a sucker and plowed through the mush brain to find the source. We coagulated one bleeder, but then another popped up. We hurriedly continued this macabre pop-a-shot game until we came to the gut-sinking revelation that the bleeding was coming from deep beyond our reach. We stuffed all manner of hemostatic material (stuff that makes blood clot) down in front of the frontal lobe to the skull base, knowing that the normal floor was blown out by the bullet.

Edward and I looked at each other. This wasn't going to work. We weren't going to get him off the table.

"Ideas?" I asked.

"No."

The bleeding slowed. We hoped the slowing was not simply because his blood pressure was bottoming out. One factor working against us was that his body had been attempting to stop the bleeding from the instant the bullet pierced the skin. The body's ability to clot blood is an absolutely remarkable system. The body has to instantly determine when bleeding is wrong and stop it. Yet it can't stop blood from flowing the normal channels, like to the heart or brain; this would cause a heart attack or stroke. This kind of injury overwhelmed all of the factors in the blood available to form a clot.

"We've got to close," I said. "Or he'll die on the table."

We placed a synthetic barrier over the brain and made no attempt to close the dura. We left the bone flap off, allowing the brain to swell outward. We began to close the skin. We had to physically stretch the skin around the swelling brain. We stapled the outer layer of the skin and then quickly placed a monitor into the other side of the head. The monitor would tell us the intracranial pressure inside the head.

His ICP was fifteen. Good.

Let's get him to the ICU.

Edward accompanied him to his room, and I went back to talk to Mom. Now we had a little more time. We went to a "quiet room" designed for just such a conversation. This time, I was able to sit down, look her in the eye, and answer all her questions more fully.

Mom was remarkably together. Her face was ashen and stained with dry tears. Family was on the way. The police had arrived and were interviewing everyone around.

We closed the door, and for the first time in an hour, there was quiet. I apologized for the brevity of our first encounter. She said she understood. I outlined her son's condition. Mikey was a healthy kid. He'd been accidentally shot by a teenager who panicked and ran away. Mikey was a happy kid who liked to sing.

I spent as much time as necessary to explain everything that happened and everything that would happen next. My job was to paint an accurate picture; I had to walk the line of being realistic without being totally devastating. At the same time, I didn't want to offer false hope. In my heart, I thought that Mikey was going to die. Mom was a rock. She asked appropriate questions. She wasn't panicked, although I could tell her heart was racing. She was young. She looked kind. She was grateful that we had tried.

We finished. I shook her hand and headed over to the ICU. Edward was there, finishing the postoperative orders and making sure everything was in order. This was the first time I actually saw Mikey's face. It was grossly swollen. I could see two black eyes—like a heavyweight fighter after a particularly brutal bout. Just above that was our gauze head wrap, with a few circles of blood seeping through. There was the ICP monitor, sticking out like a grotesque horn from the left side of his head. The breathing tube covered his mouth. The nurses continued sticking needles into his arms in an attempt to get adequate IV access.

His blood pressure was a little better. His ICP was okay.

"Well, Edward, in for a dime, in for a dollar."

Edward nodded.

I went back to the office to get a drink and sit down. We had stabilized him for now. However, this breather was just the eye of the storm.

About an hour later, Edward called.

"His ICP is in the sixties."

A new scan showed my fear—that bleeding from the base had gotten worse. Despite us removing about a third of his skull, blood was accumulating and pressing on the remaining brain. Maybe it was time to let him go.

In for a dime, in for a dollar.

"Call the OR. Let's go back."

The scrub nurses were dutifully ready. Anesthesia was ready and resigned. Edward and I were stoic.

Since we had done the dissection earlier, it only took a few minutes to expose the brain. It was swelling out at us in a sickening sorbet of blood, fluid, and grayish mush. The bleeding was major and deep. It was out of reach—out of reach unless we removed his frontal lobe.

I knew this going in. We dove into the brain with giant suckers and cautery devices in a procedure that would turn the stomach of the most rabid horror movie fan. The bullet had damaged the anterior cerebral artery, one of the two major branches of the internal carotid artery. It had also damaged a major branch of the middle cerebral artery, the second major branch. The only way to stop the bleeding was to ligate the arteries. In ideal conditions, this leads to a major stroke. In this case, we had to remove much of the brain just to get to the arteries. In an increasingly desperate attempt to help him survive until the morning, I was crippling the child.

We finished.

His ICP was better.

Mikey survived the night.

The scenario didn't improve by the morning. Mikey was requiring significant medication to support his blood pressure. His salt level was all over the map. He had *diabetes insipidus*. Despite the name, this is a completely different disease than *diabetes mellitus* (sugar diabetes). Diabetes insipidus (DI) is caused by damage to the pathway between the hypothalamus and the pituitary. It is manifest by massive fluid losses that dehydrate and, if untreated, kill the body.

The ICU team was justifiably pessimistic. We had a conference to decide if this was a futile effort. I wanted to press on. Edward and I had made that decision while I was on the highway. They consented, but I could tell they were not in agreement.

We made it through the first day. Then the second. Mikey was heavily sedated. We had a little better control of his vital signs. His ICPs were reasonably controlled. Edward and I stopped by his room every day. His mom was sitting silent vigil at his bedside. Teams of whitecoats would trundle in throughout the day, give her some information, and then move on. She would nod and thank them.

Days passed. Mikey didn't die. We'd have our daily conference with the ICU team. We'd argue. I thought we should continue to press on. Maybe I was blinded by the emotional investment that comes from operating on the child. Maybe I was just stupid. And we still had not repaired the damage to the skull base.

The bullet had completely destroyed not only his eye, but also the *skull base*—the floor of the skull that separates the brain from the nose and the mouth. This thin but remarkably effective barrier prevents all the infections in your nose and sinuses from getting to your brain, only a fraction of an inch away. That barrier also prevents the cerebrospinal fluid from leaking out the nose and the mouth. Mikey's barrier was vaporized. It was only a matter of time before he would get a massive infection. He was, however, in no condition to undergo a reconstruction surgery.

I think there are two initial phases to treating a patient with a severe head injury. The first phase is basic survival. In this phase, our goal is simply to make it to the next day. In head trauma, there is *primary* trauma. This is the direct damage caused, in Mikey's case, by the bullet. We can't do much about that. Then there's the *secondary* trauma. This is the surrounding brain that is in danger from swelling, loss of oxygen, bleeding, or stroke. Our job in this survival phase is to protect as much at-risk brain as possible.

In addition to the head trauma, Mikey was having all the problems that critically ill patients experience. He required massive blood transfusions. His salt balance was completely disrupted. If the salt level drops too low, water will leak into the brain worsening any swelling. Mikey's lungs were filling with fluid, making it difficult for the machine to force oxygen into his fragile little body. We kept Mikey in a drug-induced coma.

Since he was so sedated, we had no idea if Mikey had any functioning brain. We can control the numbers (blood pressure, ICP, oxygen level) to a point, but really, what matters is if the child wakes up. The only way to know this is to remove the sedation and see what happens. If we converted a dead child into a persistently vegetative child, then we'd have to seriously question whether we did him any good.

Two weeks later, Mikey's mom remained a noble sentinel at his bedside. She rarely bathed, slept, or ate. Mikey had remained a motionless lump under bandages and wires. There was no way to tell if he was alive or dead. I met with the ICU team, who continued to give me a constipated look. We decided to hold the sedation.

Nothing.

Hours passed. Mikey remained motionless. His damaged eye was taped shut. The swelling over the right eye had abated a little. His little face was awash in fluid leaking from his nose. As the swollen brain retracted, it opened the hole in the base of the skull.

Mikey didn't stir the next day either. Or the next. The ICU team gave me an I-told-you-so look every time we walked through the unit.

A few days later, however, Mikey began to wake up. It was gradual at first; he began to breathe faster than the settings on the ventilator. He began to react when someone placed an IV. Eventually, he began to move his right side. This was definitely progress. Within two weeks, he was moving with a purpose.

We make a distinction between movement and purposeful movement. Someone may react to a painful stimulus just based on reflexes. So if I stick someone's arm with a needle and it shakes, that's movement but not that meaningful. If the arm withdraws, that's a little better. Even better is if the patient tries to grab or swat me away; this shows that the brain has processed that something is happening and is sending the correct signals to the correct parts of the body. Just above this is movement on command. I ask the patient to show me a thumb or to hold up two fingers, and he or she does it correctly.

We have to be pretty rough to get heavily sedated patients to wake up. We pinch. We previously performed the neurosurgeon's noogie— the nipple twist. Apparently the PC police thought this was too gauche and banned the practice (although it works! Try it on people and see if they react.). It's kind of rough. We wake people up at a ridiculously early hour by strongly rubbing their chest, take our instruments and crush their fingernails, and yell, "Show me two fingers!"

Probably the first thing the patient is thinking is *Dicks*. One patient at County responded to that by flipping the double middle finger.

Slowly but surely, Mikey was coming back to life. It takes more than a bullet through the head to kill Superman.

About three weeks later, we felt he was stable enough to go through the large surgery required to fix the gaping hole in the floor of his skull. He'd been dumping spinal fluid, but we'd kept infection at bay with high-powered antibiotics. One of our challenges was to find a suitable replacement for the dura. We could directly sew a patch into the side, but there would be no way to primarily stich the undersurface where the damage was the greatest. So we mobilized the *pericrania*, the fibrous covering over the bone. This would be a nice natural barrier that we could rotate over our bony repair. We dissected out the base of the skull. This area was near his optic nerves—the nerves to the eyes that transmit vision. The left one was completely torn. The right one wasn't much better. The pituitary gland and major blood vessels were also nearby. We worked our way slowly around the gaping hole that extended to his nasal cavity. Our main goal of surgery was to create a barrier between the nose and the brain. We placed some material in the cavity to create a floor. We hoped the mucosa of the nose would overgrow and seal the area. We then cut a piece of bone from his skull flap and tailored it to the hole. We attached this with very small titanium plates and sutures. We used the pericrania to cover the floor.

After we were finished, the general surgery team placed a tracheostomy and a gastrostomy tube, for long-term ventilation and feeding. We eventually placed a shunt.

Mikey rebounded with a vengeance. He required less and less ventilatory support, to the point where he only needed a little oxygen but was breathing on his own. He moved his right side vigorously. He began to open his eyes.

Eventually, his lungs got strong enough for a speaking valve in his tracheostomy. One generally can't speak while on the ventilator. One also can't move air past the vocal cords to speak with an open tracheostomy. It takes a pretty good effort to push air hard enough to generate sound. However, if a special valve is placed, the tracheostomy can act as a de facto vocal cord. And Mikey spoke.

Boy, did he speak.

He sang loud and long, with gusto and fervor. Mikey made chicken noises (Bock, bock, bock!) with unbridled and uninhibited passion. He flapped his good arm continuously. He shouted, sang, and flapped his way into rehab.

"Mikey! *Que pasa?*"

"Ooooooooookaaaaaaaaaaaaaaayyyyyyyyyy," he would softly say in broken English. Then he'd break into a rousing session of the chicken dance. "Bock, bock, bock, cluck, cluck, cluck!" hopping up and down on his bed, flapping his wing.

"Do you have a headache?"

"Nooooooooooooooooooooooooooooo. No no no no no no no no. Bock, bock, bock!" Flap, flap, flap.

Mikey left the ICU. He eventually was able to go to a rehab facility where he instantly charmed all the workers. He was a cute little blind crooner who seemed perpetually happy.

Mikey sang. And danced. And sang some more.

The bullet had traversed the hypothalamus, a vital part of the brain that, among other things, affects sleep pattern. Mikey didn't seem to need much, if any, sleep. Like Phineas Gage and Amber, Mikey was completely disinhibited. Well into the night, the rehab was filled with the full-throated screeching of the little chicken.

Mikey progressed to the point where he could stand. He had some light perception. His speech returned, and he could answer questions (between *bock-bock clucks*).

I'd visit and talk to his blurry-eyed, exhausted mom.

"Mikey, que pasa?"

"Oooookayyyyy! Bock bock! Ai ai ai ai."

"Do you like to dance?"

"Ai ai ai ai ai ai ai ai, si si si si si si si," he would say while hopping up and down.

Mikey came back to see me about six weeks later. He had some big holes remaining in the skull. With the shunt in place, his remaining brain was collapsing. The skin was stretched over some of the jagged bone edges and metal plates. We were worried about impending skin erosion, so we decided to take him back to the OR to smooth things out and to replace some of the bone.

Mikey did not like anyone touching his head.

"Does it hurt here?"

"No no no no no no no no no!" he yelled, swatting at me with his good hand. "No no no, ai ai ai ai ai ai ai!"

"Do you feel good?"

"Si si si si si!" he sang.

Surgery went well. Some of the metal screws we had placed had pulled out and were sticking into the skin, creating the jagged feeling. We removed these, smoothed over the rough edges, and then cut a piece of titanium mesh to cover the bony defects.

Mikey loved it. His head felt better, and he sang and flapped his way home.

* * * *

Months passed. Mikey made steady progress. He could walk with his therapist. His speech was becoming clearer. He went back to school, with some significant modifications.

We then got the call that I had been dreading. Mikey was in the hospital with a high fever.

"Mikey, how are you doing?"

He just moaned.

"Mikey, can you dance for me?"

"*noooooooooooooooooo*," he whispered.

We stuck a needle into the shunt to draw off some spinal fluid. He didn't fight back. I took this as a very bad sign. The spinal fluid looked clear, which gave me a slight shot of hope. We sent it to the lab, and much to my pleasant surprise, it was clean. We decided to hold off on any surgery, hoping the fever was from something simple like a virus or sore throat.

Mikey didn't get better. He wouldn't sing. He wouldn't dance. He just moaned.

We tapped the shunt a second time. There were still no bacteria, but there was a tremendous elevation in the white blood cells. White blood cells are the microscopic soldiers that fight infection. Normally there are only one to two of these cells in a sample of spinal fluid. Mikey had hundreds. Something bad was going on. We repeated a scan and found a pocket of pus just above his face. All of Mikey's normal sinus cavities had been destroyed by the bullet. What was left was impacted and infected, right near our repair of the skull base. Well, crap.

We took Mikey to surgery to wash this all out. Eventually we removed the shunt to place a temporary drain. Mikey continued to get worse. Despite washing things out, the pus returned and spread. The small pocket of pus had broken into the large cavity left from the bullet. Mikey's entire head was filled with infection.

His mom looked at me sadly.

"I'm not sure this is going to get better."

"Is he going to die?" she asked.

I paused.

"I'm not sure. He may. This is really bad. Even if we can drain everything out, he's got so much hardware holding the skull together that he may ..." I stopped. "Plus there's the shunt. I'm not sure what we're going to do with that. He's got a temporary drain in now, but that can't last forever."

Mom understood.

"Do whatever you can."

Mikey's fever was very high. He was placed on the breathing machine. No singing. Maybe he'd never wake up. Maybe it was for the best. But we had come this far.

We decided to go back to the operating room to try to wash everything out. I shaved his head. All of his skin was covered in scar. Generally, an incision is designed so that blood supply can get to the edges, allowing healing. One does not want to cross incisions, as this cuts off all the potential blood vessels. Mikey's head was one big grid of scars.

"This is never going to heal. Ugh. What am I doing?" I said, mainly to myself. There is really no good way to fix a dead scalp flap. I felt like I was maiming a corpse.

We opened the incision, took off the bone, and began to remove clearly infected material. We got into the cavity and power-washed the area with antibiotic solution. We created a second incision within the eyebrow to drain the frontal abscess.

"Know any good prayers?" I asked Edward.

For the next few days, we peeled up the bandages to check the incision. Each day, I expected to see the skin turn black, indicating death. Each day, we said we'd check back tomorrow. Days passed. Then a week. Mikey remained asleep. But his fever was dropping.

Then, beyond all reason, Mikey opened his blind eyes.

A few days later, I walked into the ICU room with the resident team.

"Bock bock bock!"

Mikey was flapping his wing and chortling to himself.

"Mikey? How are you feeling?"

"G-g-g-g-gooooooooooooooood. Bock bock!"

Mikey was awake. His fever was gone. His skin healed. Superman was not about to go down from a sinus infection.

*   *   *   *

Mikey had recovered from two fatal problems. Now, four years later, Mikey visits me a couple times per year. While he still does the chicken dance, his repertoire has increased to include a fair amount of Beyoncé. Also, now the disinhibited adolescent boy, he's taken quite the interest in the nurses.

"Hhhheeeeeeeeellllllloooooooooo, Ladiiiieeeeeeeezzzzz!"

"Hey, Mikey!" the nurses answer. "You doing all right?"

"Si si si si si si si si si!"

CHAPTER 26

Win the Battle but Lose the War?

"Did you really make this?" I asked the small African girl sitting in the clinic.

"Oh yes, I love to knit." She smiled, sensing that I loved my gift. It was an intricate tapestry full of color, pattern, and life. It was joyous and spontaneous but with an underlying harmony—just like Kambiri. She was tiny, much smaller than a normal girl of eleven. However, her experiences (and her smile) were much, much bigger than a normal girl of eleven.

Kambiri was blind.

Kambiri was born in a small village in Africa. She was sickly and frail as a child and soon fell behind her peers. Falling behind in her rural part of Africa is dangerous, especially for a girl. Kambiri struggled, became a burden, and was eventually left in an orphanage. Somehow, Kambiri got some sort of imaging study that showed a large brain tumor.

A church group brought her to the United States where she had brain surgery somewhere in California. The surgeons did a masterful job and removed almost all of the formidable lesion. The next planned step was to do focused radiation with a *proton beam*—an exotic, highly technical treatment that could melt away the remaining tumor. Unfortunately, proton therapy is hideously expensive and way more than this blind, penniless African girl in a foreign country could afford. Kambiri was bounced between extremely gracious and extremely well-meaning church groups before eventually settling near the Baby Hospital almost two years later. Many good people tried to arrange the therapy, but, for whatever reason, it never happened.

We saw Kambiri and fell in love instantly. We called in favors. We worked the system. We may have insinuated that we had embarrassing photos of the hospital CEO. We eventually got the system to approve her as a charitable case and pay for the treatment, which would cost tens of thousands of dollars.

Kambiri had a tumor called a *craniopharyngioma*. This is a benign tumor that grows from a remnant of what forms part of your mouth. In brain surgery, *benign* does not always mean "good." *Benign* means it is unlikely to spread. Craniopharyngiomas are the cockroaches of brain tumors; they are ridiculously hard to kill, and they just keep coming back.

A craniopharyngioma usually forms in the suprasellar area, an area that is just above the pituitary gland and just below the optic nerves. Like the pituitary tumors removed by Grandpa P., craniopharyngiomas can affect the hormones and the vision. In kids, craniopharyngiomas are notorious for interrupting growth. Children are therefore usually very small. Kids also don't seem to complain about losing vision, despite the fact that most children with this tumor have lost at least some of their eye function.

The tumor itself often looks like a glistening chunk of brown soap, complete with bubbles in the form of cysts. The cysts are often filled with fluid that looks and feels like old motor oil. The tumor is greenish, brownish, and often glistens with flecks of calcium.

There are many options for treatment. Unfortunately, this means that there is not one good option. The prevailing wisdom in treatment of craniopharyngioma swings dramatically about every ten years. The only chance of cure is complete resection. A few decades ago, major surgical centers radically resected these tumors, no matter what the cost to the child. About ten years later, clinicians studied the patients. Children were often decimated. Their tumor was gone, but so were their vision and their pituitary function. The tumor often invades the hypothalamus, a basic part of the brain that controls much of your unconscious behavior. "We are not a good substitute for a functioning hypothalamus," says the Professor. Children with hypothalamic dysfunction will either eat and eat and eat until they are morbidly obese or starve themselves to emaciation. They may sleep incessantly, up to twenty hours per day. They may basically become vegetative. They need constant, precise medicine to replace their hormones; dehydration or a common cold could be life-threatening. They are often blind. Removing the tumor won the battle but lost the war.

The attitude then completely reversed. Surgeons took a more conservative approach. They began to biopsy the tumor to confirm the diagnosis and then treat with radiation. Surgical complications dropped significantly. However, radiation came at a cost, including loss of intelligence, hormone problems, and blindness. As it turned out, the ten-year survival for biopsy and radiation was exactly the same as radical resection.

Surgeons tried other, subtler means. Some patients had predominately cystic tumors. These could be drained. Some even injected toxic or radioactive material into the cysts. Many of these patients required a shunt for hydrocephalus.

*   *   *   *

Tasha was six when she had her first surgery. She was tiny for a six-year-old, but she compensated with spunk and vigor. She had limited but functional vision. She had headaches but remained active and playful. She had a CT scan, which showed a craniopharyngioma. Her tumor had a small solid portion, surrounded by large, puffy bubbles. Dr. King saw her initially. He did a biopsy of the tumor, drained one cyst, and sent her for radiation. Tasha's vision improved almost immediately.

Over the next twenty years, Tasha grew, married, divorced, graduated college, and became a fan of open-wheel racing. She had a few surgeries over the years. Thomas placed a shunt. Then another. She had a few shunt revisions and two more cyst drainage procedures. Each of these kept her in the hospital for a few days.

I met Tasha when she was twenty-seven. She was admitted to County, where Edward and the Professor were keeping watch. Tasha was admitted because she just stopped doing *anything*. It began with difficulty concentrating at work. She developed terrible headaches. Her memory seemed off. She began to lose interest in going to work. She began to sleep more. Eventually, she stopped getting out of bed at all. She refused to eat. She refused to bathe. Her mother worked diligently to get her up, but to no avail. Tasha stopped speaking. Her mother, unsure what to do, called for an ambulance.

Edward and I walked into the hospital room. Tasha was lying on the bed, staring at her feet, her head rhythmically nodding up and down like a bobblehead doll. She didn't speak. She didn't react. With an inordinate amount of effort, she would gradually move her tremulous head to the side, glance at her mom, and smile. She winced when I pressed on her abdomen, and one of her legs was grossly swollen.

Edward gave me the rundown. "She's got elevated LFTs, hypernatremia, severely low total protein, and hypothyroidism. She's also got a left-sided DVT.[129] I don't think she's eaten in over a week. Her vision is terrible. She just looks *sick*."

---

[129] LFTs, liver function tests; hypernatremia, elevated salt in the blood; low protein, a measure, in this case, of malnutrition; hypothyroid, low function of the thyroid gland, which often saps a patient's energy; DVT, deep venous thrombosis, a blood clot in the leg.

Edward used the word *sick* in a little different way than one would say someone missed work ~~to go the baseball game~~ because he or she was sick. When a surgeon says someone is *sick*, that often means the patient is spiraling down a fatal drain. Tasha was shutting down. We obtained a MRI, which showed a new large cyst forming in the back of the tumor. It dropped lazily over a gentle slope of bone called the *clivus*. This tubby water balloon was squishing her brain stem and slowly killing her.

Edward and I sat down with Tasha's mother. She was very opposed to surgery.

"I think we need to do something about the tumor or at least that cyst," I said.

"Dr. King told me that surgery was too dangerous," she said.

"Trying to resect all the tumor is dangerous, especially now that she had radiation and all her other surgeries. I'm worried that she's going to get worse if we don't do something. I think her shunt is okay. We're trying to fix all the things in her belly, but she's pretty weak from not eating for so long. Plus she has this blood clot in her leg."

"What do you recommend?"

"Well," I said, thinking through the various crappy options. "Maybe if we get her tuned up, we can just stick a catheter into that cyst and try to drain it. It'd be kind of like another biopsy, but we'd leave the catheter there in case fluid filled it up again."

Mom liked this idea. Tasha couldn't answer for herself. She looked at us through a sloe-eyed daze. We asked the general surgeons to place a PEG tube to give her nutrition. We placed her on blood thinners and eventually asked the radiologists to place a small filter in the vena cava, the major vein leading to the heart. A blood clot in the leg may be painful, but it's usually not dangerous unless it breaks off, travels up the vena cava, and lodges in the lungs. This can be immediately fatal. In fact, a classic description of this is a patient getting wide-eyed, saying, "I'm going to die," and then dying. Creepy. The filter's job was to catch any clot before it hit the lung.

Edward and I used our fancy-schmancy computer system to plot a trajectory for our catheter. No longer bound by that clunky frame from my medical school days, we were able to use the computer to hit our deep target with exquisite precision. We aspirated a satisfying rush of old motor oil.

The next day, Tasha was a new person. She was fully awake, fully cogent, and talking up a storm. She couldn't believe the month and the day; she'd lost basically six weeks of her life. Her abdomen hurt from the liver inflammation, but overall, she felt pretty good. Mom was grateful to get her daughter back. They talked like old friends, catching up at a high school reunion. Within a week, Tasha went home.

Unfortunately, victory was short-lived. Tasha returned four months later with similar symptoms and multiple new, growing cysts. The tumor, quiescent for two decades, was now rumbling back to life. I met with our radiation oncologists. They were concerned about zapping it because of its size and the way the new cysts deformed the optic nerve. They were worried that further radiation treatment would lead to blindness.

"I was always told that surgery is too dangerous," Tasha's mother said as we sat down to discuss the options.

"Surgery is dangerous, especially now. It's almost a certainty that we'll wreck whatever pituitary function she has left. Everything will be sticky from her prior radiation. There are just all kinds of potential problems, including stroke and blindness."

Tasha's mother didn't like the sound of any of this. She also didn't like seeing her daughter lying helplessly on the bed.

"What's the other option?"

"Well, not doing anything. The radiation docs won't touch her unless we debulk the tumor."

"I'm going to have to think about this."

She did. We did. Eventually, we decided to go for it.

As luck would have it, surgery went well. Edward and I worked for the better part of the day. The tumor looked like luminescent coral under the microscope, with shiny flecks of white on a base of green and brown. We gently teased tumor out of her body and systematically traveled from one cyst to another, gently popping each oil-filled balloon. Our goal was to connect all the cysts with her ventricles so any fluid could drain down the shunt.

Remarkably, Tasha recovered quite well. She was more awake the next day. We had removed virtually all of the tumor; there was only a small bit left that was tightly embedded within her hypothalamus. Overall, we were happy with the results. Tasha recovered and went home.

Two months later, Tasha developed severe, debilitating headaches. Her shunt had failed. We took her to surgery to replace the whole system. The general surgeons helped out by popping a laparoscope into her belly. They were then able to precisely place the distal catheter.

"Hey, look at this," the general surgeon said. He was a younger attending, only a year or two removed from fellowship. He was extremely facile with the laparoscope.

"Her gallbladder looks terrible."

"Wow, it sure does," I said, trying not to look stupid by asking which of the globs on the view screen was the gallbladder. Was it the black glob? I remembered my lessons from the large Czech during my intern year. Pretty sure gallbladders weren't supposed to be black. "What do we do?"

"Well, let's run some tests when we're done."

The general surgeons were quite concerned that her gallbladder, connected to the inflamed and sick liver, was failing. Their concerns were justified when a few weeks later, she again got *sick*. Her gallbladder ruptured and filled her abdomen with painful, deadly infection. Tasha had to be put back on a ventilator, and we had to relocate the shunt to her heart. Tasha was *septic*; infection filled her whole body. Her blood pressure dropped. Her breathing stopped. Whatever health reserve she stored was quickly spent.

Tasha spent months in the ICU. As soon as one problem was fixed, another one popped up. Without adequate health, all of her organs began to shut down. The skin is an organ. Soon, her recent surgical incisions began to fall apart. We had to take her back to surgery to revise her scalp. Pretty twenty-seven-year-old Tasha had her head shaved and grotesque scars crisscrossed her scalp.

Eventually, she recovered enough to come off the ventilator. Mother took her home with nursing support. Again, victory, such as it was, was short-lived. Two months later, Tasha returned, again vegetative and again septic. Her residual tumor had radically increased from the size of an almond to a growling monster.

Tasha continued her rapid spiral down the drain. Her mother grimly decided that she shouldn't have any more surgery. We agreed. Tasha died fourteen months after that first cyst surgery.

*   *   *   *

Derek was six when he was first diagnosed with a craniopharyngioma. He was a spunky little chap who liked basketball and annoying his sisters. He had a disease called pyloric stenosis as a baby, which made him vomit uncontrollably. The general surgeons worked their magic and fixed it. He began to vomit again at six, and his doctors were worried about his stomach. They investigated it, and everything seemed fine. They then looked at the head. A CT scan showed significant hydrocephalus. Derek's tumor blocked the narrow *cerebral aqueduct*, and the spinal fluid was dangerously backing up behind the obstruction.

We discussed a number of options. We discussed a biopsy and radiation treatment or an attempt at a full resection. Derek's cranio-pharyngioma was relatively small and mostly solid. The spinal fluid backup made a nice little pocket around the tumor.

"How would you take it out?" Dad asked.

"Well, I wonder if we could get it with the neuroendoscope," I said, mainly to myself.

Brian had accompanied me to this discussion.

"What's that mean?"

"We'll make a small hole and then put in the endoscope—a small device with a camera on the end. We can work through this instrument. I'm sure we could get a piece of the tumor for diagnosis and we could probably treat his hydrocephalus. I'm not sure how much of the tumor we could get out, but we could see."

"How big would the incision be?"

"About an inch."

Dad liked the sound of this.

Endoscopy procedures may be my favorite type of surgical case. After making a small hole in the skull, we pass a sheath into the lateral ventricle. We then pass the camera through this, navigate from inside the ventricle, and work away. The anatomy is beautiful. The *choroid plexus* is usually our first landmark. It looks like soft, gently oscillating seaweed. This leads us past the bright-blue road map of veins and through the passage connecting the lateral to the third ventricles. In the third ventricle, we see the gentle mounds of the mammillary bodies[130]; the thin, translucent membranous floor; and the soft red blush of the infundibular recess, the top part of the pituitary apparatus. If we look through the back of the third ventricle, we see the small cerebral aqueduct, the next passage in the spinal

---

[130] I guess so named because early anatomists thought they looked like boobs.

fluid circulation. In Derek's case, his third ventricle was filled with a jawbreaker-sized tumor.

Neuroendoscopy feels like a scuba-diving video game. If you can get through the Super Mario Galaxy disappearing green tile level on a prankster comet, you can do brain surgery. Brian and I began the surgery. I had no delusions of grandeur. We planned to treat the hydrocephalus, get a piece of the tumor, and get out. We navigated into the third ventricle, spotted the lump, and broke off a piece. This confirmed our diagnosis.

"Well, let's just see how it behaves," I said, probably to convince myself to go on. There are incredibly sophisticated tools that fit down the camera shaft. One tool looks and behaves like a little Pac-Man. We inserted this into the tumor and then gently began to gnaw away. To my pleasant surprise, the tumor seemed squishy soft. We took a little more. No bleeding. A little more couldn't hurt. Brian and I gently sucked and chomped the tumor. The more we chomped, the more the tumor delivered itself. Soon, we began to see the floor of the third ventricle.

"Whoa!" Brain yelled, as a giant red blood vessel popped into view. It was the basilar artery, the major vessel to the back of the brain and the brain stem. Injury to this vessel means instant death.

"Shit gets real when you see the basilar," I muttered.

Brian was wide-eyed. In this case, the vessel told us we were at the bottom of the tumor. We worked our way forward, and amazingly, the tumor just sort of detached. It put up less resistance than the week 12 SEC football opponents.[131]

"What just happened?" Brian asked.

"I think it's free," I said.

We attacked it with our Pac-Man.

---

[131] Presbyterian? Really?

I looked around with the scope. I could see all the normal anatomy of the third ventricle, including our newly created hole through the thin, translucent floor into the *prepontine cistern*, the home of the basilar. This serendipitously created a bypass channel for the spinal fluid flow.

"I think it's all out," I said, hardly believing my own assessment.

Sure enough, the postoperative MRI looked clean.

Derek had proton therapy for the floor of the third ventricle. His MRI is completely clean—no tumor, no hydrocephalus, no shunt— now three years after that surgery.

*   *   *   *

I think Derek is cured. Time will tell, I suppose. I'm happy with the decision and the outcome. Derek is a normal kid. He's doing well in school and perpetually annoying his sisters. What if he wasn't a normal kid? What if, during the surgery, we had injured his hypothalamus? That was definitely possible. I wasn't trying to be aggressive in his surgery; we got lucky that the tumor was so soft. What if, instead of a normal child, he became a bloated, bedridden invalid, taking multiple brittle medications? What if he was blind? What if, in order to cure him, I robbed him of a life?

Tasha had twenty good years but died in a horrible, hospitalized year. By any cancer outcome measurement, Tasha's treatment was a success. Long-term survival for brain tumor patients is usually measured in five or ten-year blocks. Is a five-year survival, starting at age six, really a success? Tasha's tumor was a dormant volcano, erupting after two decades of slumber. She had twenty good years but died brutally at age twenty-seven.

Craniopharyngiomas are benign assailants. The pendulum of thought has now swung back in most surgeons' minds. Most surgeons (including myself) recommend an attempt at rational resection. The best shot to resect is the first, when the tumor is unsullied by scar or radiation changes. But this remains a frustrating, vexing, confusing problem for me. Do we win the battle, only to lose the war?

The Baby Hospital does not give answers willingly. At least not to me.

* * * *

Kambiri smiled a huge, toothy grin. "Do you really like it?"

"Of course," I said, looking at my gift. "It's beautiful."

Kambiri was recovering from surgery. Just before she was scheduled to begin her proton therapy, she rapidly declined. Imaging showed a strikingly large, rapidly growing tumor cyst. Like with Derek, we were able to drain the cyst and remove most of the remaining tumor with the endoscope. Kambiri recovered almost instantly and now sat in my clinic, displaying her remarkable works of art.

I was curious but didn't want to offend. "Kambiri, how do you do this?" The intertwined colors on the tapestries were thematic, harmonious, and congruent. There was a true auteurship in this eleven-year-old, abandoned, tiny little blind girl.

"I feel it. I feel the colors." She smiled again.

"Well, they're lovely. Thank you so much. I feel blessed."

"I feel blessed too! I feel blessed to come to this country and have my tumor fixed and meet all the nice people. I don't worry about being blind. I can feel everything around me."

She paused.

"Every day is a blessing."

CHAPTER 27

Ellen

Ellen was twelve years old and enjoyed twelve-year-old things. She did well in school and watched Disney princess movies. She had a younger brother who did little brother things and two parents who couldn't have been any nicer.

Over about two weeks, Ellen began to have headaches. They were mild at first. But they escalated. Within a week, the headaches were daily and she began to vomit. The parents began to worry. Maybe they were migraines. But she had never had headaches before. Things got worse. She stopped going to school. She stopped getting out of bed. Two weeks earlier, she was attending basketball practice.

Ellen was evaluated by her pediatrician, who ordered a CT scan. The scan showed that the lateral and the third ventricles were grossly enlarged. They were enlarged because the cerebral aqueduct was blocked by a sickeningly large tumor. Ellen was sent to the Baby Hospital.

"How are you feeling?" I asked.

"Fine," Ellen said. A cloth covered her eyes, and the room was dark.

"Well," I said, trying to be reassuring, "if you were *fine*, you wouldn't be here talking to me."

Ellen managed a meek smile.

"I heard you started having headaches. Can you tell me about them?"

"Well, it kind of hurts all over, and I feel like I'm going to throw up."

"We're going to give you some medicine and it will help you feel better."

"Okay." Her voice was soft and weak.

I explained things to her dad and mom. The dad had a nervous smile. I liked him. I could tell that he was the cutup of their social group.

We gave her an infusion of a powerful steroid medication. This would temporarily take down any swelling in the brain and, for a short time, make her feel better. We placed her on monitors in the intensive care unit and then retreated to the offices to try to sort out what to do next.

The tumor was massive, but she was sick from the hydrocephalus. We could fix this. But what to do about the tumor? The more I looked, the more I felt a deepening sense of dread. The tumor began in the area of the *pineal gland*, right in the center of the head. It wrapped around all of the deep veins in the brain. Should I operate on it? Damage to one of those veins would mean uncontrollable bleeding and likely instant death.

"So," I said, turning to the residents. "What's our differential diagnosis?"

"Well," one of the residents said, "it looks like a PNET" (pronounced "peanut"). PNET stands for primitive neuroectodermal tumor.

"Yeah," I said. "Could it be anything else?"

He then listed all the things that could occur in that area. Most tumors in this area in kids are related to germ cells. These are some of the most primitive cells in the body. *Primitive* sort of makes the cells sound dumb, but in this case, it kind of means old. They are stem cells that can then turn into other types of cell. All the specialized cells that make up your skin, eyes, intestines, heart, and bones come from the progeny of primitive progenitor cells. Germ-cell tumors come from these basic cells. Germ-cell tumors form in the reproductive organs or in the region of the pineal gland in the brain. They tend to grow rapidly and are relentlessly aggressive. Some are exquisitely sensitive to radiation and chemotherapy.

This was her only hope. This was my only hope.

"So, let's get a piece of it."

Our plan was to place a small hole in the floor of the third ventricle to treat the hydrocephalus, similar to what we did for Derek with the craniopharyngioma. This would allow the spinal fluid to bypass the blocked cerebral aqueduct and flow normally. The advantage of this procedure is that, if successful, it would obviate the need for a shunt.

The floor of the third ventricle is a translucent membrane that is part of the hypothalamus. Our goal was to make a hole in the few millimeters between the mammillary bodies and the red blush of the infundibular recess. We had to penetrate two membranes: the floor of the ventricle called the *tuber cinereum* and a sheath of investing arachnoid called *Lilequist's membrane*. Below the floor was the formidable basilar artery.

"She's getting worse." Brian received a call that Ellen had declined. He ordered a stat CT scan.

"Damn it, she bled," he said.

The CT confirmed his conclusion. The third ventricle, our target, was now full of blood.

We trotted to the bedside. She looked worse.

"Ellen, can you hear me?"

"Yes," she said in a small voice.

"How do you feel?"

"Fine." Her voice was even weaker than before.

"You're doing great, kid," Dad said, with a valiant attempt at a smile. "She seemed fine; then she just seemed to ..." His voice trailed off as he looked for the words. "Well, she seemed to get worse."

I talked to her mom and dad. We decided that we would continue with our original plan, although the difficulty had just increased.

We took her to the operating room. The anesthesia team put her to sleep and placed lines in her veins and arteries, and we positioned her on the table. We placed a small sticker on her cheek. This would interact with a magnetic device as part of our operative navigation system. There are times where I get to play with technology that would make Captain Picard's head spin.[132]

Everything went as planned. We studied the ventricle and confirmed our location. We could see the foramen, and as expected, it was blocked with a large blood clot. The next move made me pretty nervous. We began to suck out the clot. I was worried that we might unearth a bleeding tumor vessel. I was thankful the clot sucked out nicely and we could see the whole ventricle.

We punctured a hole in the floor and then angled the scope to look at the tumor. We used a probe to bite off a few pieces. We sent one to pathology. They looked at it under the microscope and told us it was a highly undifferentiated *small blue cell tumor*. We removed the scope and passed a drainage tube into her ventricle.

She felt much better.

"How are you?"

"Fine!"

---

[132] Star Trek showed us the iPad and flip phone decades before their time. I hope I live to see that little medical device that makes the *woop woop woop woop woop* sound.

This was the first time I believed her.

We went back to the ICU where she had an uneventful night. The next day, she seemed like a normal kid. She was eating. She had no headache. She gave me a look that told me she wanted to go home.

Dad was cracking jokes, high-fiving the nurses, and generally brightening the room. Mom looked relieved. We had survived round one, but the elephant in the room was that we hadn't done anything for the tumor.

Hospital shows often vacillate between torrid sex in the locker room and fast-paced drama in the ER. They rarely show what patients and families really do all day—watch TV and try to combat boredom.

Waiting. Waiting for pathology. Waiting for the doctors. Waiting for physical therapy.

Waiting.

The first day passed. Then the second. Then the third. We were waiting for the final pathology report as I still clung to hope that this would be something we could treat with radiation or chemotherapy. Even if treatment wouldn't cure her, maybe we could shrink the thing before an attempt at surgery.

Finally, the pathology report came back: *pineoblastoma*. This is a rare and highly, highly malignant tumor.

The parents were smart and educated people. They immediately took to the Internet. I'm not sure what ran through their heads (or their hearts) when they came upon the scant few studies that reported a uniformly fatal prognosis. With full treatment, including full resection, there was a coin flip of surviving one year.

I got the news and felt defeated. Her only shot was a surgical resection. However, I was not at all sure I could do the surgery without killing her. Even if she survived, there was a good chance that she would be injured. I could take away her memory, her speech, her ability to interact with her friends. How would I even access the tumor? I scanned the schedule to figure out a day to block out for surgery.

I was on call that night. Things were busy. Around seven in the evening, Brian called and said that she had worsened again. She went from talking to completely somnolent. We ordered an emergent CT scan. This confirmed my fear; she had bled again.

I caught up to her room around midnight. Her eyes were closed. Her face was ashen. Her dad fought out a smile, but his eyes betrayed his fear. Mom was hiding her face from Ellen. She didn't want Ellen to see her cry.

"Ellen, how are you?" I asked, holding her hand.

"Fine," she said, barely audible.

She continued to slip.

I had been awake all night tending to Ellen and other patients. I had two surgeries scheduled in the morning at another hospital. By coincidence, one of the surgeries was on Brian's mother-in-law. I didn't want to leave, but I had made a commitment. I felt like I needed to be in two places at once.

My mind was on Ellen. Brian paged me about every fifteen minutes with updates. We tried all the medical tricks I knew. I didn't know what to do. I began to grasp at straws. Should we try to operate? I knew what would happen. We'd open, blood would pour out, the brain would swell, and we'd have to plow blindly into the mass in the center of her brain. The only way to stop the bleeding would be to take out the entire tumor, which I felt was unlikely.

I felt like I should be at her bedside. But two people had planned to have surgery. They were expecting it. I couldn't just abandon them. I also couldn't be so preoccupied by Ellen that I would give them anything less than my full concentration. I operated more slowly than usual, forcing myself to take care with every step. I would not rush their surgery and risk an injury.

I finished around ten thirty in the morning. I had about twelve patients scheduled to see me starting at one in the afternoon. I raced back to the Baby Hospital, parked illegally, and sprinted up to the ICU bed. There was a crowd outside her room—never a good sign.

I was sweating. I slowed to a walk and spoke to Brian.

"Your mother-in-law did fine. Things went well." It was small comfort.

As I walked into the room, the murmur of worried nurses, ICU doctors, and the family stopped. They all silently looked at me. All of them were looking for a ray of hope. A plan. Anything.

Ellen had a tube in her throat, lines in her arms, and a tube coming out of her head that was full of blood. Sitting in the room, unmistakably, was Death.

Death is something surgeons must face at one time or another. I believe the stories of animals who can sense when someone is about to die. I believe those stories, because I can do it too. I'm not sure how or why, but I can see Death. Really.

Death is not a shrouded demon with a scythe. Death is not a villain or a monster. We assign fear to Death. We popularize fear in movies, literature, and the evening news. But I've never felt fear in the presence of Death.

Death is the ending of the day, the downing of the sun, the conclusion to the story. Simple as that. It makes me sad, sometimes.

I made my way to her bed and checked the drain. Nothing. I fumbled it and immediately cursed myself in my head. The family didn't need to see anything clumsy. I held her hand.

"Ellen?"

Silence.

"Ellen?"

I touched her head and then gently opened her closed eyelids. I saw the vacant stare of enlarged pupils. Death is not passionate or demonstrative. I touched her pupils with the end of a glove, mechanically checking her corneal reflex.

Ellen's story had ended. She was fine two weeks earlier. She was a normal twelve-year-old kid who played basketball and watched Disney movies. I stared at Death for a second. He stared back. We had met before. As quickly as He came, He left.

I took a deep breath and turned around. The nurses were all still fighting back tears and hoping I had some brilliant plan. How did the room get so crowded? And hot?

Mom knew. She wept gently. It was Dad who broke the silence.

"You all have been great," he offered. Dad was a wonderful man; he was trying to make *us* feel better. "Really. We couldn't have asked for anything more. We'll just remember the good times she had. We'll remember our little girl."

Some of the nurses began to cry. The doctors spend a few minutes with each patient every day. But the nurses spend the whole day with them. They tend to their needs. They feed them. They clean them. Nurses with the strength to work in the ICU all attach to the patients. For those few days, Ellen was their daughter.

Mom's tear-filled eyes met mine. There was no anger, just sadness. We hugged. She didn't need to see me break down. I held it together but barely. I quivered as I whispered, "I wish we could have done more."

She nodded and managed a weak smile.

Dad and Mom hugged and sobbed. The sobbing grew a bit louder as I made my way to the door.

"Let's give them some time," I said to the crowd.

We began to file out. Soon the only people in the room were Ellen, her parents, and her nurse. I could hear three people weeping.

I conferred with the ICU team. We discussed the next plan and the next step in the protocol for declaring death. I looked at Brian. His eyes looked into the room for a moment. Then we walked away.

We numbly reviewed the rest of the patients and confirmed the plan, and then I headed back to see the afternoon's patients.

Ellen was gone.

Chapter 28

Yay, Ben!

The little bundle of goo was trouble from the very beginning. Ben was born, assessed, and then hustled directly toward the operating room. The general surgeons were gathering, ready to repair his defective airway and blocked intestinal system. I met them in the small staging area just outside of the operating theater. Dad could accompany the now minutes-old baby just this far.

"What's his name?" I asked, quickly assessing the child. He had a giant head with enlarged, distended veins snaking under his scalp. His soft spot was tense. His heart rate was dropping, a telltale sign of increased pressure in the head.

Dad seemed shell-shocked. The baby had been diagnosed with hydrocephalus while in utero, so this wasn't a total surprise. But still, seeing it in person, after watching his wife undergo surgery, it seemed like it was a little much.

Finally, he said, "Uh, Ben. We're naming him Ben."

The general surgeons were getting antsy.

"I'll need just a second, gents. Dad, we're going to need to tap a little of this fluid off to buy some time."

"How?" Dad asked, still staring off in the distance.

"Well ..." I said, while slathering antiseptic over the soft spot.

Dad's eyes widened. "You want to wait outside?" I asked, unsheathing a fairly sizeable needle.

"No." Dad steeled himself.

The anticipation was much worse than the procedure. His head was virtually all water, so all I had to do really was break the skin. I quickly drew off a fair amount of fluid, and the soft spot relaxed.

"We'll let them get to it," I said, motioning to the general surgeons. They whisked him off. Later, we placed a shunt that drained spinal fluid from his head to the right atrium of the heart.

*   *   *   *

Ben rallied. After his inauspicious start, he began to thrive. Each imaging study looked better. A baby's brain is much different from an adult's. The supporting cells are not mature yet. As we grow, our nerves sprout many new connections. The supporting cells (the *glia*) develop a fatty sheath that protects and nurtures the growing connections. A baby's brain does not have all this fatty supporting structure, and thus, it is very soft. It is also compressible. Ben's brain began to expand, now that we were draining the spinal fluid.

We prefer to place the end of a shunt into the belly. We can stuff extra tubing length in the abdominal cavity, anticipating the child's growth. In Ben's case, his belly was off-limits because of his abdominal problems and surgery. So we had to put it into the heart. This is a perfectly acceptable place, as the spinal fluid naturally drains into the veins. However, we can't coil up a bunch of extra tubing in the heart. So we must periodically lengthen the tubing as the baby grows.

By nine months, Ben had outgrown his tube. We decided to try to relocate it into the belly. The general surgeon popped a small endoscope into the belly and carefully cut out scar adhesions. They created a nice pocket, and we were able to pull the tube out of the heart.

Ben sprouted into a lovely little kid. His parents considered every day a blessing. Ben responded by bringing a big smile to everyone he met. He was a very positive little guy. By two years of age, he began to talk. Ben began every morning the same way; he would wake up and then, in a manner that would make Senator Stuart Smalley proud, loudly exclaim, *"Yay, Ben!"*

I'd see him periodically in clinic. He'd greet us with a big smile and give me a fist bump.

"How you doing, Ben?"

"Yay, Ben!"

*   *   *   *

At two and a half years, Ben began to get headaches. His shunt hadn't been a problem since that elective lengthening, but with headaches, our first thought is shunt malfunction.

It's always the shunt.

We scanned Ben. Each scan looked better than the last. I reassured the parents, but Ben didn't get any better. We decided to tap the shunt. Yay Ben's positive attitude quickly disappeared when he realized we were about to do something painful. Kids generally aren't too fond of us sticking needles in their head. A nurse held him down as I cleaned off his shunt and popped the needle in. The parents edged closer, expecting bad news.

"Everything looks great. We'll send some of the fluid to the lab, but I highly doubt there's any infection."

The parents sighed. Then Mom asked, "So what's wrong with him?"

It's always the shunt. Only this time, it wasn't.

"Let's see if our pediatricians can find something."

"So," the pediatric resident asked me, "is it the shunt?"

"I don't think so. His scan looks better, and the tap was fine."

"You sure it's not the shunt?"

The ER at the Baby Hospital is notorious for a quick trigger in calling neurosurgery for any child with a shunt, no matter what the problem. Headache? Call neurosurgery. Constipation? Call neurosurgery. Sprained ankle? Yes, they called a young Kendall about the shunt in a child who twisted his ankle. They called neurosurgery before the orthopedic ankle doctors.

Steve was once called to evaluate a child with cerebral palsy for shunt malfunction.

"What's the problem?" Steve asked the ER resident.

"Mom thinks he's not as active as usual."

Steve dutifully trudged to the ER. He ran his hands around the kid's head, looking for the valve. Hmmmm. Nothing. The kid didn't have a shunt.

The ER resident was chagrined. Trying to defend himself, he said, "Well, he *looked* like a kid with a shunt."

Steve scowled and headed back to the call room.

*   *   *   *

Ben didn't get better. He stopped eating and would throw up if forced. The gastrointestinal doctors were called. I tapped him a second time. The shunt was working fine.

"So, is it the shunt?"

"No."

"You sure?"

"Far as I can tell."

"Maybe it's a virus. It'll run its course."

Ugh.

It didn't run its course. Ben kept complaining of headache. No more "Yay, Ben!" in the morning.

We did further studies. One was a more detailed MRI, including his spine. Ben had a Chiari malformation. We all have a hole in the base of our skull called the *foramen magnum*. Normally, the only thing passing through the hole is the top of the spinal cord. A Chiari malformation occurs when something else sticks down through the hole, compressing the cord and blocking the normal flow of spinal fluid like the stopper in your bathtub. Usually, the offending agent is part of the cerebellum, the *"little brain"* that affects coordination. Ben's malformation wasn't bad, but it was definitely there. Maybe that was the problem.

I wasn't sure if the Chiari was the problem, but Ben was getting worse. We decided to operate. We positioned him for surgery. Before making the incision, we tapped the shunt for a third time. It was working perfectly.

Fine. It must be the Chiari.

Chiari surgery is fairly painful. We need to dissect between the major muscles of the back of the neck. This hurts. So Ben was understandably whiny after surgery. He seemed mad, especially at me. No more fist bump. Mom was getting frustrated.

"It's the day after surgery. Let's see how it goes."

Then Ben worsened. He began to yell and arch his neck in a weird fashion. We gave Ben medicine for nausea and pain. He responded a little, but he still wasn't happy.

"I thought this would fix him," Mom said, exasperated.

"Me too."

"I just want my happy little guy back."

"Me too."

He started to get better. Then he got worse. Then better. Then worse. This went on for another day.

I saw Ben late in the day. He was smiling and chowing down on some Rice Puffs. Whew, this is more like it.

"Maybe he turned the corner," I muttered hopefully.

Mom was red-eyed and tired. "Maybe."

No sooner had I said that then Ben arched his back and screamed out a bloodcurdling yell. He then seemed totally dazed. His eyes were open, but he wasn't looking at us or reacting. The lights were on, but nobody was home. After a minute or two, he seemed to wake up. Maybe he was having some weird seizure?

Mom was exasperated.

"Ben, are you okay?" I asked, holding out my fist for a reassuring bump.

Ben scowled and looked away.

"Let's scan him."

We hustled him down for a scan of his head and neck.

Damn it! It's the shunt!

His ventricles were clearly enlarged. *It's always the shunt! [Read in a Charlie Brown voice] Aaaauuuughhh!*[133]

We rushed him back to the OR. I opened the incision over his shunt. I disconnected the proximal catheter from the valve, and spinal fluid shot out under a tremendous amount of pressure. The valve wasn't working. I replaced it and checked the distal catheter. It seemed fine.

I left the OR to go to the parents' waiting room. It was now late at night, and everything was deserted. His parents popped up and dashed to me as I approached. Mom was quivering and holding back tears.

"Well, it was his shunt. I think it was working before his Chiari surgery. We must have affected the valve somehow. It was clearly not working now."

"So will he be better?"

---

[133] If ever there was a literary character who embodies pediatric neurosurgery, it's Charlie Brown.

"I hope so."

Mom wasn't reassured.

I slept for a few hours and then stopped by to see them first thing in the morning. Ben was sitting up in his high chair.

"Ben, how you feeling?"

"Yay, Ben!"

Fist bump.

CHAPTER 29

I Bless the Rains Down in Aaaaaaafrica

You now have a Toto earworm.[134]

You're welcome.

Many (most?) doctors genuinely desire to help those in need. Some of my colleagues at the Baby Hospital travel to underdeveloped nations, donating time and money to bring care to children without easy access to health care. Some remarkable people spend years in underserved areas, providing compassion and care to those suffering the ravages of poverty and war.

Neurosurgeons may do remarkable work in developed nations, but we're kind of useless in an impoverished country or in the face of a mass disaster.[135] This is because neurosurgeons are vitally dependent on advanced technology. American brain or spine surgery relies on cutting-edge imaging techniques, computer navigation, sophisticated anesthesia care, and easy access to a team of specialists. While this technology has made surgery much safer, more precise, and flat-out better, it is of little help in a country without such luxuries.

Neurosurgery is also expensive. The tests are expensive. The equipment is expensive. A very common spine surgery involves

---

[134] And if you don't, we can't be friends.
[135] Sorry Sanjay, nobody in the know thinks you saved Haiti.

placing screws to fuse together a joint. Each screw, although not fundamentally different from something you'd buy at a hardware store, costs hundreds if not thousands of dollars. In many nations, those funds are better spent on vaccines and clean water.

The neurosurgeons who can make a difference are those who treat children. In Africa, the population is heavily skewed toward children. Pediatric neurosurgeons may make a lasting difference by treating children afflicted by spina bifida, hydrocephalus, and brain tumors. In fact, a few remarkable surgeons (such as Benjamin Warf and A. Leland Albright) have established hospitals, provided care, and trained local surgeons. Their lasting contribution to worldwide health is laudable and remarkable.

I was fortunate enough to meet Dr. Joe Mamlin, an internist with a vision of a lasting, sustainable health-care system in Kenya. He left a prestigious, successful, *comfortable* American practice and traveled to Africa with the goal of establishing a medical school. He partnered with a local hospital and has dedicated the latter part of his career training Kenyans to become doctors. I believe his accomplishments are exemplary; under his leadership, the school was vital in the response to the African HIV/AIDs epidemic. These efforts were recognized with a nomination for a Nobel Peace Prize in 2007.[136]

Dave and I benefitted from the herculean, groundbreaking efforts of Dr. Mamlin. Dave was the neurosurgery chief resident. He was a tall, gangly, sharp-featured chap who fit in perfectly with the skull-base cowboys. He was a gifted surgeon, but he had an abrasive edge and sometimes brutal honesty. These traits reminded me a little of a young Professor, although Dave lacked the mirth. As a junior resident, Dave clashed with the attendings on other services. His review from the general surgeons read simply: "Worst intern ever." I found this

---

[136] For further information, http://www.ampathkenya.org.

interesting and a little amusing, because two of his cointerns did not speak English; they were fired midway through the year. Apparently Dave was worse than either of them. Everything about Dave was deadly serious, and I somehow found this hilarious. I liked him immediately.

Despite his gruff exterior, Dave sincerely wanted to help the less fortunate, including those in other nations. He was inspired by other missionaries from his church and first suggested that we travel to Kenya. Dr. Mamlin hosts many doctors, students, and residents at his hospital, but Dave and I were the first neurosurgeons from our program. We contacted the local doctors, gathered as many supplies as we could carry, and planned our trip.

"Are we nuts for doing this?" I asked as we drove to the airport. I was completely unsure what we were getting into or if I would be of any service to the people. My picture of Africa, skewed through the lens of Hollywood, was a continent of lions carrying grenade launchers.

"Maybe. Too late to back out now."

We stuffed as much equipment as we could into a trunk and carried it to the airport. Eighteen short hours later, we landed in Kenya. As we left the airport, I mentally prepared myself for the ensuing quest for survival—man against nature—in the bush. Instead, I lounged in a very comfortable taxi, which drove us down the highway toward a beautiful, modern cosmopolitan city. It was exactly like an American city, except it was cleaner, the people were nicer, and everyone spoke much better English.

We hoped the local plane to Eldoret. Eldoret was a little more rural but seemed to be a comfortable, midsized city. The town was dusty, but the people were kind.

Our biggest adjustment was the roads. Streets were narrow without sidewalks or shoulders. Also, there were no speed limits. Instead, the roads were littered with *governors*, basically large speed bumps that would trash a car's chassis if the driver took them too fast. We checked into the gated compound established by Dr. Mamlin and then went to the hospital.

The Kenyan medical students were meticulously dressed, with crisp white shirts, dress shoes, and ties. The hospital was a series of spread out buildings, with open-air walkways and windows.

Janitors swept the ubiquitous dust off the floors. Patient cots were organized in long open rooms. There were scant few nurses for the number of patients.[137] The patients' families were thus put to work, helping with hygiene and medical care. The hospital only had four ventilator machines. If a patient required long-term ventilation, the family would be tasked with squeezing a bag for each breath, rather than utilize one of the few machines. Gauze, tape, and linens—material that Americans would casually throw away—were carefully cleaned and reused.

Dave and I were taken to the operating theater, where we met the attending neurosurgeon, Dr. K. He was a large, regal man with a meaty handshake and a warm smile. He was kind and dedicated, but I got the distinct impression that he'd be very good in a fight. He had trained in parts of Africa, Japan, and India. We introduced ourselves, thanked him for the opportunity to visit, and took a tour. The theater had closed windows and Spartan equipment. There was very little lighting and none of the opulent technology in my normal OR. But the equipment was clean and well maintained.

The best part of the operating theater was that cooks brought amazingly good food into the staging area for our lunch. We also had teatime. Dave and I were introduced to *ugali* (cornmeal), goat,

---

[137] Soapbox aside, if you ever hear a hospital administrator say the hospital is full and there are "no beds," I'll wager he or she really means there are not enough nurses. Regulations limit the number of patients per nurse, so, even though there may be *floors* of empty rooms in an American hospital, the hospital has "no beds." In Africa, patients get piled in and the nurses do the best they can. In America, we think it's better to block them from entering the hospital. We suck.

Kenyan pilau (spiced rice), *wali wa nazi* (coconut rice), and my favorite, chapati bread. We ate with our OR team, relaxed, and mentally prepared for the next case. I felt this practice was joyous and conducive to a team spirit. This contrasted with the rough and hurried hospital lunch in America, where I would sprint to my office to hide and catch up on dictating my EMR charts. Teatime felt kind of dignified.

Dr. K. had lined up multiple surgical patients for our trip. We evaluated them and introduced ourselves with Dr. K. as the translator, if needed. Most of the people spoke English. Dr. K. had one trainee, a perpetually smiling, enthusiastic young man named Godfrey. In Kenya, the residents must pay for surgical training. This is a tremendous disincentive for any prospective surgeon. Godfrey not only volunteered for training, but he had to pay his own way.

Over the next week, Dave and I operated on a number of fascinating adults and children.

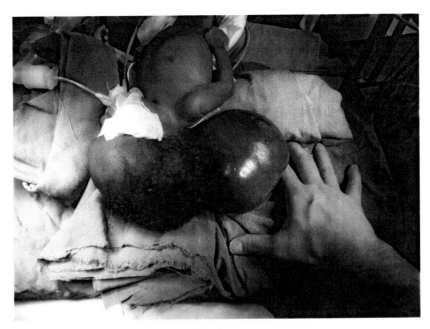

Egads …

We treated adults with brain and spine tumors, children with spina bifida and hydrocephalus, and a teenager with a particularly difficult craniopharyngioma.

Dr. K. tried to translate the results for the teenager's family. Dave and I noticed that the other Kenyans seemed nervous around them. They kept their distance and avoided eye contact.

"He is a *Maasai*, cattle people. His people believe that all cattle on earth are given to them by God and that they have the right to take them. If they come to take your cattle and you try to stop them, they may kill you."

Dave and I assessed his family. They looked fierce. We were quite thankful that the teenager did well with the surgery. We were even more thankful that we weren't carrying any cows.

"Many people here live off their animals," Dr. K. continued. "Farmers will build a nice home for their animals, but the farmers will sleep in a little shack. The farmer is more worried about the safety of the animals than his own."

"Maasai women are also married to *all* the men. Not just one husband. So if a man lives with the woman and his friend wants to be with her, the man has to leave." Dr. K. shook his head disapprovingly. This practice encouraged the transmission of HIV.

For the next week, Dave and I dressed in our nicest shirts and ties and arrived in the hospital early each morning. The protocol was to change into crisp white scrubs and our designated OR shoes. We would then be in theater all day. We scrubbed with alcohol ("spirit") and picked out the few instruments we recognized. The patient's imaging studies were usually two to three months old. We taped these printed films to the light. No fancy-schmancy computer-generated images sullied with screen savers!

The journey to the hospital was arduous for the patients. They would often have to walk, sometimes hundreds of miles, and leave behind their homes and jobs. Many families traveled together. Some had to abandon the family farm. Patients only came to the hospital for life-threatening events. Despite all their hardships, the families were unfailingly grateful. I couldn't help but contrast the sacrifice these families would make with the selfish dirtbagitude of people like Jocelyn.

The hospital threw a large celebration during the week. Dave and I were a little embarrassed about the fuss, but we soon we began to enjoy the food and company. The Kenyan staff was reserved but unfailingly kind and polite. Once they relaxed, however, they were filled with an unbridled joy. After the party, we retreated to a nearby golf club.

"Do you play golf?" I asked Dr. K.

"No time. I work and then tend my farm."

We happened to be in the country during the summer Olympics. All the Kenyans gathered around the television to watch the distance-running events. The contests started, and the reserved, dignified doctors began shouting like a drunken Jets fans. They yelled and cheered. They smacked each other on the back. They personally knew many of the runners, as the elite often trained in the area.

"You see, this is the strategy …" Dr. K. said, grabbing me in a hearty embrace. "This one is *the rabbit.*"

Strategy? Don't you just run fast?

He realized I had no idea about the intricacies of distance running and began to laugh. He had a full, rich, booming laugh. He looked at me with a little pity, realizing I was uneducated in the art of the track. He explained how the runners worked as a team. He explained each of the athlete's jobs. For some Kenyans, running was life.

Godfrey said, "When I was little, I used to run to school. We had an hour for lunch, so I would run home. Then I'd run back. Then we'd race home after school. It was great!"

"How far away was your school?" I asked.

"About six kilometers."

The Kenyans took great pride in their athletes, and I felt a thrill when a local runner won one of the women's events.

After our time of surgeries, Dave and I went on safari. Kenya is spectacular. Dr. K. arranged for two gents to drive us to a scenic vista overlooking the Great Rift Valley. There was a small but fancy inn at the top of this peak. We saw many European runners in uniforms. This area was a favored training destination for elite runners because of the altitude and tradition. The valley had clearings and a few farmhouses, but I felt like I was looking back in time. There were no gauche lights or tacky postcards. There was just ancient nature. We also saw many wild monkeys doing their business, completely unafraid of people.

Spectacular!

We drove to the rift in a vintage Toyota. The road was dusty and filled with governors. We were stopped twice for stalled vehicles, and our car overheated. Our guides remained in good spirits despite the stalls. They spoke reasonable English, but they really shined in singing along to their music of choice: old American country music. They crooned happily and lustily with Chet Akins, Mickey Gilley, and Johnny Cash.

I showed them pictures of my kids, and they nodded and smiled with approval. "Very strong looking! Healthy!"

"This is my father," the leader of the two said. He showed me a picture of a man surrounded by three women. He pointed to the oldest woman. "She is my mother. But my father grew wealthy, so he figured he could afford another wife. That is her. Then he grew even more wealthy so he got a third."

I'm not sure how my Lovely Wife would react to that idea. I think I'll ask.

As we flew back to the States, I felt both happy and guilty. I was happy for the experience and grateful for the hospitality. Dave and I realized that we would likely never again see some of the surgical pathology that we treated. We felt proud to operate like the Old Dogs—reliant on anatomic knowledge and surgical training rather than technology. We felt happy to experience the exotic land and meet the people. We were buoyed by their kindness and passion.

But I felt guilty. I felt guilty that I would complain about my call schedule. Dr. K. was the only practicing neurosurgeon in the northern half of the country. In fact, when we asked him what he needed most, he answered, "A vacation." I'm not sure Godfrey slept the entire time we were there. This young man, paying his own salary, stayed in the hospital every night, tending to his patients.

I also felt a letdown the next time I had an adult clinic. I realized the hardships that families in Kenya endured to get their loved one to the hospital. There was a period of adjustment for me, where I struggled to find meaning in a young healthy male belligerently demanding disability paperwork for back pain.

I also returned with an idea that I believe should be mandatory in all American hospitals:

Let's put it right outside the CEO's office.

Chapter 30

The Fall of Thomas

Thomas stared across his office, helpless behind a mountain of charts. He still insisted on writing a complete, full-page note by hand and then reading it to a dictation machine. This process took hours, and he was behind by months.

"I think the only reason I have a car is to transport charts."

Thomas was on vacation that week, so naturally, he was in the office and had three scheduled surgeries.

"Are you doing anything fun on your week off?" I asked.

"Does dictating count?"

"No."

He paused. "Well then, no."

"Are you at least going to get out of here early?"

"Then I'd have to go home. Home is a vacation from the office, but the office is a vacation from home." He looked sad and frailer than usual.

"Problems at home?" I asked.

Thomas sighed deeply and looked down.

His pager went off. He recognized the number as one of the adult patients. "I'll bet she lost her meds again."

"How do you know that?" I asked.

"Because she paged me about five times throughout the night."

"I thought you weren't seeing adults anymore? I can take over her care."

Thomas sighed again, too tired to throw me a quick quip or joke. "I'm really not feeling so good."

The charts were no mere annoyance. Thomas was no longer part of a family; he was part of a business. If the chart wasn't completed, the group and the hospital couldn't bill the patient. Thomas didn't care one whit about who was billed, but both the group and the hospital did. Also, the government cared. If the billing was not supported by the dictation on a Medicare or a Medicaid patient, Thomas had technically committed Medicare fraud. The suits were concerned and angry. Thomas was way behind, because his method was so labor intensive.

Thomas got paged again. Someone on the other end asked him for money.

"The beauty of spending all my money is that soon I won't have any for people to ask for."

"That doesn't sound like a good retirement plan," I said.

"I'm really hoping my lottery investment will pay off. I really feel I have a good shot; I'm just as qualified as anyone else." He chuckled to himself. He pulled out a ketchup packet, opened it, smeared it on his index finger, and licked it. I wondered if that would be the only thing he'd eat that day.

"What would you do if you won the lottery?"

"Probably lose it all."

Thomas was paged again. Another patient.

"Enjoy your vacation," I muttered.

*   *   *   *

Thomas began to have meetings with corporate and the hospitals. He had to get his dictations done. He doggedly insisted on his out-dated, time-intensive way of handwriting. He tried to explain why to me once—something about being worried that the dictating service would lose what he said. I retorted that he always remembered every-thing anyway, so in the rare event that this happened, he could just do it again. That logic seemed foreign to him. He couldn't figure out the new computer system, especially since there were multiple systems for multiple hospitals and none interfaced. He started to give up. He couldn't make himself care about business. All he wanted to do was help the sickest children.

Thomas drifted further down. We rallied together to remind him to change his scrubs. His hair suggested "mountain man writing a manifesto" rather than "experienced neurosurgeon." The residents and the office staff would bring him food and implore him to eat something. His spindly limbs moved slower. He walked with a shuf-fling gait, head cocked to one side, thinking about whatever geniuses think about.

When he was at the office, he felt guilty about not being home. When he was home, he wanted to be at the office. He stayed awake much of the night, writing his charts and answering the ever-insistent pager. He talked less. He sighed more.

The new department chairman called me into his office.

"What's happening with Thomas?" he asked.

"He's at a low point. He does this sometimes."

"The dean has taken notice. You know Thomas is not tenured. He could be fired."

I wondered why he wasn't tenured. His academic rank hadn't changed in decades. I'd guess it was because he never got around to filling out the paperwork.

The chairman continued, "People have noticed his health, his dress. A lot of people are worried about him. Worried about more than his charts. You've known him for a while. What do you think?"

Steve's words echoed in my thoughts: *You can't fix Thomas.*

"I think Thomas can be very passive-aggressive. He needs to be nurtured. If you push him, he'll resist. In fact, I sometimes think he wants to be fired. It would give him an excuse to throw away the pager."

"Can you talk to him?"

"I'll try," I answered.

"This isn't the first time Thomas's been in trouble."

"I know."

"But we're all under a microscope here. Some of this is out of my hands. If he can't catch up on his charts, the hospital is going to suspend his privileges. They feel that they are at legal risk and won't tolerate it. I want you to take some of his patients until he's caught up."

"I can do that."

The chairman thought for a while. "So does he have any financial savings?"

"I doubt it. Thomas says all his money is invested in 'consumer goods.'" I smiled.

The chairman didn't get the joke.

"Uh, because his various hangers-on spend all his money on stuff. Thomas's joke, not mine."

The chairman was not amused.

"What's his retirement plan?"

"I really don't think he has one. Quite honestly, I don't ever see him retiring."

"He has to retire sometime."

"Well, when I was in Japan, there was a word called *karoshi*. This meant someone who literally worked himself to death. Sometimes I think that's Thomas's retirement plan."

The chairman looked disturbed. He sighed and folded his arms. "We need to think of something."

* * * *

Thomas accepted the transfer of a child with a large brain tumor. The child was evaluated, imaged, treated, and taken to surgery the next day. I had a case in another room. Thomas looked haggard.

"You cool to do this case?" I asked him in the morning.

"Oh yeah," Thomas said reassuringly.

"Did you eat something?"

"I had a salad last night. It was really good. Really. Except there was one bad tomato. I always eat the cherry tomatoes first. You know these things? I figure three good ones aren't worth one bad one, so I eat them first to get the bad one out of the way."

"How about today?"

"Coffee."

"Need any help?"

"Nah, I'm golden."

I started my case. I was worried about Thomas, but right then, the patient on the table demanded my full attention. Luckily, it was a short surgery and things were going well.

Dana popped into the room.

"How much longer do you have?" she asked. This was an unusual question. Usually it means that someone needs the operating room for an emergency. But I wasn't in the emergency room. "Not long."

She looked frightened. This was also unusual for her. She had been through the trials of complex surgeries on deathly ill children. She rarely lost her cool or gave any hint of losing control. After all, she had smoothly and expertly navigated the operative chaos of the first night with Mikey.

"Thomas may need your help."

"Ah. Well, I'm almost done. I can stop by in a little bit."

"Okay," she said, unsure of what to do next. She hesitated, I think somehow hoping I could come now. But she knew I couldn't leave the current surgery. She shuffled out of the room.

I looked at my scrub nurse. We didn't say a word, but we were both thinking the same thing: *We'd better get this case done quickly.*

I finished and walked out of the room, intent on going to see the parents of my patient and then checking on Thomas.

"Anesthesia stat to room 5."

Suddenly the hallway was filled with people literally sprinting to room 5. This announcement is a true emergency. "Code calls" are announced in the hospital all the time. I would tend to listen for the room number before I got worried. If the following room number was in a zone with sick kids—the ICU, the cardiac floor, the neurosurgery ward—my heart rate would shoot up and I'd run to the area. Much more commonly, the "code" announced the lobby or the cafeteria, usually indicating that someone fainted. But everything is an emergency inside the operating room suites. That announcement meant a child was dying—usually.

In this case, my stomach dropped and a wave of panicked nausea swept over me.

Thomas.

I ran down to room 5. It was packed with people, such that I couldn't open the door. Everyone had a look of frightened concern. I made eye contact with Brian. His face was covered by his surgical mask and all I could see was his wide, alarmed eyes.

I elbowed my way in to survey the room. A child was on the table with a surgically exposed brain. The anesthesia resident was behind the drapes, and Brian was standing motionless. The crowd was away from the patient, surrounding Thomas, who was still gowned, lying on the ground, trying desperately not to touch anything with his hands. The senior anesthesiology attending was kneeling beside him.

"Can you hear me, Thomas?"

Thomas had a vacant look in his wild eyes, and he was shaking.

"Let's get a blood pressure. He's breathing. Hook him up to the pulse ox."

The scrub nurse was gowned but holding Thomas's hand. I think she tried to catch him when he fell. Dana was hovering, feeling the horrible helpless feeling that a parent gets when her child is hurt.

I grabbed her, hopefully kindly but firmly, on the arm. "Let's go."

We hurriedly left the room and scrubbed. She went in first and switched back into command mode. I gowned and surveyed the child. As much as I wanted to help Thomas, I felt that my first duty was to the child.

"Hey, how's it going?" I asked Brian, hoping to lighten the mood.

"Fine," he halfheartedly answered.

"Well, let's see what's going on."

I removed the towel that the resident had placed over the sterile field. I was filled with dread. I worried that I would find some horrible injury in this poor kid's brain.

"No bleeding. That's a good start." I was relieved. They hadn't gotten very far. I could just see the tumor, and the surrounding brain looked fine.

"Well, maybe we should take this thing out."

Brian relaxed. Dana got laser focused, and we began to operate, trying desperately to block out the noise behind us.

I focused on the task at hand but could hear Thomas coming to.

"No, I feel fine. Really, let me up!" he insisted firmly.

"Just stay down, Thomas," the anesthesiologist ordered.

Thomas began ripping off his gown and trying to sit up. He began fighting with the crowd holding him in place.

"Let me up!"

"Just stay down. We're getting a gurney."

"I don't need a gurney! I'm fine! I feel okay! I need to get back to the case!"

"We're going to start an IV."

"I don't want a damn IV! I'm fine!" Thomas was getting more and more agitated. He was struggling but to no avail.

The anesthesia team was nonplussed. "His pressure is better."

"Room 3 is open," one of the technicians announced.

"Okay, let's get him there. I'll start a line," the anesthesiologist ordered.

"I don't want a damn line!"

"Thomas, I'm not asking. This is what we're going to do. We're calling cardiology."

"I don't need a cardiologist! I need to get back to surgery!"

The group brought in a gurney, picked up the kicking skeleton, and hustled him out of the room. The surroundings instantly went from a cacophony of noise to an unsettling silence. Only the steady beep of the monitor was heard.

After working for a while, I looked at Brian.

"What happened?"

"I don't know. He stood up, wobbled for a bit, and then went down."

"Anything bad happen to the kid?"

"I don't think so."

After about an hour, Thomas burst back into the room, trailed by a few of the OR staff, trying to restrain him.

"We've got it covered," Dana said.

Thomas was not going to be denied; he hustled to the sink despite the protests of the staff around him. He pushed his way to the scrub station and washed his hands, muttering that he was "fine" the whole time.

Thomas came back into the room in a ball of fury, hands dripping, eyes angry and defiant. Dana looked at me silently, asking if she should gown him. I gave a curt affirmative nod.

Thomas elbowed Brian out of the way. He was breathing hard. He was clearly furious. I'm not sure at what. He grabbed a sucker and then dangerously and recklessly thrust it into the field.

"Whoa!" I said, grabbing his hand. I needed to calm him down.

"Can you bring in the microscope please?" I asked. This gave us a few minutes. "Let me catch you up on the case."

Thomas looked around at the group of OR staff and anesthesiologists who had assembled behind him. He wanted to lash out at them. "I'm fine!" He seemed as dangerous as a wounded animal. "I'm fine!"

I looked at Brian. "Will you go check on my patient? Also, I never was able to go talk to the family …"

"I'll do it," Brian said. I think he was relieved to have an exit strategy.

The microscope was prepared. "Can we get two sitting stools?" I asked.

"I don't need to sit!"

Thomas was lashing out at anything that dared suggest he couldn't do the case. He had a feral look in his eyes. He felt angrily emasculated at the anesthesia team for resuscitating him. I'll bet he was angry with Dana and me. I can't begin to understand his thought processes, but I'll bet he was angry at the betrayal of his own worn body. After years of patchy sleep and ketchup packets, the body was going on strike. He was angry that people—who loved him—were hovering behind him.

"I know, but *I* need to sit. I don't have your stamina. I get tired during these cases," I said.

"I'll keep standing," Thomas hissed.

I lowered the bed as far as it would go and then brought the microscope as low as it would go. I placed it lower than I normally would, putting myself in an uncomfortable position. There was no way Thomas could see without sitting. Begrudgingly, he sat in a huff.

He stuck his sucker back into the wound. I grabbed his hand again.

"Let me show you around first," I said, "you know, to get you oriented."

This seemed to make sense to him.

I maneuvered the microscope around, showing Thomas the relevant anatomy, continuing to operate the whole time. We settled with the scope in a more normal position where we were both comfortable. I kept my hands between his and the patient and kept quietly commenting about the tumor, the borders, the blood supply, and the surrounding brain. Thomas began to lose himself in the surgery. His tense arms relaxed. His back, rigid and bracing for a fight, softened.

Gradually, slowly, Thomas came back to us.

"I hope this isn't interrupting your day," he said in the kind voice I knew and loved. When he said this, Dana visibly relaxed.

"Well, it's almost one. The Professor and I were set to tee off at noon," I joked.

Thomas laughed.

I jumped into my imitation of the Professor's voice: "Thomas, I putt *like a god*."

Thomas laughed again. I kept going, imitating the Professor talking smack about the other attendings.

Still in Professor voice, I said, "And so Dr. Montgomery called me into the room and asked me what he should do with the aneurysm. I said, 'You should dissect it out and clip it.' He didn't like that answer! *Hehehehehehehe!*"

Thomas was amused at my imitation. I don't like to brag,[138] but I was pretty good at mimicking the Professor's laugh. I wasn't as good as Bryce, but I was in the neighborhood. Dr. Montgomery, like the Professor, was Jewish.

"I had a kid with an aneurysm that I sent to the adult side," Thomas said, now back in relaxed story mode. "Dr. Montgomery was upset that I sent the patient to the Professor instead of him. I said, 'Well, I told them to send him to the old bald Jewish guy, and I guess they got the wrong one!'"

Dana got the hint and jumped into the conversation. She knew and loved the Professor. "What was that thing you had him do the other day?"

"Thomas, you'll like this," I began. "So I had a kid with a shunt infection—"

"I don't like it so far ..."

"Right. Anyway, we were putting the shunt back and the Professor happened to call. He has some Hebrew chant he does to ward off infection. So we put him on speakerphone and asked him to do it."

"It was awesome!" Dana added.

"And?" Thomas asked.

"No infection! The Professor is magic."

Thomas was now relaxed, looking like a puppy after getting the Cesar Milan treatment. The case continued. Thomas took the hint and didn't reach into the wound. He folded his arms and then began telling stories. The anesthesia team filtered out, satisfied that Thomas was out of danger.

The tumor finally popped out. I inspected the area and was happy with the result. Thomas was impressed. We closed and woke the child up. He was fine.

---

[138] Editor's note: total lie.

We left the room happy, but then a dread began to sink in. There was no way to cover this up. There was no way the dean and the chairman were going to be kept in the dark.

Thomas seemed happy as we talked to the family. He explained that he felt sick and asked me to help. The family seemed initially baffled, but Thomas's reassuring kind words helped. They seemed okay with things. I told them that Thomas and I would work together in the postoperative care of their child. The postoperative imaging showed that we had achieved complete removal of the tumor, and after the expected recovery time, the child was discharged home in very good condition.

Thomas was smiling as we walked back to the office.

"Thanks," he said.

"No problem," I said. We parted. I was happy with the case but worried. There was no way around it—we were going to lose Thomas.

CHAPTER 31

The Prom Queen

"Daaaaaaaaaaaad, I have a headache!"

"I'm watching football."

"But it huuuuuuuuuuuurts!"

Sigh.

Six-year-old plants himself directly in my line of sight, his hobbit hair completely obscuring the television. I heroically resist the urge to scream obscenities while looking over the kid to see this crucial second-quarter play. It is the fourth game of the season after all.

"You want some Tylenol?"

No. He just wanted attention.

"Can we play catch?"

"Sure, just as soon as this game, uh, and the next one are over. Four hours max. Maybe five. Go find your mother."

Typical fall Sunday ...

*   *   *   *

She was six, and she was beautiful. Her name was Katie, and she had fair skin with freckles and strawberry-blond hair like her mother. She danced. She watched TV, and she played.

She began having headaches. I imagine they were pretty innocuous at first. Tylenol fixed them. Then it didn't. Then the headaches became more frequent and she started to see funny. She got glasses. They didn't help. In the miasma of everything a single mom has to do in a day, this was really getting to be a bother.

The little girl kept dancing. She tilted her head a lot. Her headaches were more frequent. She stopped dancing.

Groceries, bills, football—suddenly it didn't matter. Those are things that matter when nothing is wrong. Well, we all have our issues. But now Katie wasn't dancing, watching TV, or playing. Something was wrong—not complain-to-your-friends wrong but *wrong* wrong. The pediatrician sensed her mom's alarm and ordered an MRI. The technician sensed that something was wrong and called his radiologist boss during the scan. The radiologist knew something was wrong and called me. I went to talk to Mom while Katie was still in the scanner.

"She was fine ... really." Mom paced around the waiting room with nervous energy. Multiple phone calls and a surgeon coming to see you during the scan are not normal, right? Mom's dad sat with a stern, angry look. "We got the glasses; we, uh, we were doing what we could ..." She wouldn't sit. She paced, perhaps recalling some genetic instinct to fight anything that threatened her child.

"We need to find a quiet spot," I said.

"This is quiet!" Granddad shouted loudly, eliciting odd looks from the other people in the room.

"Maybe a more private spot," I ventured.

We walked to an empty room near the scanner. An MRI makes a lot of noise. There's a mechanical whir followed by a click as each picture is taken. It's remarkable technology, really. But it's big and frightening. An entire room is strictly maintained for a giant machine with a hole in the middle. Patients must be absolutely still, so the head is often strapped to a holder. Right in the center of this huge, loud, angry-sounding machine were two tiny dancing feet.

"How much longer?" Mom asked.

The technician didn't meet her eyes. "About thirty minutes. The radiologist wants to check her spine."

"Spine? She has a headache!"

Since the child was still in the scanner, the only place for us to look at the images together was in the control room. We tried to block out the sound, and I pulled up the first pictures.

Granddad was pacing.

"Here," I said, pulling up a wheeled chair. "Have a seat."

"Don't wanna."

"Please."

Katie had a brain tumor. It expanded a part of her brainstem called the *pons*. The pons is normally jovially round, the gentle pot-belly of the brainstem. Katie's was swollen beyond belief, nauseatingly infested with tumor. The tumor had angrily exploded out the side and spewed onto the surrounding nerves, blood vessels, and cerebellum.

I looked in the window of the MRI scanner and saw the two little feet moving rhythmically. She did like to dance. The head holder in the Baby Hospital was rigged so that a child could watch a movie during the procedure. They must have gotten to a musical number. I imagined Katie smiling and imagining dancing along with whatever talking animals were singing on the screen.

I took a deep breath. The diagnosis was clear. Only one thing— one horrible, unrelenting thing—looked like this.

Katie was going to die.

Soon.

This was a *diffuse intrinsic pontine glioma* or DIPG. The brainstem is divided into three main parts—the midbrain, the pons, and the medulla. These areas control the basic functions of being alive. A *glioma* is a tumor growing from the supporting cells around the nerves. It can be high-grade or malignant. A malignant glioma (glioblastoma mutliforme) killed Merlin. A low-grade glioma may be cured if we can resect it.

A low-grade glioma in the midbrain, a scant half-inch above Katie's tumor, usually grows in a discrete ball. It's tricky, but it can be removed and cured. A glioma in the medulla, a scant half-inch below Katie's, can sometimes be resected and usually is very indolent. But the exact same tumor in the pons intertwines with all the nerves and relentlessly progresses. Children die usually within a year. And there's nothing we can do about it. In Katie's case, the tumor was not only growing in the pons but growing fast enough to spread. That's pretty rare and even worse.

We try to treat it. She wouldn't survive the surgery if we tried to resect it. So we try radiation. We try chemotherapy. This tumor is unusually cruel. It *responds* to treatment. It will shrink. It may even look like it's going away. But then, almost sadistically, it always comes back. Treatment buys some time but never cures it.

Our ability to treat this entity has not really changed much in the past fifty years or so. Maybe we can diagnose it earlier with modern imaging. There's a controversy in pediatric neurosurgery regarding biopsy. A biopsy is normally done to confirm or provide a diagnosis. We can do that on MRI. Nothing looks quite like a DIPG. A biopsy may also be used to grade the aggressiveness of a tumor. The grading of a DIPG is tricky. Based purely on findings on the pathology slide, the tumor may be low grade or slow moving. Sometimes it looks more aggressive. But in this case, it doesn't matter. If the biopsy shows a high-grade tumor, we know the child will likely die within a year. If the biopsy shows a low-grade tumor, we know the child will likely die within a year.

For me, this is the worst diagnosis to have to explain to a mom. Horrible as it is, parents can wrap their brain around trauma. People understand that there's a bad problem if the child is vomiting or losing consciousness. Katie had headaches and double vision. That's it. And now I'm supposed to tell her mom that she's got less than a year to live and we can't do anything?

I hate that tumor.

I went over the films, explained why we had to check her spine,[139] and showed Mom and Granddad the tumor. Mom sat stone-faced. Granddad got up and paced, furious.

"So nothing you can do?" he hissed.

"We're going to call our oncologists. We'll need to bring her into the hospital. We'll make a plan, and we'll do the best we can."

"But it won't work?" he demanded.

"I can't tell you how Katie will react to treatment, but if we have a large group of kids, very few survive past one year."

"Well, that's just not acceptable."

"I agree," I said.

"Well, we'll just take her to a better hospital. I'm just not going to give up!"

"We're not giving up. We'll do everything we can."

"I don't care where we have to go; we'll find someone who cares about my granddaughter enough to do something!"

I didn't say anything. Mom's eyes never left me. The buzzzzzzz-click of the machine continued.

"This is just ... This is just ... *She's just a little girl!*" Granddad paced more furiously, wringing his hands and looking for something to punch. "You mean to tell me *nothing* will help her? This is amateur

---

[139] To see if the tumor had spread downward.

hour!" His voice dropped from angry ranting to seething hatred. "We'll find someplace that can treat her."

I didn't say anything.

Unfortunately, this was not my first time discussing this diagnosis. Granddad's reaction is pretty typical. I'd be angry too. I *was* angry, and I hadn't even met the little girl. The only thing I really knew of her was her tapping feet. It's natural for doctors to take offense at a parent accusing us of incompetence or of not caring. I've seen doctors argue back, and that really doesn't help anything. Maybe the best thing I can do for this family is be a target for their anger.

People commonly want to go "someplace else." Merlin used to say that a specialist was a doctor who was more than an hour's drive away. I just gave the family the diagnosis. From then on, Mom and Granddad would associate me with the worst news of their entire lives. Chemotherapy is the same, regardless of the hospital. There's no advantage to going anywhere for chemotherapy. Radiation is also pretty much the same. There are some places with a noted surgeon. Sometimes that's worth a trip. Often it's not. Some of the most famous surgeons in this country are hacks who publish a lot. In this case, it didn't matter. Surgery wouldn't help.

The MRI finished, and I got to meet Katie.

"Hello," she said with a matter-of-fact tone.

"What were you watching?"

"*Mulan.*"

"Did you like Mushu?"

She smiled. One side of the face went higher than the other. "Have you seen it?"

"Only about a hundred times." I began singing, "Aaaaaahhhlll maaake a maaaaaaan out of you!"[140]

---

[140] I defy you to name a movie that couldn't be improved by adding Donny Osmond.

She grinned. We had connected. I showed her my penlight. She tried to follow it, but her eyes wouldn't work together and she got frustrated. She had good strength in her arms, but one side was a little better than the other. She didn't look sick. Without knowledge of subtle cranial nerve findings, one would say she looked normal.

"I liked the bug," she said to no one in particular.

"Me too. We could all use a lucky bug."

* * * *

Katie began chemotherapy and radiation therapy. She was treated with Botox for double vision. Did you know there are actual uses for Botox rather than turning once pretty ladies into soulless mannequins with faces of desperation?

The tumor grew relentlessly. It didn't even have the decency to shrink initially to give false hope. The oncologists asked me to resect part of it to see if it was some other horrible tumor mimicking a DIPG. There was a nodule on the back of the cerebellum, away from the inoperable part. It was reasonably easy to remove. The diagnosis was confirmed. This was a letdown. Although we knew the diagnosis, we were hoping it was a pathologically different tumor that we could treat.

Katie slowly got worse. The one weak side became totally paralyzed. Her eyes dropped to the point where she couldn't open one of them without using her one good hand. I would see her from time to time in the hospital.

"Hi, Katie. How are you?"

"Fine." She would then sigh. "I can't dance."

"Really? Not even a little bit?"

She sighed again. "No."

"How about like this?" I then broke into an awkward white guy

overbite ~~convulsion~~ dance.[141] My dancing is like a jalapeño slider—
horrible, instantly regrettable, and sure to cause nausea and time on
the toilet. Tragically, I didn't have to exaggerate for comedic effect.

Katie giggled. "I guess I could do *that*."

She shimmied her one good arm and bobbed her head. She had a
big, happy grin on half of her face.

"Perfect!" I said. "You are *almost* as good as me."

*   *   *   *

The oncologists threw everything they had at her. They delved into
experimental protocols. Nothing worked. The tumor kept spreading.

Two months later, Katie was vomiting terribly. We checked a CT
scan. Her ventricles were grossly enlarged and pushing on her surrounding brain. Her one eye was completely closed. The other one
was closing. Her pupils weren't reacting. Somehow, she was awake.

"Katie? How are you?"

"Fine."

"Do you feel sick?"

She sighed. "Yes. But I'm fine."

Granddad was seething again. Mom was quiet. I took them to
another room.

"We can place a shunt, drain her spinal fluid," I offered.

"Will that help?" Mom asked.

"In the short term. She'll feel better. I think she's sicker because
the spinal fluid is building up."

"Okay."

"Now, I hesitate to bring this up, but I need to tell you about the

---

[141] I wanted to insert a link to the video of me dancing at my wedding, but for some
reason, the Lovely Wife burned all the copies. Can't imagine why.

other option." I really didn't want to say this with Granddad around, but I felt it was my duty. "We could *not* place a shunt."

"And what would happen?" Mom asked quietly.

Granddad's face began to flush red.

"She'd die."

Granddad stormed out of the room. Mom didn't react. She thought for a while.

"How much time would the shunt buy us?"

"That will depend on the tumor. It will fix what's making her sick right now but not the real problem."

She thought again.

"Do it."

We took her to surgery and placed the shunt. Katie felt better. Three days later, her shunt failed. Thomas fixed it in the dead of night, and she felt better again. Katie finished all chemotherapy options and went home.

I saw her back in clinic a few weeks later. Her incisions were all healed. One eye was closed. The other was slightly open. It was probably for the best because the eye muscles weren't working. One eye closed prevented double vision, which can be very uncomfortable. She was in a wheelchair. She looked like a fragile porcelain doll.

Mom was smiling gently, comfortingly. Granddad was seething.

"Hi, Katie. How are you?"

"Fine."

Granddad burst in. "What else can you do?" he shouted.

"*Dad*!" Mom yelled, grabbing his arm.

"Don't tell me that *God* will take care of things! Don't tell me that! How can a 'god' let this happen to a little girl? Tell me that!" He stormed out of the room, eyes flooding with tears.

Katie didn't move. Mom sighed and smiled again. I wasn't sure what to do next.

Mom broke the silence. "Katie, should we ask the doctor to dance again?"

Katie smiled her sickly half smile and giggled. "No!"

"Katie, should we show him the pictures?" Mom asked, gently placing her hand on Katie's. Katie's face brightened. *"Yes!"*

"Do you want to tell him what you did?"

"I went to prom!"

Katie's mom produced her phone and started scrolling through a bunch of pictures. There was Katie's school, decorated in tinsel and streamers, with a group of schoolkids—some Katie's age, some looking like they were in high school—all dressed in gowns and tuxedos. There were teachers. There was Katie getting lifted out of her chair by two dashing high school students.

They were dancing. Katie was smiling. There were action shots of the gents twirling her around. Then she was sitting on a throne with a crown. The school had thrown a special prom. Katie was the prom queen.

"You were dancing ..." I whispered. Barely. I could barely speak.

"I was dancing," Katie said softly, smiling.

Mom smiled too. She knew.

"You are a beautiful dancer," I said.

Katie paused.

"Better than you!"

I couldn't argue with that.

"You really are a beautiful prom queen," I said.

Katie smiled.

She died within the week.

*   *   *   *

How do you answer Granddad's question? How do you justify a loving God with the relentless destruction of a six-year-old child? The greatest philosophers in history have wrestled with this question for centuries. I don't know the answer. But sometimes I have to *give* an answer. Sometimes Granddad doesn't storm out but stares at me expecting me to say something.

Is there a God? Should we start with this? Is it okay for a doctor to share his or her personal beliefs? Should religion ever play a part, or is medicine a calculated agnostic endeavor?

It's hard *not* to ask the God question, working at the Baby Hospital. I think it's a myth that doctors (scientists for that matter) are all atheists. I've found the opposite to be true. Most of the doctors at the Baby Hospital are religious to some degree. I also think it's a myth that "scientists" are universally atheists. Sure, many are. But not all.

I have a simpleton's interest in theoretical physics. Physicists are enamored with finding the TOE—the "theory of everything." They have a fundamental belief that there is a TOE that will explain everything. Maybe string theory or M theory or cosmic expansion or whatever is the hot topic of the day. Religious or agnostic, I've found that scientists believe that such a theory exists.

Why?

Why should it exist? Why does it matter? Why does the most hard-core atheist physicist believe that there *needs* to be a theory of everything?

I think there's a fundamental knowledge (not belief) that there is an underlying harmony in the universe. I can't look into the night sky without being awed by the beauty. I can't study theoretical physics without being astounded by the resonance. I love reading amateurishly about string theory, the theory that everything—space, time, matter, atoms, quarks, penguins, *everything*—is composed of the interaction of tiny vibrating violin strings. I love that thought.

Music.

The universe is made of music. The universe is the song of God.

I have more higher education than one person should ever have. I've studied in labs and published many scientific papers. The more I study the brain, the more I'm convinced of one thing: it's beautiful.

The world is beautiful. The sky is beautiful. The brain is beautiful. How is that not evidence of God? Sometimes I'll be shaken out of my football coma and actually look at my child. I'll see his wide wet eyes and moppet hair, gloriously uncombed and tangled. I'll see his wide smile with the wonky teeth and pure joy if I leave the couch. I'll be so overcome with love that I feel short of breath. How do we explain love without a basis in something other than chance?

I don't know the answers to Granddad's question, but I know there's a God. Not a God characterized by the vomitus politics of the day. But a God characterized by love. A Creator. A Songwriter.

What about a six-year-old with a horrible, fatal tumor?

I don't know. I really don't. I could tell Granddad some esoteric, flaccid explanation about big-picture and perspective, but that's all hollow. I just don't know.

But that last clinic appointment, that last time I saw Katie, I could look at her and see heaven. I don't ask you to understand or even believe me, but I could see it. Just as clear as I can see Death. I saw heaven through Katie. It's not that I think I see it; I *know* I see it, just as I see heaven in the eyes of my bratty kid or any of my other hundreds of patients. I know there's value. I know there's love. I know that there's a loving God welcoming Katie into heaven. I could see it. I can't explain it. I can't begin to ease the stabbing hurt in Katie's family. I won't even try. But there is heaven.

It's a nice place. There's no cancer. Katie dances there.

CHAPTER 32

Is It Worth It?

Thomas stumbled into his office, accidentally scattering a pile of charts that were haphazardly stacked by his desk. He arrived in a rush and then slumped in his chair, looking smaller than ever. He grimaced in anguish and then tried to log on to his computer. It wasn't working. Exasperated, he stared at it for a while. Then he began to speak softly to it, hoping it would be the one thing in his life that would help him.

"Boss?" I started.

Thomas sighed deeply, eyes transfixed on the black screen.

I continued, "You don't look too hot."

"Oh, I was here until two,[142] then had to go home and my girl-friend wanted to watch a movie, then I had to get up to fix breakfast, and now ..."

"And now your computer doesn't work."

"And now my computer doesn't work," his voice trailed. The world was betraying him.

"Let me take a look." I reached over and summoning all the technical expertise that an engineering degree from Golden U had to offer, made the genius move of turning it off and then on again.

---

[142] I knew he meant *a.m.*

It began to boot up. His background photo—his kids in happier times—popped up.

"Thanks. They're meeting today."

"The hospital committee?" I asked.

"Yep. They're going to decide if I can operate or not."

He looked frail. Like a nursing home patient.

My grandmother, God rest her soul, suffered from Alzheimer's disease late in life. She declined slowly, almost imperceptibly at first. Exquisitely cultured, she made up for lack of memory with smiles, nods, and good manners. It was honestly years before anyone noticed she was really slipping. She was happy during these years. Rather than being scared for the future, she was living in the past.

As her memory continued to fade, she traveled further and further back in time. She became a child again. She was a child of the Great Depression. Fairly wealthy in later life, she began in poverty, as did many in small-town Indiana during this time. So, she instinctively did her chores, including starting the house fire for warmth. My mother moved in with my grandmother to help. My grandmother spent most of her day puttering about the yard, looking for suitable kindling to start the fire to cook dinner.

Thomas was reverting to instinct. He was unable to see into the future because all it held was blackness. We had adapted to the new rules and new EMR. Each day, all of us got new e-mails of different training modules and regulations and required classes and yearly sensitivity training and all the other rot the vast bureaucratic hordes could crap out. Thomas couldn't handle it. He began to snap at the office staff, yelling, pouting, and then almost aggressively volunteered for more work. He saw more and more patients, cared for more and more sick kids, got more and more behind on his charting, and became more and more desperate.

My grandmother declined, as all Alzheimer's patients do.

Eventually, she was moved to a nursing home. She didn't recognize her family. She became a frail, gnarled Oliver Twist. She would sneak around, stealing other the residents' pudding and looking for kindling. Eventually she became wheelchair- and then bed-bound. She was happy, but as soon as one of the nurses moved her, she grew violently angry and lashed out.

"Stopitstopitstopit! You leave me alone!"

"You need a bath, Ms. Nixon."

"Nononononono!"

She didn't know. She didn't understand. She was scared.

The office manager was growing exasperated.

"Thomas, we can't schedule your procedure until you do the dictation!"

Thomas bristled. "Well, I'll tell you what; here's the deal. Last night, I had to take my son to his show, and then I got called from the ER. I wasn't on call, but I came in anyway, then I got called from a mom in Goshen, then I got home, then I had to make breakfast, then ..."

"I understand all that, Thomas, but I still *can't* schedule the surgery until you enter the orders and do the dictation!"

"This kid is a ward of the state, and I have set out the day ..."

"Thomas, you're not listening! It's not that I don't *want* to schedule the case; it's that I *can't* schedule the case!"

Thomas began to quiver in rage. When he got angry, his voice grew pressured and his eyes became frighteningly wild. I'm sure he knew she was correct, but he was angry. And scared.

"You need a bath, Ms. Nixon. We're going to move you."

"Nononononoyoustopityoustopit!"

"You need to finish your dictations, Thomas."

*   *   *   *

I find it amazing how an epoch can end so unceremoniously. One day, Thomas was the heart and soul of the Baby Hospital. And with the meeting of one committee, he was out. Just out.

"What do you think will happen?" Elizabeth asked, standing in the door of my ~~closet~~ office.

"I don't know."

"Do you think they'll let him operate again?"

"No. Maybe minor cases, but I doubt it. I think this is it."

Elizabeth sighed.

"What do you think he'll do?"

"I don't know. Go on disability, I guess. He's got a valid case—pacemaker and all that."[143]

"I talked to him the other day. I said, 'Thomas, do you even know how much money you spend in a year?' I said, 'How many people are you supporting?'" She then listed all the various people Thomas supported. "I mean, what are all these people going to do once he has no income? I think disability ends at sixty-five."

Elizabeth paused and stared off into space. We were both thinking the same thing.

She continued, "I asked him about his retirement plan. I said, 'Thomas, what's your retirement plan?' He had no idea. He made some joke about the lottery. I really think he's penniless. He cashed in his pension to pay for a house. Now his youngest is going off to college. How is he going to pay for that with no job? ... I swear—it's like I'm watching someone drive a truck off a cliff! I can't hit the brakes for him; all I can do is yell for him to stop."

We paused.

"Maybe he doesn't want to stop," I said softly.

---

[143] Thomas had a pacemaker inserted after he passed out in the OR.

"What?" she said, eyes initially wide and then narrowing in dawning comprehension.

"Maybe he doesn't want to stop," I said again. "Maybe his retirement plan is to die."

While this plan had been obvious to me for years, it was a revelation for Elizabeth. I could see her mind working and coming to the conclusion that this was the only thing that made sense.

"His whole identity is wrapped up in being a doctor," she said. "His whole identity. The Baby Hospital is his home. This is where he comes to get away from——"

"The world," I said, finishing her sentence.

I was resigned. *You can't fix Thomas.*

*   *   *   *

"How are you feeling?" I asked Thomas as he was cleaning out his desk.

"Pretty good. Really. My pacemaker keeps going off, but I guess that's what it's there for. My voice is a little better."

"Think it'll keep getting better?" I asked hopefully.

"I'm not sure. I feel pretty good. But I'm pretty sure I'm as old as I've ever been."

Fair point.

"What are you going to do?"

"I don't know."

*   *   *   *

So is it worth it?

I became a board-certified pediatric neurosurgeon *seventeen years* after medical school.[144] I get to go to meetings with Johnny Spine and worry about EMR, lawsuits, and CEOs who think firing four hundred nurses makes good business sense. Each day brings the possibility of another Ellen or Katie and the gut-punching feeling of losing a child.

Thomas fought that good fight every day for twenty-seven years. Then he broke. The heart and soul of the Baby Hospital was dismissed in a committee meeting. In some ways, he was the embodiment of the lessons the hippie classes tried to instill in us early on. His main strength—unbridled altruistic caring for his patients—didn't coexist with modern medicine.

Is that our fate? Is that my fate? Is Thomas a warning, a view into a self-destructive, self-loathing future? Was Handsome Dan's warning correct?

I spent the next few weeks after Thomas's departure in a twilight depression. His office was the first in the little chain of rooms leading to my office, a converted storage closet.[145] I passed it every day. It was still full of his undictated charts, scattered haphazardly on the floor. There were a few old pictures and many dog-eared chess books. There was a plaque memorializing recognition as one of the state's "top physicians." The office was full but empty. Much in the way a corpse is not a person, the office was a room without a soul. So was the Baby Hospital.

"We got a 'presence of shunt' consult," Brian said glumly.

"What's the story?"

"Ten-year-old myelo. Febrile. Last shunt revision was three years ago by Thomas. Probably a kidney infection." The resident emotionlessly ticked off the pertinent information.

We reviewed the films and then headed to the room to check on the kid. Patients with spina bifida are a setup for urinary tract

---

[144] To be fair, including the time in the military.
[145] Sadly, not a joke.

infections. Virtually all of the patients with open spina bifida (my-elomeningocele) have a neurogenic bladder, meaning the nerves that normally tell the bladder to empty don't work. So urine pools and is an inviting spa for bacteria. This child had a classic story for *pyelone-phritis*—kidney infection. It probably wasn't the shunt.

"I knew it wasn't the shunt," Mom said. "But they called you anyways. I guess they think it's always the shunt."

"Yep."

Mom was in her late forties, attractive, and well kept. She lived in an upscale part of town, and her husband was a computer designer. She was affluent. She was educated and competent and seemed like a nice person. She clearly loved her daughter and knew her condition quite well.

"Well, we agree with you. Her CT scan and x-rays look fine. I don't think her shunt is the problem," I said.

The child was somewhat ashen and didn't want to move. She'd been vomiting. "Is Thomas here?" she asked with a weak voice.

"No, I'm sorry. I'm one of his partners," I said.

"Oh." She was disappointed.

"Thomas has been her doctor since she was born," Mom said with a smile. "Do you think he'll be around? She would love to say hello."

"Well, Thomas is out right now. Medical reasons. Honestly, I'm not sure if he's going to be back," I said.

"Oh," Mom said. She absorbed the news, and for a pregnant moment, nobody said anything. Two tears silently trickled out of her eyes. She took a deep breath. She didn't sob, and she turned so her daughter couldn't see her face. She composed herself and said, "Thomas has been her doctor since she was born." She looked up and sighed, and then she found her voice. "I was worried about him at our last clinic appointment. He was so frail."

She continued, "I had an ultrasound when I was about twenty

weeks pregnant, and they found the spina bifida and hydrocephalus. I saw a bunch of doctors. Every single one of them told me all the things that were wrong with my daughter. Some people told me to abort her—you know—my child. All of these doctors told me all the problems we were going to have.

"Then she was born and the doctors told me about the lesion on her back and the size of her head. She was going to be taken to the Baby Hospital away from me, and she needed surgery. All I could think about was everything wrong with her and maybe I'd made a mistake keeping her.

"Then Thomas came into my room. Do you know what he said? He said, 'What a beautiful baby!'" She paused. "No one else had called her a *baby*."

She sat down. For a moment, we both stared at nothing.

She dried her tears, composed herself, and stood up again.

"Well, will you please give him our best?"

"Definitely."

"Is he all right?"

"I think so. Just needs some time off."

This seemed to comfort her. She walked over to her sick child. The little girl would recover with some time and antibiotics.

"He was the only one who called her a baby. My baby. All the other doctors thought she was a *problem*."

I have the honor of working with people with amazing technical skills. Some of my mentors are masters of brain surgery. Some can make radiation beams dance to melt an abnormal blood vessel or neuter a tumor. Johnny can reconstruct a spine in a patient with advanced arthritis, trauma, or scoliosis. This restores function, relieves crushing pain, and gives people their lives back. Some of my mentors—the Professor, Merlin, Grandpa P.—bubbled with a passion and joy for teaching that inspired generations of students.

If any of the rest of us stopped going to work, our patients might be disappointed or even sad, but would anyone spontaneously cry? This mom was not one of Thomas's histrionic, crazy patients. She was a good, solid, well-educated mother of a child with spina bifida. And Thomas gave her hope with the simple act of recognizing the beauty of her baby.

The gravity of his job pressed on him, as it does on me and everyone else who takes care of kids like Katie and Ellen. I saw another child with a DIPG as a resident. Like Ellen, that child declined quickly.

"How do you deal with this?" I asked Thomas.

Asking Thomas a question is an invitation for a bad pun about food or complete sexual depravity. But it's also an invitation for wisdom.

"I think you have to take so much joy in the children who do well that it blocks out the pain from the ones who don't."

The advice was simple and perfect.

Thomas could not exist in today's medical world. That is today's world's loss. Doctors are succumbing to burnout, losing faith in their jobs and their futures, and losing empathy for humanity. I can see the wisdom of trying to combat this in medical school, but that effort is failing. Ignoring the problem simply condemns a group of students to enter the real world without preparation. Suicide among physicians is an epidemic no one wants to talk about.[146]

So it begs the question: Is it worth it?

Someday, I'm going to meet another Ellen or Katie or Mikey or Ben. I hope I'll be able to help some. I won't be able to help others, and they'll die on my watch. Someday, I'm going to get behind in the ever-important doctor responsibilities of charting, billing, dictating, testifying, and attending meetings upon meetings, insipid and boring.

---

[146] Again, enough doctors commit suicide each year to fill an entire school's medical school class. Yikes.

Someday, some powerful figure will calculate that the revenue I generate is not worth the expense I incur.

I don't want to fix Thomas. I want to fix everything else.

*   *   *   *

We are all called to something. I'm called to take care of children. It's horrible that beautiful little kids like Ellen or Katie will suffer. But they will. There will be another child with a tumor. There will be another horrible car accident. I will have to tell someone's family that their beautiful child was maimed or killed or will be born with a birth defect or may never talk. These children and families will need someone.

The Baby Hospital forces you to ask the big question. It forces you to ask about Death and heaven and God.

> "Truly I say to you, whatever you did for one of the
> least of these brothers and sisters of mine, you did it
> for Me" (Matthew 25:40).[147]

Some of the children at the Baby Hospital certainly qualify as the "least of these."

> "Let's not get tired of doing what is good" (Galatians
> 6:9).[148]

It's a privilege to care for children. It's a privilege to be called during the worst time in a family's life. It's a privilege to be entrusted with the life of a baby. It's a privilege to be expected to study, to

---

[147] New International Version.
[148] New Living Translation.

364

overcome the bureaucracy of medicine, and to feel capable of commanding an OR. It's a privilege to operate on the central nervous system.

I can see Death. And I can see Heaven. I wish I could understand the tapestry of the universe, of existence, of nature. But I can't. But I can see some things. I can see that there is a Song of Creation. I can even hear it. I can hear it in a child's laugh, my favorite sound. It's beautiful.

Yes. It's worth it. Because of this: